Caves to Cathedrals

Visual Arts in Ancient and Medieval Texts

Revised Second Edition

Written and edited by
Lee Ann Turner

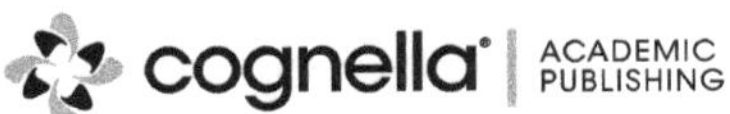

Bassim Hamadeh, CEO and Publisher

Carrie Montoya, Manager, Revisions and Author Care

Kaela Martin, Project Editor

Berenice Quirino, Associate Production Editor

Jess Estrella, Senior Graphic Designer

Natalie Lakosil, Licensing Manager

Bryan Mok, Interior Designer

Natalie Piccotti, Senior Marketing Manager

Kassie Graves, Director of Acquisitions and Sales

Jamie Giganti, Senior Managing Editor

Cover images: copyright © Depositphotos/loriklaszlo.

Birdseye view of *Rome from the Très Riches Heures de duc de Berry* by the Limbourg Brothers, 1411-1416, Musée Condé, MS. 55, f. 141. Copyright in the Public Domain.

Printed in the United States of America.

ISBN: 978-1-5165-3164-6 (pbk) / 978-1-5165-3165-3 (br)

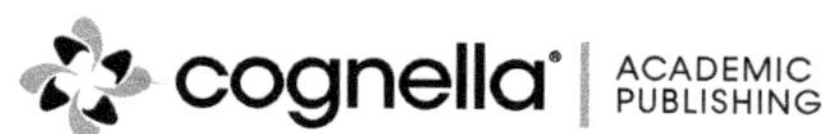

Contents

The Ancient Near East

11

Ancient Egypt

19

The Ancient Aegean

39

Classical Greece

51

The Etruscans   91

The Roman World   105

Early Christianity   149

The Byzantine World   159

The Art of Islam 179

Early Medieval Europe 203

The Romanesque Period   231

The Gothic Period   249

Acknowledgments   269

Preface to the
Second Edition

The title of this small volume, *Caves to Cathedrals*, is the nickname for an introductory art history class that surveys the artistic monument of the Western world from the Paleolithic caves through the Gothic cathedrals. As a collection of translated ancient and medieval texts on artistic production, it is meant as a supplement to the textbook for such a class. While I primarily use *Gardner's Art through the Ages*, this anthology should work with other textbooks such as those authored by Janson, Stockstad, Adams, or Honour and Flemming. All these books follow subdivisions similar to those used here: Stone Age, Ancient Near East, Egypt, and the Aegean, followed by Classical Greece and Rome, Early Christianity, Byzantium, the Islamic World, Early Medieval Europe, then the Romanesque and Gothic Periods, stopping around 1300 CE. Note that my adoption of BCE and CE rather than BC and AD follows the usage in the most recent editions of Gardner.

There are other anthologies in print similar to this one, most notably Linnea H. Wren's *Perspectives on Western Art: Source Documents and Readings from the Ancient Near East through the Middle Ages* (Westview Press, 1987). There are also more specific source books such as Caecilia Davis-Weyer's *Early Medieval Art, 300–1150: Sources and Documents* (Toronto, 1986), Teresa G. Frisch's *Gothic Art 1140-c.1450: Sources and Documents* (Toronto, 1987), Miriam Lichtheim's *Ancient Egyptian Literature* in three volumes (University of California Press, 1973-1980), Cyril Mango's *The Art of the Byzantine Empire 312–1453: Sources and Documents* (Prentice Hall, 1972), Michael Maas's *Readings in Late Antiquity: A Sourcebook* (Routledge, 2010 2nd edition), J. J. Pollitt's *The Art of Ancient Greece: Sources and Documents* (Prentice Hall, 1965) and *The Art of Rome: Sources and Documents* (Prentice Hall, 1966), James B. Pritchard's *The Ancient Near East: A New Anthology of Texts and Pictures* (Princeton University Press, 1958), and Kay Slocum's *Sources in*

Medieval Culture and History (Prentice Hall, 2011), to name a few. Moreover, many textbooks, such as Janson's, include primary texts as well.

What may distinguish this collection is that, rather than attempting to paint a picture of a culture or period, the selected texts are concretely tied to either a particular monument, a specific event associated with artistic production or display, an individual portrayed in art, terminology, or contemporary thoughts on art and architecture. Texts that describe daily life or are an example of a seminal work of the period (e.g., *Beowolf*) are not included. There are already many compilations of such works associated with courses in history, humanities, and Western civilization; D. Brendan Nagle and Stanley M. Burstein's *The Ancient World, Readings in Social and Cultural History* (Prentice Hall, 1995) is one example.

Perhaps due to my own background in Classical archaeology, I've always taken a very practical, concrete, and almost literal approach to text selection. I also embrace a broad view of the visual arts which allows for the inclusion of more ephemeral but highly interesting aspects of visual culture, such as fashion, stage scenery, tents, and public displays. Furthermore, in the second edition I've endeavored to include texts related to, if not the actual voices of, less represented populations in source documents, such as women, Jewish explorers, and Africans traveling abroad. There was also a conscious effort to include humorous and even, occasionally, somewhat shocking selections. Anything to make the past come to life, at least a little, for the reader. My aim is always to keep this collection as readable and unintimidating as possible for the student. The texts are generally short. My introductions are also quite brief, only contextualizing the author and the text, and their pertinence to the visual arts.

New to the second edition are images. They are not numerous and are meant to complement the readings and not overlap with those in the primary textbook. The number of readings has also increased from 64 to 89; most sections have additional texts, but the Etruscan and Islamic chapters were revised the most. Besides primary texts, several more recent sources that demonstrate the continuing influence of the ancient world are included, such as Keats' *Ode on a Grecian Urn* and Nietzsche's introduction to *The Birth of Tragedy*. I also tried to provide as wide a selection of authors and text types as possible—hence the addition of a hagiography from *The Golden Legend* and examples of *ekphrases* by Callistratus and Philostratus. Notably, the new texts include readings I use in classes beyond the survey, so I don't necessarily recommend assigning every reading in this collection to students in an introductory class. Rather, my hope is that this collection may remain useful for students and instructors in more advanced coursework.

In selecting texts, I endeavored to find readings that were more than mere footnotes to what is stated or pictured in the main textbook. For instance, proof that parchment was invented in Pergamon consists of two sentences in Pliny, and evidence of the fourteenth-century mutilation of the Sphinx's face by a man named al-Dahr—and not Napoleon—is a single short passage in al-Maqrizi's

Marvels of Construction. Even some longer texts add very little to what the primary textbooks say, such as the description of the collapse of the Hagia Sophia dome (Agathias, and Theophanes) and Constantine and Helena's patronage in the Holy Land (Eusebius, and Sozomen, respectively). I also opted to avoid as many lists as possible, such as additional church inventories (e.g., Centula) or the layout of cities like Alexandria (Strabo, and *Expositio Totius Mundi*), sixth-century Rome (Zachariah of Mytilene's *The Syriac Chronicle*), and Constantinople (Procopius, and *Chronicon Pachale*), since the latter are really just inventories of buildings. I had wanted to include a description of Alexander the Great's tomb and its visitors, but the numerous very short scattered statements (Strabo, Plutarch's *Life of Alexander*, Diodorus Siculus, Suetonius' *Caesar*, Lucian, Dio Cassius, etc.) rendered the selection virtually unreadable. Other texts were too long and required too much additional information, such as the stories of Brutus and Lucretia (Livy) and Romulus and Remus (Livy, Plutarch, Dionysus of Halicarnassus). Some texts were quite interesting to me but in actuality peripheral to the main narrative and, therefore, potentially confusing to students: Theodore Ducas Lascaris' thirteenth-century description of the Pergamon acropolis ruins, Seneca's sermon against luxury (*Epistle 90*), Sidonius Apollinaris' letter describing the outlandish dress of a Frankish prince, early Arab geographers' description of the enormous stones at Baalbek (Masudi, Muqaddasi etc.), or a letter from a female pilgrim to the Holy Lands in the fourth century (*Peregrinatio Etheriae* or *Itinerarium Egeriae*).

The source for each of the included 89 texts, and other information used in their introductions, is cited after the title. Occasionally I cite other sources of information in footnotes, but I tried to keep those to a minimum. The majority of translations, and all the images, are in the public domain. While this did help to keep copyright costs down, it also means that some of the language in the translations can be rather old fashioned. I did modernize the language when needed but tried to do so with a light touch. The main benefit of using public domain texts is that almost all of them can be found online in their entirety. Students, if interested, can very easily find the complete text and explore it further. An online location for either the translation used here or another translation that happens to be available on the Internet is noted after the bibliographical citation. The addresses for the main Internet sites referenced in this collection are listed below.

In the end, this small book is the result of many years of teaching the first half of the survey of Western art, utilizing at one point or another almost every main textbook for the class. I would certainly welcome comments, corrections, and suggestions for additional readings from other instructors of this class.

Lee Ann Turner
History of Art and Visual Culture
Art Department
Boise State University
Boise, Idaho 83725
May 2017

Websites

- Cuneiform Digital Library Initiative: cdli.ucla.edu (not used, but a good resource to know)

- Documenta Catholica Omnia: www.documentacatholicaomnia.eu

- Google Books: books.google.com

- HathiTrust Digital Library: www.hathitrust.org

- Internet Archive: www.archive.org

- Internet Ancient History Sourcebook: sourcebooks.fordham.edu/ancient/asbook.asp

- Internet Medieval Sourcebook: sourcebooks.fordham.edu/sbook.asp

- JStor (most university libraries subscribe to this collection of journals)

- LacusCurtius: penelope.uchicago.edu/Thayer/E/Roman/home.html

- Oriental Institute of the University of Chicago: oi.uchicago.edu

- Perseus Project: www.perseus.tufts.edu

- Project Gutenberg: www.gutenberg.org

- Project Gutenberg Australia: www.gutenberg.net.au

- Smithsonian Institution Libraries: library.si.edu/digital-library

- Theoi Project: www.theoi.com

- The Stoa Consortium: www.stoa.org

- The Stoics: www.stoics.com

- Wikimedia Commons: commons.wikimedia.org

- Wikisource: wikisource.org

The Manuscript Tradition: A Very Brief Overview

The majority of the texts translated in this collection did not reach us in their original form. Only texts that were inscribed (i.e., etched, engraved, or carved) on a hard surface like stone have survived the passage of time. Hence, the Law Code of Hammurabi (#4) and inscriptions from Egyptian funerary contexts (#7, #8, #9, #15) are original texts, as are the much more recent writings of Shelly (#14), Keats (#28), Nietzsche (#31), and Lawrence (#34). All the rest are the end result of centuries of hand copying Latin and Greek manuscripts.

The very word 'manuscript' is derived from the Latin words 'manu' or 'hand' and 'scribere' or 'to write.' Abbreviated MS (plural MSS), a manuscript is any hand-written text. In antiquity, literary texts were written on papyrus which is a reed that grows in marshy places, particularly Egypt. Pages of papyrus would be glued together to form a scroll. Occasionally ancient papyrus scrolls or their fragments are unearthed at places like Pompeii or Egypt, but even these texts are already copies, for the most part, of much older writings. Later, during the Roman Empire, perhaps due to the rise of Christianity and the need to preserve scripture, sturdier sheep/goat (parchment) and calf (vellum) skins were used. Certainly after the fall of the Western Roman Empire and by the time of the Arab invasions in the seventh century, papyrus was rarely available or used. The pages of parchment and vellum would be stitched together in a book called a codex (plural codices). An illuminated manuscript is simply one that has been illustrated.

Of course a codex comprised of parchment and vellum was expensive to produce. Vastly cheaper paper—made from the pulp of fibrous plants, usually cotton and linen and hemp rags—was invented in China possibly as early as the second century BCE. The technology reached the Arab world and its center of learning in Baghdad by the eighth century and was in use in the

Byzantine world and Moorish Spain by the eleventh century. The production of paper, the word is actually derived from the word papyrus, later spread to Italy and by the fourteenth and fifteenth century was in wide use in most of Western Europe. Modern paper utilizing wood pulp was not developed until the nineteenth century.

Regardless of the base material, all texts were hand-copied until the introduction of the printing press to Europe by Johannes Gutenberg in the fifteenth century. Anyone who has ever hand copied a text on their own, perhaps hard to imagine in this day of quick cell phone photographs, soon realizes how many errors can be introduced in even a first generation copy, especially if the original handwriting is difficult to cipher. Imagine centuries of this, and copies of a copy of a copy. Another level of complexity arises when one or even the only surviving copy of a text is a translation into another language. The collation of all the extant copies, variant readings, and translations of a particular text, in the attempt to reconstruct what the original text actually said, is called the text's manuscript tradition.

Typically the copying and translating of texts occurred at centers of learning. These centers of learning changed over time, depending on population concentration, fiscal support, and political stability. In the Hellenistic and Roman eras, Athens, Pergamon, and Alexandria housed famous libraries. Scholars gathered there to utilize the collections and were already aware of variations between different scrolls of the same text. In the fourth century, when the Christian church was coming to the fore, schools at Alexandria, Athens, Beirut, Constantinople, and Gaza supported the need for an expanded educated Roman civil service. Elsewhere, both Christian and Classical texts were being translated into Syriac (also known as Syria Aramaic) and even into Armenian at this time. As disruptions and invasions increased in the fifth and sixth centuries, which ultimately resulted in the fall of the western half of the Roman Empire in 476, there is a narrowing in the range of literature referenced and a drastic reduction in the numbers of schools. In the continuing eastern Byzantine half of the empire, Arab incursions and Iconoclasm further disrupted Classical learning into the 9th century. If one wants to use the term 'Dark Age,' this is the period (sixth through eighth centuries) in which to apply it. In the Muslim Near East, however, Baghdad became a great center of learning, and texts from antiquity, especially those of scientific, medical, mathematical, or philosophical merit, were translated into Arabic, largely from existing Syriac versions. One translator, Hunain ibn Ishaq (809-873), reported that he had searched for Greek manuscripts in Mesopotamia, Syria, Palestine, and Egypt. He would then collate the existing Syriac and Arabic versions against as many Greek manuscripts as he could find and produce a revised rendering.

The ninth century finally saw revivals of Classical learning in both the East and West. During the Middle Byzantine period, the imperial university at Constantinople was revived, and scholars searched for books preserved in isolated monasteries. It is at this time that Photios (see reading #58) summarized in his *Bibliotheca* some 280 Classical, heretical, and Christian texts that he had read, many of which are now lost. It speaks to the number and types of texts that had survived despite unsettled times and instances of book burnings and censorship. As a result of Photios' salon and different schools, there is nearly a continuous tradition thereafter of Classical studies in Byzantium—until, that is, the sack of Constantinople by the fourth Crusade in 1204 (see #60). It is believed that all the rare and now unknown texts that Photios described were probably lost at that time.

In the west during the ninth century, the court of Charlemagne introduced Classical texts preserved in Rome to the Frankish kingdom and established schools at Aachen, Tours, Reims, Metz, and Corbie. In no small way, the Carolingian revival was beholden to such earlier scholarly efforts as Isidore of Seville (see reading #73), the Venerable Bede (#70, #72), St. Augustine, and the industry of Irish copyists at Iona, Lindisfarne, and St. Gall. Still the importance of the Carolingian court for the preservation of Latin Classical texts cannot be overstated. In many cases, a single badly-damaged copy of an author's text had survived into the ninth century only to be copied, finally, at one of the Carolingian schools. Even then, some of the great Latin authors were still but a single copied manuscript stored on a shelf. The slightest accident could have robbed us of Petronius (#44) for instance, or five books of Livy (#36), before their ultimate rediscovery and dissemination some 400 or more years later during the Renaissance.

In the tenth century, the Greek East and Latin West intersected somewhat with the dynastic marriages between the Byzantine and Ottonian empires. In the eleventh century the Benedictine monastery at Montecassino (#75) emerged as a great center of learning, and by the end of the century the First Crusade was launched. The intellectual map of Europe truly began to change in the twelfth century with the final Norman conquest of Byzantine- and Islamic-influenced southern Italy and Sicily and the gradual re-conquest of Moorish Spain when Toledo emerged as a center where Arabic science and scholarship was made readily available to the West. By 1200, the first Western university was evolving in Paris and by 1300 the Renaissance, that great period of rediscovery of the Classical past and the time of Petrarch and Boccaccio (#88, #89), had started. If a Classical manuscript had survived to that point, it is most likely known to us today and has been, or can be, translated into English and included in collections like this one.

Sources and further reading:

Michelle P. Brown, *Understanding Illuminated Manuscripts, A Guide to Technical Terms*, London, The J. Paul Getty Museum and The British Library Board, 1994.

Raymond Clemens and Timothy Graham, *Introduction to Manuscript Studies*, Cornell University Press, 2007.

L. D. Reynolds and N. G. Wilson, *Scribes and Scholars: A Guide to the Transmission of Greek and Latin Literature*, 3rd edition, Oxford University Press, 1991 (a 2014 fourth edition is now available).

A good online resource is www.digital-scriptorium.org.

For an engaging and award-winning read on the importance of the rediscovery of a particular text, Lucretius' *On the Nature of Things (De rerum natura)*, take a look at Stephen Greenblatt's The *Swerve: How the World became Modern*, New York, W.W. Norton & Co., 2011.

Image List

Introduction

Each translated text or reading is numbered and is referenced throughout the volume by its number preceded by the number symbol or hashtag (#). The source for the translations, both print and digital when available, is noted below the title. This is followed by a brief introduction in italics. Within the translated document, square brackets indicate text inserted either by myself or other editors to aid in reading or provide additional information. Three dots indicate an ellipsis where a portion of the text has not been reproduced. The spellings of translations from the United Kingdom (e.g., theatre, colour) have been changed to American spellings (i.e., theater, color). Occasionally, when an older translation is used, the language may be somewhat modernized. The numbers that sometimes follow the title of the original text in parentheses reference the universal numbering system (usually book, chapter, section/line) used in the multiple editions of these texts.

1

The Ages of Man, from Hesiod's *Works and Days* (lines 110–179)

Hesiod, the Homeric Hymns and Homerica, translated by Hugh G. Evelyn-White, Loeb Classical Library, Cambridge, Harvard University Press, first printed 1914, pp. 11, 13, 15.

Available online at Perseus Project and Internet Archive

Credit: Hesiod, "The Ages of Man," *Works and Days*, trans. Hugh G. Evelyn-White. Copyright in the Public Domain.

Hesiod, one of Greece's earliest poets, probably wrote sometime between the second half of the 8th century and first quarter of the 7th century BCE. Works and Days *is a didactic poem, often with a rather cranky moralizing tone, offering advice on living a life of honest hard work. The passage reproduced here recounts the myth of the five ages of man. It is an ancient concept (compare the Bible's Daniel 2:31–45) which, while probably not originating with Hesiod, is one of the traditions behind our present division of antiquity into the Bronze and Iron Ages.*

First of all the deathless gods who dwell on Olympus made a golden race of mortal men who lived in the time of Cronos when he was reigning in heaven. And they lived like gods without sorrow of heart, remote and free from toil and grief: miserable age rested not on them; but with legs and arms never failing they made merry with feasting beyond the reach of all evils. When they died, it was as though they were overcome with sleep, and they had all good things; for the fruitful earth, unforced, bore them fruit abundantly and without stint. They dwelt in ease and peace upon their lands with many good things, rich in flocks and loved by the blessed gods.

But after the earth had covered this generation—they are called pure spirits dwelling on the earth, and are kindly, delivering from harm, and guardians of mortal men; for they roam everywhere over the earth, clothed in mist and keep watch on judgments and cruel deeds, givers of wealth; for this royal right also they received;—then they who dwell on Olympus made a second generation which was of **silver** and less noble by far. It was like the golden race neither in body nor in spirit. A child was brought up at his good mother's side a hundred years, an utter simpleton, playing childishly in his own home. But when they were full grown and were come to the full measure of their prime, they lived only a little time and that in sorrow because of their foolishness, for they could not keep from sinning and from wronging one another, nor would they serve the immortals, nor sacrifice on the holy altars of the blessed ones as it is right for men to do wherever they dwell. Then Zeus the son of Cronos was angry and put them away, because they would not give honor to the blessed gods who live on Olympus.

But when earth had covered this generation also—they are called blessed spirits of the underworld by men, and, though they are of second order, yet honor attends them also—Zeus the Father made a third generation of mortal men, a brazen race, sprung from ash-trees; and it was in no way equal to the silver age, but was terrible and strong. They loved the lamentable works of Ares and deeds of violence; they ate no bread, but were hard of heart like adamant, fearful men. Great was their strength and unconquerable the arms which grew from their shoulders on their strong limbs. Their armor was of bronze, and their houses of bronze, and of bronze were their implements: there was no black iron. These were destroyed by their own hands and passed to the dank house of chill Hades, and left no name: terrible though they were, black Death seized them, and they left the bright light of the sun.

But when earth had covered this generation also, Zeus the son of Cronos made yet another, the fourth, upon the fruitful earth, which was nobler and more righteous, a god-like race of hero-men who are called demi-gods, the race before our own, throughout the boundless earth. Grim war and dread battle destroyed a part of them, some in the land of Cadmus at seven-gated Thebes when they fought for the flocks of Oedipus, and some, when it had brought them in ships over the great sea gulf to Troy for rich-haired Helen's sake: there death's end enshrouded a part of them. But to the others father Zeus the son of Cronos gave a living and an abode apart from men, and made them dwell at the ends of earth. And they live untouched by sorrow in the islands of the blessed along the shore of deep-swirling Ocean, happy heroes for whom the grain-giving earth bears honey-sweet fruit flourishing thrice a year, far from the deathless gods, and Cronos rules over them; for the father of men and gods released him from his bonds. And these last equally have honor and glory.

And again far-seeing Zeus made yet another generation, the fifth, of men who are upon the bounteous earth. Thereafter, would that I were not among the men of the fifth generation, but either had died before or been born afterwards. For now truly is a race of iron, and men never rest from labor and sorrow by day, and from perishing by night; and the gods shall lay sore trouble upon them. But, notwithstanding, even these shall have some good mingled with their evils.

The Stone Ages

2

A description of a Paleolithic cave, from Francois de Belleforest's *The universal Cosmography of the whole World (La cosmographie universelle de tout le monde, Paris, 1575, volume II, p. 198)*

Francois de Belleforest's La Cosmographie universelle *from 1575 is a French translation and expansion on the* Cosmographia *of Sebastian Münster (1544). This somewhat fanciful description of a cave, probably the Grotte de Rouffignac in the Dordogne region of southwest France, may be the earliest recorded reference to a Paleolithic cave painting.*

Also near Miramont, which is a small village in the Perigord, one can see a cavern or grotto five to six leagues long, which the local residents call *Cluzeau*. Those who have entered describe great wonders; beautiful rooms and chambers paved with thin stones of different colors as in a mosaic; stone altars; paintings in several places and foot-prints of many animals large and small. Those who have entered say that there are several springs and streams, including one that is a hundred to a hundred twenty feet wide, and which runs with great strength and speed, being besides very deep. No one dares to go beyond it, although the cave extends much further, nor does anyone enter except in large groups and with a great many torches, candles, and lanterns (because there is no glimmer except from the entrance), and carrying provisions they can use in case they get lost.

3

Stonehenge in the medieval tradition, from Geoffrey of Monmouth's *History of the Kings of Britain (Historia Regum Britanniae 8.10–12)*

Six Old English Chronicles, edited with notes by J. A. Giles, London, Henry G. Bohn, 1848, pp. 215–217.

Available online at Google Books and Wikisource

The Historia Regum Britanniae *was written in 1136 and relates the mythical history of Britain. It was very influential in later periods, particularly in terms of the legend of King Arthur. In this excerpt we are told that Stonehenge was originally built by giants in Ireland for healing baths. It was moved to Salisbury by Merlin to be used as a burial memorial (see Fig. 1). This is clearly fanciful. Arthur, a Christian ruler, postdates the Roman departure from England in the 5th century CE, some two thousand years after the construction of Stonehenge. On the other hand, the bluestones of Stonehenge did in fact travel a great distance, but they were brought from Wales, not Ireland.*

"If you are desirous," said Merlin, "to honor the burying-place of these men with an everlasting monument, send for the Giant's Dance, which is in Killaraus, a mountain in Ireland. For there is a structure of stones there, which none of this age could raise without a profound knowledge of the mechanical arts. They are stones of a vast magnitude and wonderful quality; and if they can be placed here, as they are there, round this spot of ground, they will stand forever.

At these words of Merlin, Aurelius burst into laughter, and said, "How is it possible to remove such vast stones from so distant a country, as if Britain was

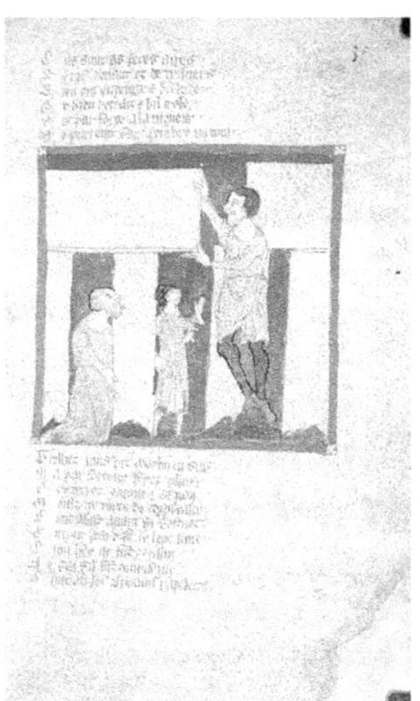

Fig. 1 Oldest known illustration of Stonehenge, shows Merlin assisting in its construction, 14th century (Egerton 3028, folio 30R).

not furnished with stones fit for the work?" Merlin replied, "I entreat your majesty to forbear vain laughter, for what I say is without vanity. They are mystical stones, and of a medicinal virtue. The giants of old brought them from the farthest coast of Africa, and placed them in Ireland, while they inhabited that country. Their design in this was to make baths in them, when they should be taken with any illness. For their method was to wash the stones and put their sick into the water, which infallibly cured them. With the like success they cured wounds also, adding only the application of some herbs. There is not a stone there which has not some healing virtue." When the Britons heard this, they resolved to send for the stones, and to make war upon the people of Ireland if they should offer to detain them. And to accomplish this business, they made choice of Uther Pendragon, who was to be attended with fifteen thousand men. They chose also Merlin himself, by whose direction the whole affair was to be managed. A fleet being therefore got ready, they set sail, and with a fair wind arrived in Ireland...

After the victory they went to the mountain Killaraus, and arrived at the structure of stones, the sight of which filled them both with joy and admiration. And while they were all standing round them, Merlin came up to them and said, "Now try your forces, young men, and see whether strength or art can do the most towards taking down these stones." At this word they all set to their engines with one accord, and attempted the removing of the Giant's Dance. Some prepared cables, others small ropes, others ladders for the work, but all to no purpose. Merlin laughed at their vain efforts, and then began his own contrivances. When he had placed in order the engines that were necessary, he took down the stones with an incredible facility, and gave directions for carrying them to the ships, and placing them therein. This done, they with joy set sail again, to return to Britain, where they arrived with a fair gale, and repaired to the burying place with the stones.

Image credits

Fig. 1: British Library, "Oldest illustration of Stonehenge: British Library Egerton 3028," https://commons.wikimedia.org/wiki/File:BLEgerton3028Fol30rStonehenge.jpg. Copyright in the Public Domain.

The Ancient Near East

4

Excerpts from the Law Code of Hammurabi

The Code of Hammurabi, translated by L. W. King, with commentary from Charles F. Horne and the Eleventh Edition of the Encyclopaedia Britannica by Claude Hermann Walter Johns, 1915, reprinted BiblioBazaar 2007, pp. 45–54.

Available online at the Internet Ancient History Sourcebook

Hammurabi, who reigned from 1792–1750 BCE, formulated one of the earliest written law codes known to us. It was inscribed in thirty-five hundred lines of cuneiform characters on a 7' 4" tall diorite/basalt stele. The stele itself was found at Susa, brought there as spoils by some Elamite raider as a trophy of war. It is now in the Louvre. Other copies, however, are also known. What follows are some excerpts, sometimes with parallel Old Testament references noted.

128. If a man takes a woman to wife, but has no intercourse with her, this woman is no wife to him.

129. If a man's wife is caught with another man [*in flagrante delicto*], both shall be tied and thrown into the water, but the husband may pardon his wife and the king his subject. [Deut. 22:22]

130. If a man violates the wife [betrothed or child-wife] of another man, who has never known a man, and still lives in her father's house, and he sleeps with her and is caught, this man shall be put to death, but the wife is blameless. [Deut. 22:23–27]

132. If the "finger is pointed" at a man's wife about another man, but she is not caught sleeping with the other man, she shall jump into the river for her husband. [Num. 5:11–31]

133. If a man is taken prisoner in war, and there is sustenance in his house, but his wife leaves his house and court, and goes to another house: because this wife did not keep her court, and went to another house, she shall be judicially condemned and thrown into the water.

134. If a man is captured in war and there is no sustenance in his house, if then his wife goes to another house this woman shall be held blameless.

135. If a man is taken prisoner in war and there is no sustenance in his house and his wife goes to another house and bears children; and if later her husband returns and comes to his home: then this wife shall return to her husband, but the children follow their father.

136. If any one leaves his house, runs away, and then his wife goes to another house, if then he returns, and wishes to take his wife back: because he fled from his home and ran away, the wife of this runaway shall not return to her husband.

137. If a man wishes to separate from a woman who has born him children, or from his wife who has born him children: then he shall give that wife her dowry, and a part of the usufruct [use and enjoyment] of field, garden, and property, so that she can rear her children. When she has brought up her children, a portion of all that is given to the children, equal as that of one son, shall be given to her. She may then marry the man of her heart.

138. If a man wishes to separate from his wife who has born him no children, he shall give her the amount of her purchase money and the dowry which she brought from her father's house, and let her go.

195. If a son strikes his father, his hands shall be hewn off. [Exod. 21:15]

196. If a man puts out the eye of another man, his eye shall be put out.

197. If he breaks another man's bone, his bone shall be broken. [Exod. 21:23–25; Lev. 24:19–20; Deut. 19:21]

198. If he puts out the eye of a freed man, or breaks the bone of a freed man, he shall pay one gold mina.

199. If he puts out the eye of a man's slave, or breaks the bone of a man's slave, he shall pay one-half of its value.

200. If a man knocks out the teeth of his equal, his teeth shall be knocked out.

201. If he knocks out the teeth of a freed man, he shall pay one-third of a gold mina.

209. If a man strikes a free-born woman so that she loses her unborn child, he shall pay ten shekels for her loss.

210. If the woman dies, his daughter shall be put to death.

5

The tower of Babel, from the Book of Genesis (11:1–9)

Holy Bible, King James Version, 1987 printing

Available online at http://www.biblegateway.com

Credit: "Genesis 11:1-9," *Holy Bible*, King James Version. Copyright in the Public Domain.

King James I of England authorized a new translation of the Bible into English in 1604. It was finished in 1611 and quickly became the standard for the English-speaking world. Below is the story of the tower of Babel which explains why there are so many languages in the world. The idea of such a tower made of brick has sometimes been associated with some earlier incarnation of the great ziggurat of Babylon dedicated to Marduk. The tower tends to be imagined by artists, however, in terms of architectural modes familiar in their day (see Fig. 2 and 3).

[1]And the whole earth was of one language, and of one speech.

[2]And it came to pass, as they journeyed from the east, that they found a plain in the land of Shinar; and they dwelt there.

[3]And they said one to another, Go to, let us make brick, and burn them thoroughly. And they had brick for stone, and slime had they for mortar.

[4]And they said, Go to, let us build us a city and a tower, whose top may reach unto heaven; and let us make us a name, lest we be scattered abroad upon the face of the whole earth.

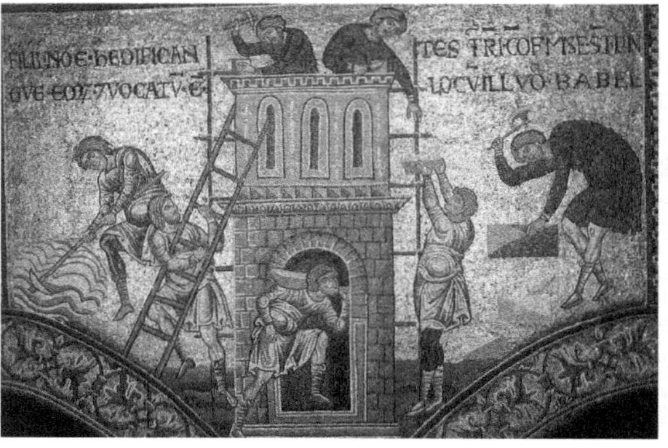

Fig. 2 Tower of Babel imagined in a mosaic from the nave of Monreale cathedral, 12th century, Sicily.

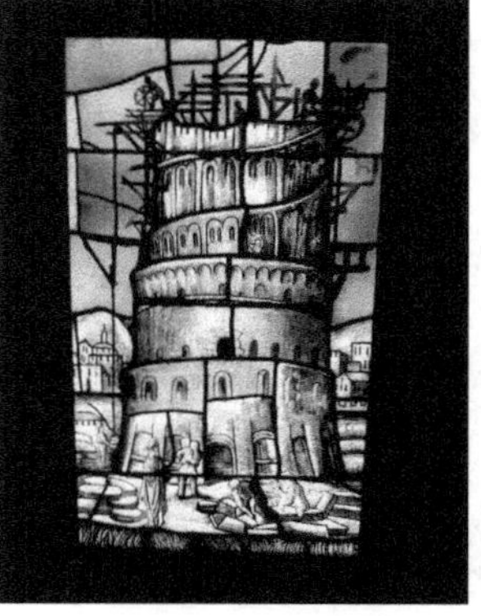

Fig. 3 Tower of Babel imagined in a 15th century stained glass window from the Milan cathedral.

[5]And the Lord came down to see the city and the tower, which the children of men built.

[6]And the Lord said, Behold, the people is one, and they have all one language; and this they begin to do: and now nothing will be restrained from them, which they have imagined to do.

[7]Go to, let us go down, and there confound their language, that they may not understand one another's speech.

[8]So the Lord scattered them abroad from thence upon the face of all the earth: and they left off to build the city.

[9]Therefore is the name of it called Babel; because the Lord did there confound the language of all the earth: and from thence did the Lord scatter them abroad upon the face of all the earth.

Image credits

6

The Hanging Gardens of Babylon, from Diodorus Siculus' *Library of History (Bibliotheca historica 2.10)*

Diodorus Siculus, *Library of History*, volume I, translated by C. H. Oldfather, Loeb Classical Library, Cambridge, Harvard University Press, first printed 1933, reprinted 1968, pp. 385, 387.

Available online at LacusCurtius

The Hanging Gardens of Babylon were considered one of the Seven Wonders of the Ancient World. They were built within the walls of the royal palace at Babylon, the work probably of King Nebuchadnezzar II (reigned 604–562 BCE). No certain traces of the gardens have been found, so we rely on ancient authors for a sense of their magnificence. The following is one such description by the Greek historian Diodorus of Sicily (mid-first century BCE), who could never have seen the gardens but probably based his description on an earlier, now-lost account.

There was also, besides the acropolis, the Hanging Garden, as it is called, which was built, not by Semiramis, but by a later Syrian king to please one of his concubines; for she, they say, being a Persian by race and longing for the meadows of her mountains, asked the king to imitate, through the artifice of a planted garden, the distinctive landscape of Persia. The park extended four plethera on each side, and since the approach to the garden sloped like a hillside and the several parts of the structure rose from one another tier on tier, the appearance of the whole resembled that of a theatre. When the ascending terraces had been built, there had been constructed beneath them galleries which carried the entire weight of the planted garden and rose little by little one above the other along the approach; and the uppermost gallery, which was fifty cubits high, bore the highest surface of the park, which was made level with the circuit wall of the battlements of the city. Furthermore, the walls, which had been constructed at great expense, were twenty-two feet thick, while the passageway between each two walls was ten feet wide. The roofs of the galleries were covered over with beams of stone sixteen feet long, inclusive of the overlap, and four feet wide. The roof above these beams had first a layer of reeds laid in great quantities of bitumen, over this two courses of baked brick bonded by cement, and as a third layer a covering of lead, to the end that the moisture from the soil might not penetrate beneath. On all this again earth had been piled to a depth sufficient for the roots of the largest trees; and the ground, which was leveled off, was thickly planted with trees of every kind that, by their great size or any other charm, could give pleasure to beholder. And since the galleries, each projecting beyond another, all received the light, they contained many royal lodgings of every description; and there was one gallery which contained openings leading from the topmost surface and machines for supplying the garden with water, the machines raising the water in great abundance from the river, although no one outside could see it being done. Now this park, as I have said, was a later construction.

Ancient Egypt

7

A letter from Pepi II regarding a Pygmy, from the tomb of Harkhuf

James Henry Breasted, *Ancient Records of Egypt: Historical Documents from the Earliest Times to the Persian Conquest, volume I*, Chicago, University of Chicago Press, 1906–7, pp. 160–161

Available online at Internet Archive

When the pharaoh Pepi II was 8 or 9 years old, (Dynasty VI, around 2270 BCE), he received a letter from Harkhuf, a caravan leader, describing a dancing pygmy he was bringing back from his fourth expedition abroad. Harkhuf recorded on the walls of his tomb Pepi's response which is translated below. Although Breasted, in the below text, translates the term used as dwarf, the Egyptians did differentiate between the two and, in fact, the term for pygmy is used here.[1] Both categories of short-statured people appear to be viewed positively in Egypt, especially during the Old Kingdom (see Fig. 4), and the excitement of the little king is hard to miss.

Royal decree (to) the sole companion, the ritual priest and caravan-conductor Harkhuf.

I have noted the matter of your letter, which you sent to the king, to the palace, in order that one might know that you have descended in safety from Yam with the army that was with you. You said [in] this letter, that you have brought

---

[1] Warren R. Dawson "Pygmies and Dwarfs in Ancient Egypt" *The Journal of Egyptian Archaeology*, 24:2, 1938, pp. 185–189. Chahira Kosma, "Historical Review, Dwarfs in Ancient Egypt", *American Journal of Medical Genetics*, 140A, 2006, pp. 303–311.

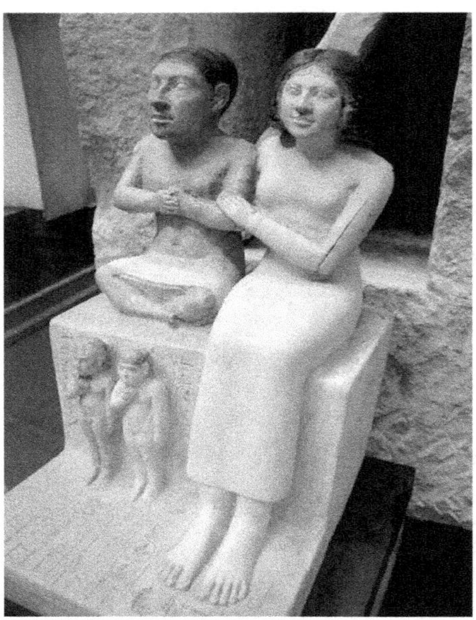

Fig. 4 The Dwarf Seneb and his family, Giza, Dynasty IV or V.

all great and beautiful gifts, which Hathor, mistress of Imu has given to the king of Upper and Lower Egypt, Pepi, who lives forever and ever. You said in this letter, that you brought a dancing dwarf of the god from the land of spirits, like the dwarf which the treasurer of the god Burded brought from Punt in the time of king Isesi (Dynasty V). You said to my majesty: "Never before has one like him been brought by any other who has visited Yam."

Each year you do what your lord desires and praises; you spend day and night in doing that which you lord desires, praises, and commands. His majesty will award you many excellent honors to be an ornament for the son of your son forever, so that all people will say when they hear what my majesty does for you: "Is there anything like this which was done for the sole companion, Harkhuf, when he descended from Yam, because of the vigilance he showed, to do that which his lord desired, praised, and commanded."

Come northward to the court immediately; bring this dwarf with you, alive, prosperous and healthy from the land of spirits, for the dances of the god, to rejoice and [gladden] the heart of the king of Upper and Lower Egypt, who lives forever. When he goes down with you into the vessel, appoint excellent people, who shall be beside him on each side of the vessel; take care lest he fall into the water. When he sleeps at night appoint excellent people, who shall sleep beside him in his tent, inspect him ten times a night. My majesty desires to see this dwarf more than the gifts of Sinai and of Punt. If you arrive at court with this dwarf alive, prosperous and healthy, my majesty will do for you a greater thing than that which was done for the treasurer of the god Burded in the time of king Isesi, according to the heart's desire of my majesty to see the dwarf.

Image credits

8

An Egyptian Artist Statement from Irtisen's funerary stele

Translated by J. A. Wilson, "The Artist of the Egyptian Old Kingdom", *Journal of Near Eastern Studies* 6, 1947, Chicago, p. 245, note 68.

Available online at JStor

This text is from the Middle Kingdom funerary stele (Louvre C 14) of Irtisen, an artisan probably specializing in relief sculpture. It is also the oldest known artist's statement in Western art. What is perhaps most striking is Irtisen's claim that he knows how to express the movements of certain figures, such as "the pose of the arm" of someone harpooning a hippopotamus. This appears to be a verbal reference to being adept at the accepted canonical ways of rendering specific Egyptian subject matter.

The overseer of the Craftsmen, the Painter and Sculptor Irtisen says:

I know the mysteries of the divine word and the conducting of ritual. All prepared magic, it belongs to me, without [any] thereof passing me by. Moreover, I am a craftsman successful in his craft, one who comes out on top through that which he knows.

I know [how to reckon] the levels of the flood, how to weigh according to rule, how to withdraw or introduce when it goes out or comes in, in order that a body may come in its place.

I know [how to express] the movement of a figure, the stride of a woman, the positions of one instant, the cringing of the solitary captive, how one eye looks at another, how to make frightened the face of the outlaw, the pose of the arm of him who harpoons the hippopotamus, and the pace of the runner.

I know how to make things of paste and inlaid things, without letting the fire melt them, nor do they wash off in the water either.

There is no one who can reveal it to anybody except for me alone and my eldest son of my body. The god has commanded that he do [it] and that I reveal it to him. I have seen the products of his hands in acting as Overseer of Works, in every noble costly stone, beginning with silver and gold and going down to ivory and ebony.

9

On moving a colossal stone for a statue, from the tomb of Thuthotep

James Breasted, *Ancient Records of Egypt: Historical Documents from the Earliest Times to the Persian Conquest*, volume I, Chicago, University of Chicago Press, 1906–7, pp. 306–312.

Available online at Internet Archive

This text is from the tomb of Thuthotep (=Djehutihotep) at Deir el-Bersha (Dynasty XII, reign of Sesostris III) and was next to a painted scene showing 172 men in four rows pulling by ropes a colossal statue on a sledge (Fig. 5). The translator, James Breasted, estimated that Thuthotep's stone, which was 13 cubits long or some 22 feet, would weigh around 60 tons. Note that a nome is a division of Egypt that we might equate with a state. Thuthotep was nomarch, which would be similar to a governor.

Following a statue of 13 cubits, of stone of Hatnub [alabaster]. Lo, the way, upon which it came, was very difficult, beyond anything. Lo, the dragging of the great things upon it was difficult for the heart of the people, because of the difficult stone of the ground, being hard stone.

I caused the youth, the young men of the recruits to come, in order to make for a road, together with shifts of necropolis miners and of quarrymen, the foremen and the wise. The people of strength said: "We come to bring it;" while my heart was glad; the city was gathered together rejoicing; very good it was to see beyond everything. The old man among them, he leaned upon the

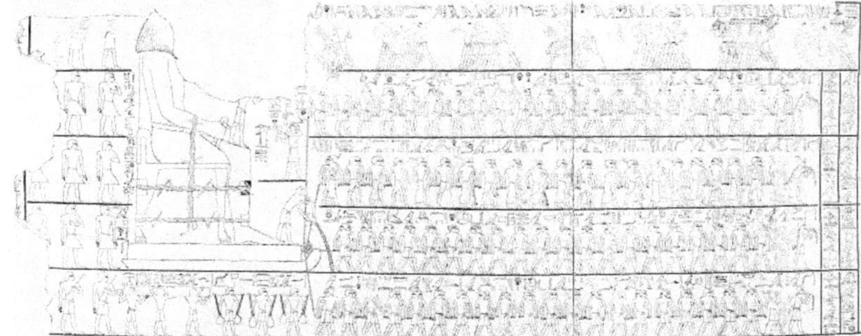

Fig. 5 Drawing of a relief depicting the transportation of a colossal statue, Tomb of Thuthotep (Djehutihotep), Dynasty XII, at Deir el-Bersha.

child; the strong armed together with the tremblers, their courage rose. Their arms grew strong; one of them put forth the strength of 1000 men.

Behold, this statue, being a squared block on coming forth from the great mountain, was more valuable than anything. Vessels were equipped, filled with supplies, in advance of my army of recruits, the youth bore in advance of it. Their words were laudation, and my praises from the king. My children adorned were behind me. My nome shouted praise. I arrived in the district of this city, the people were gathered together, praising; very good it was to see, beyond everything … . Their hearts had not thought of this which I had done … after that this my tomb was complete in its everlasting work.

Image credits

Fig.5: Percy E. Newberry, "Transportation of a Colossal Statue, Tomb of Thuthotep," https://commons.wikimedia.org/wiki/File:Transportation_of_statue_of_Djehutihotep_II.jpg. Copyright in the Public Domain.

10

The great Sphinx speaks to Thutmosis IV, from the Dream Stele

James Breasted, *Ancient Records of Egypt: Historical Documents from the Earliest Times to the Persian Conquest*, volume II, Chicago, University of Chicago Press, 1906–7, pp. 320–324.

Available online at Internet Archive

An inscribed stele found between the paws of the great Sphinx of Khafre (Dynasty IV) at Giza records a dream that the future Dynasty XVIII pharaoh Thutmosis IV had as a boy. In it, the Sphinx as Harmakhis (the rising sun) tells him essentially that he will be pharaoh if he clears away the sands swallowing the statue. There are, however, errors and irregularities in the writing that are inconsistent with this date. It is possible that the text is an attempted restoration of a damaged original that belonged to Thutmosis IV. Someone, at least, did excavate the area around the sphinx, built a wall to hold back the sand, and set up this stele (Fig. 6).

One of those days it came to pass that the king's son, Thutmosis, came, coursing at the time of midday, and he rested in the shadow of this great god. A vision of sleep seized him at the hour the sun was in the zenith, and found the majesty of this revered god speaking with his own mouth, as a father speaks with his son, saying: "Behold me! See me! My son, Thutmosis, I am your father, Harmakhis-Khepri-Re-Atum, who will give you my kingdom on earth at the head of the living. You will wear the white crown and the red crown upon the throne of Keb, the hereditary prince. The land will be yours in its length and breadth, that which the eye of the All-Lord shines upon.

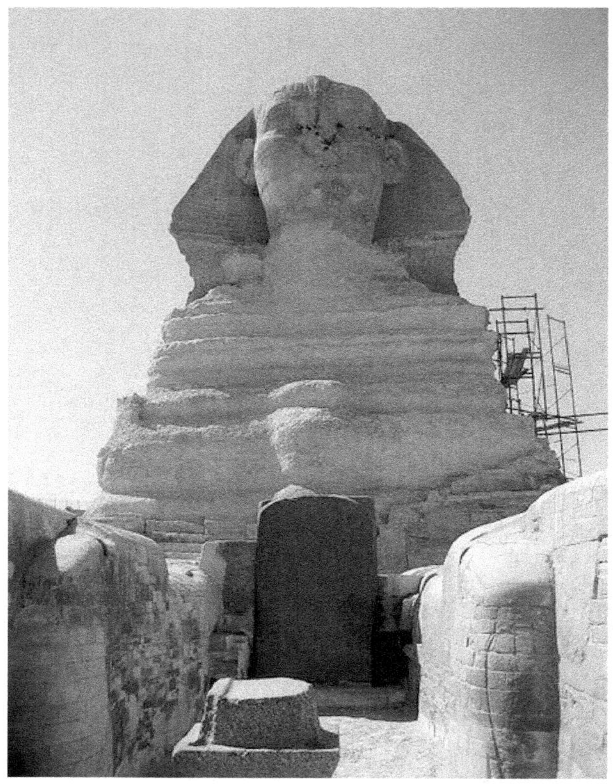

Fig. 6 Dream stele of Thutmosis IV (Dynasty XVIII) between the paws of the Great Sphinx at Giza (Dynasty IV).

The food of the Two Lands will be yours, the great tribute of all countries, the duration of a long period of years. My face is yours, my desire is toward you. You will be to me a protector [for] my manner is as if I were ailing in all my limbs. The sand of this desert upon which I am, has reached me; turn to me, to have that done which I have desired, knowing that you are my son, my protector, come hither, behold, I am with you, I am your leader." When he had finished this speech, this king's son awakes hearing this.

Image credits

Fig. 6: Chanel Wheeler, "Great Sphinx with the Dream Stele," https://commons.wikimedia.org/wiki/File:Great_Sphinx_with_Stelae.jpg. Copyright in the Public Domain.

11

On Mummification, from Herodotus' *The Histories* (2.86–89)

Herodotus, *The Histories*, translated by Aubrey de Sélincourt, revised edition, London, Penguin Classics, 1972, pp. 160–161.

A different translation is available online at Perseus Project

Herodotus, often called the Father of History, wrote in the fifth century BCE, primarily about the wars between Greece and the Persian Empire. He was, however, curious about all aspects of the human condition and traveled widely as a young man. His description of the process of mummification reproduced here is one of the most complete to survive.

Mummification is a distinct profession. The embalmers, when a body is brought to them, produce specimen models in wood, painted to resemble nature, and graded in quality; the best and most expensive kind is said to represent a being whose name I shrink from mentioning in this connection; the next best is somewhat inferior and cheaper, while the third sort is cheapest of all. After pointing out these differences in quality, they ask which of the three is required, and the kinsmen of the dead man, having agreed upon a price, go away and leave the embalmers to their work. The most perfect process is as follows: as much as possible of the brain is extracted through the nostrils with an iron hook, and what the hook cannot reach is rinsed out with drugs; next the flank is laid open with a flint knife and the whole contents of the abdomen removed; the cavity is then thoroughly cleansed and washed out, first with palm wine and again with an infusion of pounded spices. After that it is filled with pure bruised myrrh, cassia, and every other aromatic substance with the exception of frankincense, and sewn up again, after which the body is placed in *natrum* [a type of salt], covered entirely over, for seventy days—never longer. When this period, which must not be exceeded, is over, the body is washed and then wrapped from head to foot in linen cut into strips and smeared on the underside with gum, which is commonly used by the Egyptians instead of glue. In this condition the body is given back to the family, who have a wooden case made, shaped like the human figure, into which it is put. The case is then sealed up and stored in a sepulchral chamber, upright against the wall.

When, for reasons of expense, the second quality is called for, the treatment is different: no incision is made and the intestines are not removed, but oil of cedar is injected with a syringe into the body through the anus which is afterwards stopped up to prevent the liquid from escaping. The body is then pickled in *natrum* for the prescribed number of days, on the last of which the oil is drained off. The effect of it is so powerful that as it leaves the body it brings with it the stomach and intestines in a liquid state, and as the flesh, too, is dissolved by the *natrum*, nothing of the body is left but the bones and skin. After this treatment it is returned to the family without further fuss.

The third method, used for embalming the bodies of the poor, is simply to clear out the intestines with a purge and keep the body seventy days in *natrum*. It is then given back to the family to be taken away.

When the wife of a distinguished man dies, or any woman who happens to be beautiful or well known, her body is not given to the embalmers immediately, but only after the lapse of three or four days. This is a precautionary measure to prevent the embalmers from violating the corpse, a thing which is said actually to have happened in the case of a woman who had just died. The culprit was given away by one of his fellow workmen.

12

The Opening of the Mouth and Eyes, from the *Book of the Dead* (chapter 23)

The Egyptian Book of the Dead, translation and commentary by Sir P. Le Page Renouf, continued and completed by Prof. E. Naville, printed for The Society of Biblical Archaeology by Harrison and Sons, London, St. Martin's Lane, 1904, p. 62.

Available online at the Internet Archive

The Book of the Dead is a New Kingdom compilation of spells meant to help the deceased in his or her transition to the afterlife. It is the successor of the Middle Kingdom Coffin Texts and the Old Kingdom Pyramid Texts. The opening of the mouth ceremony, attested as early as the Old Kingdom and continuing through Roman times, was a funerary ritual performed on statues and mummies to animate them so that they could see, and receive air and food (Fig. 7). It reveals something of the extraordinary role of imagery in ancient Egypt. Compare aspects to Psalm 51.

Let my mouth be opened by Ptah, and let the muzzles which are upon my mouth be loosed by the god of my domain.

Then let Thoth come, full and equipped with Words of Power, and let him loose the muzzles of Sutu [Seth] which are upon my mouth, and let Tmu [Atum] lend a hand to fling them at the assailants.

Let my mouth be given to me. Let my mouth be opened by Ptah with that instrument of steel wherewith he opened the mouths of the gods.

I am Sechit Uat'it [Sekhmet-Wadjet] who sits on the right side of Heaven; I am Sahit encircled by the Spirits of Heliopolis.

And all the Words of Power, and all the accusations which are uttered against me—the gods stand firm against them; the cycles of the gods unitedly.

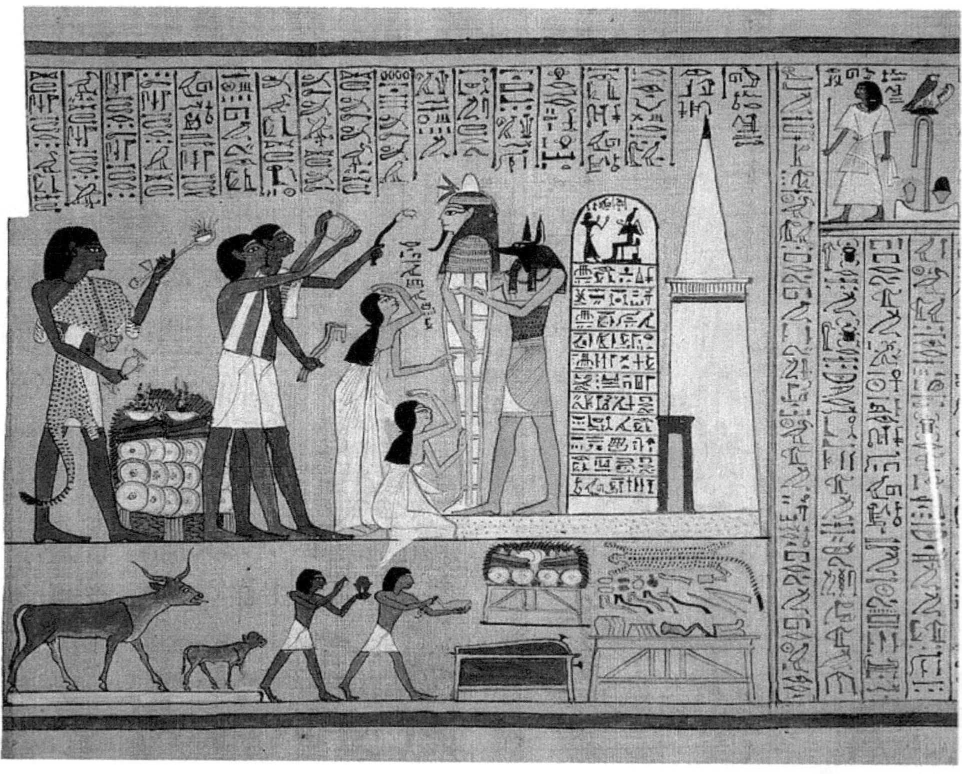

Fig. 7 The opening of the mouth ceremony, Book of the Dead of Hunefer, Dynasty XIX, from Thebes.

Image credits

13

The Colossus of Memnon, from Callistratus' *Descriptions of Statues (Ekphraseis or Statuarum descriptiones* 9)

Philostratus: Imagines, Callistratus: Descriptiones with an English translation by Arthur Fairbanks, New York, Putnam Sons, 1931, pp. 407, 409.

Available online at Internet Archive

Memnon was a legendary king of Ethiopia who helped defend the city of Troy. Son of the mortal man Tithonus and the goddess of the dawn Eos, he was ultimately slain far from home by the Greek hero Achilles. A millennium later, in the first century BCE, Memnon became associated with one of the two colossal statues that mark the entrance to the funerary complex of the Dynasty XVIII pharaoh Amenhotep III. We are told that after the statues were damaged in an earthquake (Strabo 17.46), one of them began to make a sound at the time of sunrise—perhaps due to the breeze that often arises with the change in temperature. So the legend arose that it was Memnon greeting his mother, the goddess of the dawn, each day. Pausanias (1.42.2) likens the sound the statue made to the twang of a broken harp string, Strabo to a slight blow, and Pliny (36.11) to a creak. The 'singing' statue drew tourists during the next two centuries, many of whom left graffiti on the statue base. Sometime after Emperor Septimius Severus visited the statue, the Romans repaired it and, sadly, it never made a sound again. Callistratus, a Greek writer of the third century CE, riffs on the wonder of this statue in the following exercise of expository writing, called ekphrasis (for further discussion of this term see #42).

I wish to describe to you the miracle of Memnon, for the art it displayed was truly incredible and beyond the power of human hand. There was in Ethiopia an image of Memnon, the son of Tithonus, made of marble; however, stone though it was, it did not abide within its proper limits nor endure the silence imposed on it by nature, but stone though it was it had the power of speech. For at one time it saluted the rising Day, by its voice giving token of its joy and expressing delight at the arrival of its mother; and again, as day declined to night, it uttered piteous and mournful groans in grief at her departure. Nor yet was the marble at a loss for tears, but they too were at hand to serve its will. The statue of Memnon, as it seems to me, differed from a human being only in its body, but it was directed and guided by a kind of soul and by a will like that of man. At any rate it both had grief in its composition and again it was possessed by a feeling of pleasure according as it was affected by each emotion. Though nature had made all stones from the beginning voiceless and mute and both unwilling to be under the control of grief and also unaware of the meaning of joy, but rather immune to all the darts of chance, yet to that stone of Memnon art had imparted pleasure and had mingled the sense of pain in the rock; and this is the only work of art of which we know that has implanted in the stone perceptions and a voice. Daedalus did indeed boldly advance as far as motion, and the products of his art had power to transcend the materials of which they were made and to move in the dance; but it was impossible and absolutely out of the question for him to make statues that could speak. Yet the hands of Ethiopians discovered means to accomplish the impossible, and they overcame the inability of stone to speak. The story runs that Echo answered this Memnon when it spoke, uttering a mournful note in response to its mournful lament and returning a mimicking sound in response to its expressions of joy. The statue in question both lulled to rest the sorrows of Day and caused her to abandon her search for her son, as though the art of the Ethiopians were compensating her by means of the statue for the Memnon who had been snatched away from her by fate.

14

A poem inspired by a statue of Ramesses II, Percy Bysshe Shelley's *Ozymandias*

This sonnet by Shelly was originally published in 1818. The title, Ozymandias, *is the Greek name for Ramesses II (Dynasty XIX). Though the actual statue that inspired Shelley is uncertain, the end of the poem does paraphrase an inscription found on the base of a statue at the Ramesseum, the pharaoh's funerary temple located across the Nile from Luxor (Fig. 8). Diodorus Siculus (Library of History, 1.47.4, also the source for #6) records the inscription as: "King of Kings am I, Ozymandias. If anyone would know how great I am and where I lie, let him surpass one of my works."*

I met a traveler from an antique land
Who said: Two vast and trunkless legs of stone
Stand in the desert. Near them, on the sand,
Half sunk, a shattered visage lies, whose frown
And wrinkled lip, and sneer of cold command
Tell that its sculptor well those passions read
Which yet survive, stamped on these lifeless things,
The hand that mocked them and the heart that fed.
And on the pedestal these words appear:
"My name is Ozymandias, king of kings:
Look on my works, ye Mighty, and despair!"
Nothing beside remains. Round the decay
Of that colossal wreck, boundless and bare
The lone and level sands stretch far away.

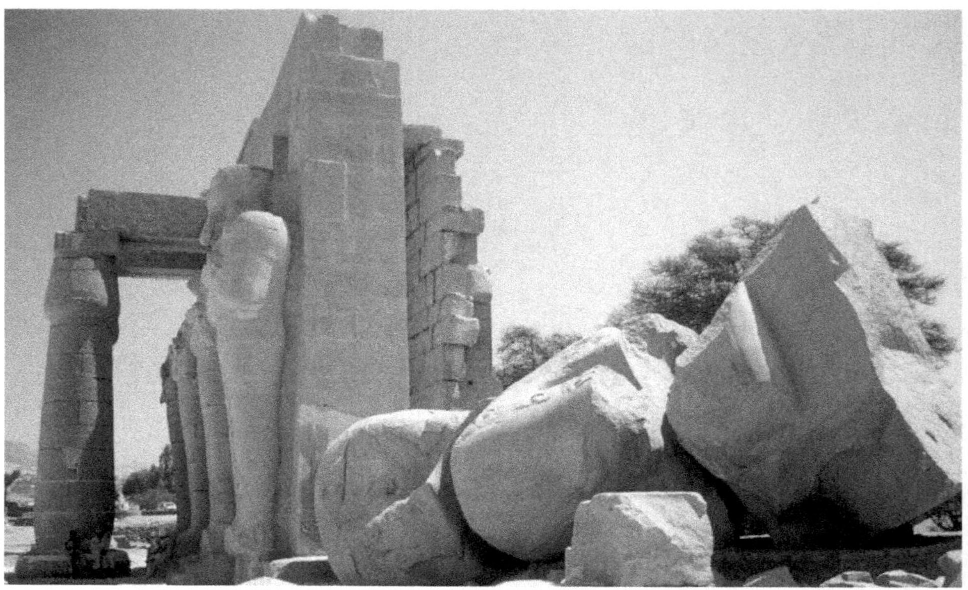

Fig. 8 The fallen statue of Ramesses II at the Ramesseum (Luxor, Egypt) that inspired Shelley's poem Ozymandias.

Image credits

Fig. 8: Copyright © Charlie Philips (CC BY-SA 2.0) at https://commons.wikimedia.org/wiki/File:The_%22Ozymandias_Collossus%22,_Ramesseum,_Luxor,_Egypt.jpg.

15

Ramesses III versus the Sea Peoples, an inscription from Medinet Habu

William Edgerton and John *Wilson, Historical Records of Ramses III: The texts in Medinet Habu*, volume I, Chicago, 1936, pp. 53–56.

Available online at the Oriental Institute of the University of Chicago

Credit: William Edgerton and John Wilson, "Ramesses III Versus the Sea Peoples," *Historical Records of Ramses III*, volume I: The texts in Medinet Habu, pp. 53-56. Copyright in the Public Domain.

Like so many pharaohs before him, Ramesses III recorded his reign's accomplishments on the walls of his funerary temple. Among these, inscribed on the second Pylon at Medinet Habu, is a long description of his battle with a group he identifies as the peoples of the sea. The Sea Peoples, we are told, came from various lands and banded together to ravage much of the Near East before attacking Egypt around 1188 BCE. The nearby pictorial relief portrays people in varying dress, armor, and hairstyles. Accompanying them are carts carrying women and children indicating more of a migration rather than invasion by an army. While Egypt won this battle, it will essentially lose the war since the New Kingdom collapses about 100 years later, marking the end of the great Bronze Age civilizations.

Year 8 under the majesty of Horus ... King of Upper and Lower Egypt, Lord of the Two lands ... Son of Re, Ramesses...

...The foreign countries made a conspiracy in their islands. The lands were removed and scattered in the fray at one time. No land could stand before their arms, from Hatti, Kode [Turkey], Carchemish [Syria], Arzawa, and Alashiya [Cyprus] on, cut off at one time. A camp [was set up] in one place in Amor [Amorite kingdom in northern Lebanon]. They desolated its people, and its land was like that which has never come into being. They were coming forward toward Egypt, while the flame was prepared before them.

Their confederation was the Peleset, Theker, Shekelesh, Denyen, and Weshesh, lands united. They laid their hands upon the lands to the [very] circuit of the earth, their hearts confident and trusting: 'Our plans will succeed!"

Now the heart of this god, the Lord of the Gods, was prepared, ready to ensnare them like birds. He made my strength to exist, while my plans succeed... I organized my frontier in Zahi, prepared before them the princes, the commanders of the garrisons, and the warriors. I caused the Nile mouth to be prepared like a strong wall with warships, galleys, and coasters, equipped, for they were manned completely from bow to stern with valiant warriors, with their weapons; the militia consisting of every picked man of Egypt, were like lions roaring upon the mountain tops. The chariotry consisted of runners, of picked men, of every good and capable chariot-warrior. Their horses were quivering in every part of their bodies, ready to crush the countries under their hoofs. I was the valiant Montu (i.e., warrior god), standing fast at their head, so that they might gaze upon the capturings of my two hands, King of Upper and Lower Egypt ... son of Re, Ramesses.

I am one who acts unrestrainedly, conscious of his strength, a hero, rescuing his army on the day of the fray.

As for those who reached my frontier, their seed is not, their heart and their soul are finished forever and ever. As for those who came forth together on the sea, the full flame was in front of them at the Nile mouths, while a stockade of lances surrounded them on the shore, (so that they were) dragged (ashore), hemmed in, prostrated on the beach, slain, and made into heaps from tail to head. Their ships and their goods were as if fallen into the water.

I made the lands turn back from mentioning Egypt; for when they pronounce my name in their land, then they are burned up. Since I have sat upon the throne of Harakhte and the Great Enchantress (crown) was fixed upon my head like Re, I have not let the countries behold the frontier of Egypt, to boast thereof to the Nine Bows (i.e., the enemies of Egypt). I have taken away their land, their frontiers being added to mine. Their chiefs and their tribespeople are mine with praise, for I am upon the ways of the plans of the All-Lord, my august, divine father, the Lord of the Gods.

Rejoice ye, Egypt, to the height of heaven, for I am the Ruler of the Two Lands upon the throne of Atum. The gods made me to be King in Egypt, to strengthen her, to repel for her the plans and hill-countries.

The Ancient Aegean

Although the people of Minoan Crete and Late Helladic Greece did have writing (Linear A and B), no truly literary texts have been discovered thus far in the Bronze Age Aegean. Aspects of these cultures, however, do seem to be remembered in myths written down by the Greeks hundreds of years later. In the myths below regarding Crete, a dim memory of the labyrinthine plan of the palaces, the importance of the bull, and the eventual fall of the Minoans to people from the Greek mainland can be detected.

16

Pasiphae and the Bull, from Apollodorus' *The Library* (*Bibliotheca* 3.1.3–4)

Apollodorus, *The Library*, volume I, translated by Sir James George Frazer, Loeb Classical Library, Cambridge, Harvard University Press, first printed 1921, reprinted 1967, pp. 303, 305, 307.

Available online at Perseus Project

The Bibliotheca *or* Library *of Apollodorus is a comprehensive summary of Greek mythology that dates to the second-first centuries BCE. The excerpt below recounts the Cretan story of King Minos' wife Pasiphae and the bull sacred to Poseidon (see Fig. 9). The craftsman and builder Daedalus, in particular, is remembered in later periods: for instance, the earliest Greek stone sculptural style, Daedalic, is named after him, and Gothic builders often incorporated a labyrinth pattern in the interior pavement of churches partially in his honor as the first architect.*

Asterius dying childless, Minos wished to reign over Crete, but his claim was opposed. So he alleged that he had received the kingdom from the gods, and in proof of it he said that whatever he prayed for would be done. And in sacrificing to Poseidon he prayed that a bull might appear from the depths, promising to sacrifice it when it appeared. Poseidon did send him up a fine bull, and Minos obtained the kingdom, but he sent the bull to the herds and sacrificed another. (Being the first to obtain the dominion of the sea, he extended his rule over almost all the islands.)

But angry at him for not sacrificing the bull, Poseidon made the animal savage, and contrived that Pasiphae should conceive a passion for it. In her love

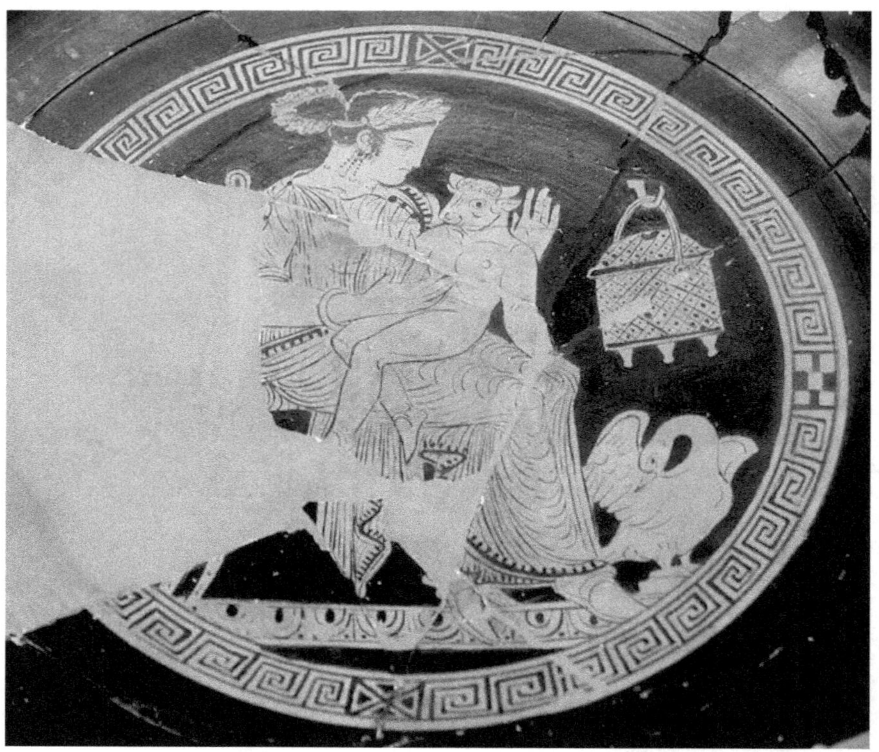

Fig. 9 Pasiphae holding baby Minotaur, red-figure kylix from Vulci, 4th century BCE, Paris, Cabinet des Médailles.

for the bull she found an accomplice in Daedalus, an architect, who had been banished from Athens for murder. He constructed a wooden cow on wheels, took it, hollowed it out in the inside, sewed it up in the hide of a cow which he had skinned, and set it in the meadow in which the bull used to graze. Then he introduced Pasiphae into it; and the bull came and coupled with it, as if it were a real cow. And she gave birth to Asterius, who was called the Minotaur. He had the face of a bull, but the rest of him was human; and Minos, in compliance with certain oracles, shut him up and guarded him in the Labyrinth. Now the Labyrinth which Daedalus constructed was a chamber "that with its tangled windings perplexed the outward way."

Image credits

Fig. 9: Bibi Saint-Pol, "Pasiphae and the Baby Minotaur," https://commons.wikimedia.org/wiki/File:Pasiphae_Minotauros_Cdm_Paris_DeRidder1066_detail.jpg. Copyright in the Public Domain.

17

Theseus and the Minotaur, from Apollodorus' *The Library* (*Bibliotheca* 3.15.8-E.1.10)

Apollodorus, *The Library*, volume II, translated by Sir James George Frazer, Cambridge, Harvard University Press, 1921, reprinted 1970, pp. 119, 123, 133, 135, 137.

Available online at Perseus Project

In this second passage from Apollodorus (see #16 as well) we are told how the Athenian hero Theseus goes to Crete and slays the Minotaur, perhaps a memory of the fall of the Minoan civilization. His father, Aegeus, gives his name to the Aegean Sea and the region that rings it.

[The Athenians] inquired of the oracle how they could be delivered; and the god answered them that they should give Minos whatever satisfaction he might choose. So they sent to Minos and left it to him to claim satisfaction. And Minos ordered them to send seven youths and the same number of damsels without weapons to be fodder for the Minotaur.

Aethra bore to Aegeus [the king of Athens] a son Theseus, and when he was grown up, he pushed away the rock and took up the sandals and the sword [tokens of his paternity left by his father Aegeus], and hastened on foot to Athens ... But Medea, being then wedded to Aegeus, plotted against him [Theseus] and persuaded Aegeus to beware of him as a traitor. And Aegeus, not knowing his own son, was afraid and sent him against the Marathonian bull. And when Theseus had killed it, Aegeus presented to him a poison which he had received the selfsame day from Medea. But just as the draught was about to be administered to him, he gave his father the sword, and on recognizing it Aegeus dashed the cup from his hands. And when Theseus was thus made known to his father and informed of the plot, he expelled Medea. And he [Theseus] was numbered among those who were to be sent as the third tribute to the Minotaur; or, as some affirm, he offered himself voluntarily. And as the ship had a black sail, Aegeus charged his son, if he returned alive, to spread white sails on the ship. And when he came to Crete, Ariadne, daughter of Minos, being amorously disposed to him, offered to help him if he would agree to carry her away to Athens and have her to wife. Theseus having agreed on oath to do so, she besought Daedalus to disclose the way out of the labyrinth. And at his suggestion she gave Theseus a clue when he went in; Theseus fastened it to the door, and, drawing it after him, entered in. And having found the Minotaur in the last part of the labyrinth, he killed him by smiting him with his fists; and drawing the clue after him made his way out again. And by night he arrived with Ariadne and the children at Naxos. There Dionysus fell in love with Ariadne and carried her off ... In his grief on account of Ariadne, Theseus forgot to spread white sails on his ship when he stood for port; and Aegeus, seeing from the acropolis the ship with a black sail, supposed that Theseus had perished; so he cast himself down and died.

18

The Funeral of Patroclus, from Homer's *Iliad* (23.131–262)

The Iliad of Homer, translated by Richmond Lattimore, University of Chicago Press, 1951, pp. 453–457.

A different translation is available online at Perseus Project

Homer is traditionally believed to have been an eighth century BCE poet who created The Iliad *and* The Odyssey. *These two epic poems relate events, personalities, and society of the Mycenaean or Late Helladic period. The* Iliad *in particular concerns a six-week period during the tenth year of the Trojan War when Achilles, insulted by Agamemnon, withdraws from the battlefield. One result is that Achilles' closest friend Patroclus is killed by the great Trojan warrior Hector. Most of book 23, portions of which are excerpted below, describes the funeral, burial, and games held in honor of Patroclus. These rites were not only often emulated in later centuries but the tradition of funeral games was largely responsible for the rise of athletic competitions in the Western world.*

...And they rose up and got into their armor
and stepped up, charioteer and sideman, into the chariots
with the horsemen in front, and behind them came on a cloud of foot-soldiers
by thousands; and in the midst his companions carried Patroclus.
They covered all the corpse under the locks of their hair, which they cut off
and dropped on him, and behind them brilliant Achilles held the head
sorrowing, for this was his true friend he escorted toward Hades....

...the close mourners stayed by the place and piled up the timber,
and built a pyre a hundred feet long this way and that way,
and on the peak of the pyre they laid the body, sorrowful
at heart; and in front of it skinned and set in order numbers
of fat sheep and shambling horn-curved cattle; and from all
great-hearted Achilles took the fat and wrapped the corpse in it
from head to foot, and piled up the skinned bodies about it.
Then he set beside him two-handled jars of oil and honey
leaning them against the bier, and drove four horses with strong necks
swiftly aloft the pyre with loud lamentations. And there were
nine dogs of the table that had belonged to the lord Patroclus.
Of these he cut the throats of two, and set them on the pyre;
and so also killed twelve noble sons of the great-hearted Trojans
with the stroke of bronze, and evil were the thoughts in his heart against them,
and let loose the iron fury of the fire to feed on them...

[The next day] with gleaming wine they put out the pyre that was burning,
as much as was still aflame, and the ashes dropped deep from it.
Then they gathered up the white bones of their gentle companion,
weeping, and put them into a golden jar with a double
fold of fat, and laid it away in his shelter, and covered it
with a thin veil; then laid out the tomb and cast down the holding walls
around the funeral pyre, then heaped loose earth over them
and piled the tomb, and turned to go away. But Achilles
held the people there, and made them sit down in a wide assembly,
and brought prizes for games out of his ships, cauldrons and tripods,
and horses and mules and the powerful high heads of cattle
and fair-girdled women and grey iron. First of all
he set forth the glorious prizes for speed of foot for the horsemen...

19

Polyphemus attacks Odysseus, from Homer's *Odyssey* (9.471–542)

The Odyssey *of Homer (who also wrote the* Iliad, *see #18) recounts the ten years of wanderings endured by the Greek hero Odysseus as he journeyed home to Ithaca after the fall of Troy. In the episode related below, a one-eyed giant or Cyclops called Polyphemus shuts Odysseus and his men into his cave with a giant stone and begins to eat them. In order to escape, the men blind the Cyclops (Fig. 10) and, the next day, strap themselves to the underbellies of Polyphemus' sheep, which he lets out each morning, and slip out of the cave undetected. Polyphemus pursues, hurling giant boulders after the fleeing men. Today, architecture incorporating boulders so large that only a giant could lift them is called cyclopean masonry.*

Quickly they went aboard the ship and sat to the oarlocks,
and sitting well in order dashed the oars in the gray sea.
But when I was as far from the land as a voice shouting
carries, I called aloud to the Cyclops, taunting him:
"Cyclops, in the end it was no weak man's companions
you were to eat by violence and force in your hollow
cave, and your evil deeds were to catch up with you, and be
too strong for you, hard one, who dared to eat your own guests
in your own house, so Zeus and the rest of the gods have punished you."

So I spoke, and still more the heart in him was angered.
He broke away the peak of a great mountain and let it
fly, and threw it in front of the dark-prowed ship by only
a little, it just failed to graze the steering oar's edge,
but the sea washed up in the splash as the stone went under, the tidal
wave it made swept us suddenly back from the open
sea to the mainland again, and forced us on shore. Then I
caught up in my hands the very long pole and pushed her
clear again, and urged my companions with words, and nodding
with my head, to throw their weight on the oars and bring us
out of the threatening evil, and leaned on and rowed hard.
But when we had cut through the sea to twice the previous distance,
again I started to call to Cyclops, but my friends about me checked me,
first one then another speaking, trying to soothe me:
"Hard one, why are you trying once more to stir up this savage
man, who just now threw his missile in the sea, forcing
our ship to the land again, and we thought once more we were finished;
and if he had heard a voice or any one of us speaking,
he would have broken all our heads and our ship's timbers
with a cast of a great jagged stone, so strong is his throwing."
So they spoke, but could not persuade the great heart in me,
but once again in the anger of my heart I cried to him:
"Cyclops, if any mortal man ever asks you who it was
that inflicted upon your eye this shameful blinding,
tell him that you were blinded by Odysseus, sacker of cities.
Laertes is his father, and he makes his home in Ithaca." ...

So I spoke, but he then called to the lord Poseidon
in prayer...

...and the dark-haired god heard him.
Then for the second time lifting a stone far greater
he whirled it and threw, leaning into the cast, his strength beyond measure,
and the stone fell behind the dark-prowed ship by only
a little, it just failed to graze the steering oar's edge,
and the sea washed up in the splash as the stone went under; the tidal
wave drove us along forward and forced us onto the island...

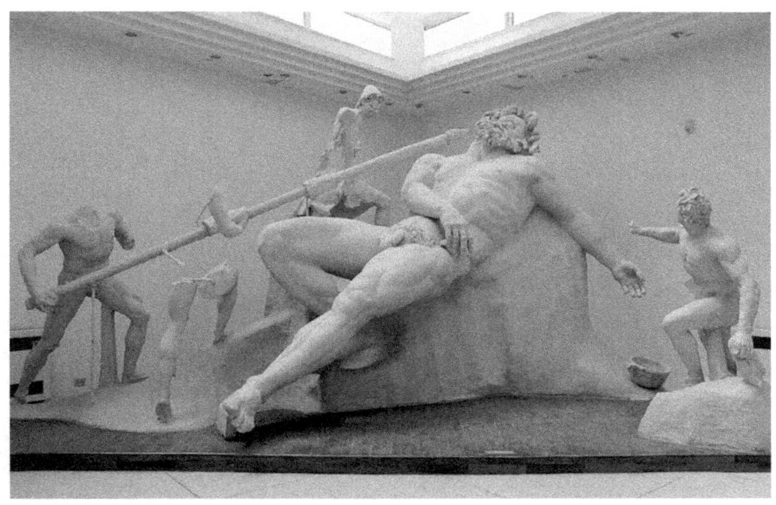

Fig. 10 Odysseus blinding the cyclops Polyphemus. Sculptural group from the grotto of Tiberius at Sperlonga, Italy (see also reading #43 Tiberius)

Image credits

Fig. 10: Copyright © Carol Raddato (CC BY-SA 2.0) at https://commons.wikimedia.org/wiki/File:The_Blinding_of_Polyphemus,_cast_reconstruction_of_the_group,_Sperlonga_(15155709202).jpg.

Classical Greece

20

On proportions and the Architectural Orders, from Vitruvius' *On Architecture (De architectura 3.1.3 and 4.1.3–10)*

Vitruvius, *The Ten Books on Architecture,* translated by Morris Hicky Morgan, Cambridge, Harvard University Press, 1914, reprinted Dover 1960, pp. 72–73, 102–106.

Available online at Perseus Project

Credit: Vitruvius, "On Proportions and the Architectural Orders," *The Ten Books on Architecture,* trans. Morris Hicky Morgan. Copyright in the Public Domain.

Active during the first century BCE, Vitruvius was an architect and engineer who dedicated his ten books On Architecture *to the Roman emperor Augustus. This treatise, after its rediscovery in the fifteenth century, was enormously influential—perhaps most famously for its inspiration of Leonardo Da Vinci's drawing of the Vitruvian Man (Fig. 11). In the ancient world man was, indeed, the measure of all things, right down to measurements in feet, palms, fingers, and cubits (the distance between the elbow and tip of the middle finger). Reproduced here are the sections that 1) inspired Leonardo's drawing and 2) explain the origins, again in terms of the human body, of the Classical architectural orders.*

ON PROPORTIONS AND THE VITRUVIAN MAN (3.1.3)

Similarly, in the members of a temple there ought to be the greatest harmony in the symmetrical relations of the different parts to the general magnitude of the whole. Then again, in the human body the central point is naturally the navel. For if a man be placed flat on his back, with his hands and feet extended, and a pair of compasses centered at his navel, the fingers and toes of his two hands and feet will touch the circumference of a circle described there from. And just as the human body yields a circular outline, so too a square figure may be found from it. For if we measure the distance from the

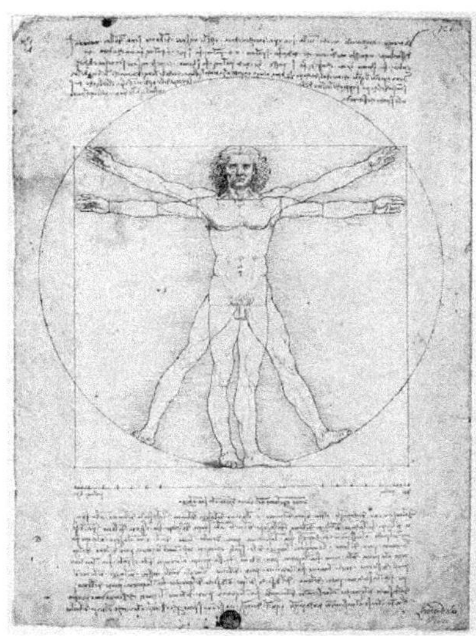

Fig. 11 Vitruvian Man by Leonardo Da Vinci (circa 1490), Academia of Venice.

soles of the feet to the top of the head, and then apply that measure to the outstretched arms, the breadth will be found to be the same as the height, as in the case of plane surfaces which are perfectly square.

ON THE COLUMNS OF THE DORIC, IONIC, AND CORINTHIAN ORDERS (4.1.3–10)

To the forms of their columns are due the names of the three orders, Doric, Ionic, and Corinthian, of which the Doric was the first to arise, and in early times. For Dorus, the son of Hellen and the nymph Phthia, was king of Achaea and all the Peloponnesus, and he built a fane [temple or sacred place], which chanced to be of this order, in the precinct of Juno at Argolis, a very ancient city, and subsequently others of the same order in the other cities of Achaea, although the rules of symmetry were not yet in existence. Later, the Athenians, in obedience to oracles of the Delphic Apollo, and with the general agreement of all Hellas, dispatched thirteen colonies at one time to Asia Minor, appointing leaders for each colony and giving the command-in-chief to Ion... Now these cities, after driving out the Carians and Lelegans, called that part of the world Ionia from their leader Ion, and there they set off precincts for the immortal gods and began to build fanes: first of all, a temple to Panionion Apollo such as they had seen in Achaea, calling it Doric because they had first seen that kind of temple built in the states of the Dorians. Wishing to set up columns in that temple, but not having rules for their symmetry, and being in search of some way by which they could render them fit to bear a load and also of a satisfactory beauty of appearance, they measured the imprint of a man's foot and compared this with his height. On finding that, in a man, the foot was one sixth of the height, they applied the same principle to the column, and reared the shaft, including the capital, to a height six times its thickness at its base. Thus the Doric column, as used in buildings, began to exhibit the proportions, strength, and beauty of the body of a man.

Just so afterwards, when they desired to construct a temple to Diana in a new style of beauty, they translated these footprints into terms characteristic of the slenderness of women, and thus first made a column the thickness of which was only one eighth of its height, so that it might have a taller look. At the foot they substituted the base in place of a shoe; in the capital they placed the volutes, hanging down at the right and left like curly ringlets, and ornamented its front with cymatia and with festoons of fruit arranged in place of hair, while they brought the flutes down the whole shaft, falling like the folds in the robes worn by matrons. Thus in the invention of the two different kinds of columns, they borrowed manly beauty, naked and unadorned, for the one, and for the other the delicacy, adornment, and proportions characteristic of women. It is true that posterity, having made progress in refinement and delicacy of feeling, and finding pleasure in more slender proportions, has established seven diameters of the thickness as the height of the Doric column, and nine as that of the Ionic. The Ionians, however, originated the order which is therefore named Ionic.

The third order, called Corinthian, is an imitation of the slenderness of a maiden; for the outlines and limbs of maidens, being more slender on account of their tender years, admit of prettier effects in the way of adornment. It is related that the original discovery of this form of capital was as follows. A freeborn maiden of Corinth, just of marriageable age, was attacked by an illness and passed away. After her burial, her nurse, collecting a few little things which used to give the girl pleasure while she was alive, put them in a basket, carried it to the tomb, and laid it on top thereof, covering it with a roof-tile so that the things might last longer in the open air. This basket happened to be placed just above the root of an acanthus. The acanthus root, pressed down meanwhile though it was by the weight, when springtime came round put forth leaves and stalks in the middle, and the stalks, growing up along the sides of the basket, and pressed out by the corners of the tile through the compulsion of its weight, were forced to bend into volutes at the outer edges. Just then Callimachus ... passed by this tomb and observed the basket with the tender young leaves growing round it. Delighted with the novel style and form, he built some columns after that pattern for the Corinthians, determined their symmetrical proportions, and established from that time forth the rules to be followed in finished works of the Corinthian order.

Image credits

21

On women's clothing: the Peplos and the Chiton, from Herodotus' *The Histories* (5.87)

Herodotus, *The Histories*, translated by Aubrey de Sélincourt, revised edition, London, Penguin Classics, 1972, p. 372.

A different translation is available online at Perseus Project

Herodotus, who wrote the passage on mummification (#11), here anecdotally explains why Athenian women stopped wearing the Dorian peplos and started wearing the chiton, which was popular in the eastern portion of the Greek world known as Ionia. Interestingly, after the Persian Wars there seems to have been a backlash against things associated with the east, and Greek women reverted back to the plainer peplos.

The Athenians admit that [after a battle with the people of Aegina] only one of their men returned to Attica alive... and even that sole survivor soon came to a bad end; for when he reached Athens with a report of the disaster, the wives of the other men who had gone with him to Aegina, in grief and anger that he alone should have escaped, crowded round him and thrust the brooches, which they used for fastening their dresses, into his flesh, each one, as she struck, asking him where her husband was. So he perished, and the Athenians were more horrified at this fate than at the defeat of their troops in Aegina. The only way they could punish their women for the dreadful thing they had done was to make them adopt Ionian dress; previously Athenian women had worn Dorian dress, very similar to the fashion at Corinth; now they were made to change to linen tunics, to prevent them from wearing brooches.

22

Pheidias' statue of Zeus Olympios, from Pausanias' *Description of Greece* (5.11.1–11)

Pausanias Description of Greece, volume II, translated by W.H.S. Jones, and H. A. Ormerod, Loeb Classical Library, Cambridge, Harvard University Press, 1918, reprinted 1966, pp. 437–445.

Available online at Perseus Project.

Pausanias was a Greek travel writer during the second century CE, nicknamed the Ancient Baedaker by modern scholars. Pheidias was famous for creating the gold and ivory (i.e., chryselephantine) statues of Athena Parthenos for the Athenian Parthenon and Zeus Olympios for the temple of Zeus at Olympia. The latter was considered one of the Seven Wonders of the Ancient World. Neither statue exists today, but textual descriptions, such as what follows by Pausanias, help us to visualize these masterpieces.

The god sits on a throne, and he is made of gold and ivory. On his head lies a garland which is a copy of olive shoots. In his right hand he carries a Victory, which, like the statue, is of ivory and gold; she wears a ribbon and—on her head—a garland. In the left hand of the god is a scepter, ornamented with every kind of metal, and the bird sitting on the scepter is the eagle. The sandals also of the god are of gold, as is likewise his robe. On the robe are embroidered figures of animals and the flowers of the lily. The throne is adorned with gold and with jewels, to say nothing of ebony and ivory. Upon it are painted figures and wrought images. There are four Victories, represented as dancing women, one at each foot of the throne, and two others at the base of each foot. On each of the two front feet are set Theban children ravished by sphinxes, while under the sphinxes Apollo and Artemis are shooting down the children of Niobe. Between the feet of the throne are four rods, each one stretching from foot to foot. The rod straight opposite the entrance has on it seven images; how the eighth of them disappeared nobody knows. These must be intended to be copies of obsolete contests, since in the time of Pheidias contests for boys had not yet been introduced. The figure of one binding his own head with a ribbon is said to resemble in appearance Pantarces, a stripling of Elis said to have been the love of Pheidias. Pantarces too won the wrestling-bout for boys at the eighty-sixth Festival. On the other rods is the band that with Heracles fights against the Amazons. The number of figures in the two parties is twenty-nine, and Theseus too is ranged among the allies of Heracles. The throne is supported not only by the feet, but also by an equal number of pillars standing between the feet. It is impossible to go under the throne, in the way we enter the inner part of the throne at Amyclae. At Olympia there are screens constructed like walls which keep people out...

On the uppermost parts of the throne Pheidias has made, above the head of the image, three Graces on one side and three Seasons on the other... The footstool of Zeus, called by the Athenians *thranion*, has golden lions and, in relief, the fight of Theseus against the Amazons, the first brave deed of the Athenians against foreigners. On the pedestal supporting the throne and Zeus with all his adornments are works in gold: the Sun mounted on a chariot, Zeus and Hera, Hephaestus, and by his side Grace. Close to her comes Hermes, and close to Hermes Hestia. After Hestia is Eros receiving Aphrodite as she rises from the sea, and Aphrodite is being crowned by Persuasion. There are also reliefs of Apollo with Artemis, of Athena and of Heracles; and near the end of the pedestal Amphitrite and Poseidon, while the Moon is driving what I think is a horse. Some have said that the steed of the goddess is a mule not a horse, and they tell a silly story about the mule.

I know that the height and breadth of the Olympic Zeus have been measured and recorded; but I shall not praise those who made the measurements, for even their records fall far short of the impression made by a sight of the image. Nay, the god himself according to legend bore witness to the artistic skill of Pheidias. For when the image was quite finished Pheidias prayed the god to show by a sign whether the work was to his liking. Immediately, runs the legend, a thunderbolt fell on that part of the floor where down to the present day the bronze jar stood to cover the place.

All the floor in front of the image is paved, not with white, but with black tiles. In a circle round the black stone runs a raised rim of Parian marble, to keep in the olive oil that is poured out. For olive oil is beneficial to the image at Olympia, and it is olive oil that keeps the ivory from being harmed by the marshiness of the Altis. On the Athenian Acropolis the ivory of the image they call the Maiden is benefited, not by olive oil, but by water. For the Acropolis, owing to its great height, is over-dry, so that the image, being made of ivory, needs water or dampness. When I asked at Epidaurus why they pour neither water nor olive oil on the image of Asclepius, the attendants at the sanctuary informed me that both the image of the god and the throne were built over a cistern.

23

On the Periclean Building Program, from Plutarch's *Life of Pericles* (12.3–13.3)

Plutarch's Lives, volume III, translated by Bernadotte Perrin, Loeb Classical Library, Cambridge, Harvard University Press, 1916, reprinted 1958, pp. 37, 39, 41.

Available online at Perseus Project and LacusCurtius

In the latter part of the first century CE, Greek historian Plutarch wrote a series of parallel biographies that paired Greek and Roman historical figures on the basis of character. For instance, the fifth century BCE Greek statesman and general Pericles is compared to the third century BCE Roman politician and general Fabius Maximus. The section reproduced below describes what is arguably one of the most important contributions to Western art: the Periclean building program on the Athenian acropolis.

For his part, Pericles would instruct the people that it owed no account of their moneys to the allies provided it carried on the war for them and kept off the Barbarians; 'not a horse do they furnish,' said he, 'not a ship, not a hoplite, but money simply; and this belongs, not to those who give it, but to those who take it, if only they furnish that for which they take it in pay. And it is but meet that the city, when once she is sufficiently equipped with all that is necessary for prosecuting the war, should apply her abundance to such works as, by their completion, will bring her everlasting glory, and while in process of completion will bring that abundance into actual service, in that all sorts of activity and diversified demands arise, which rouse every art and stir every hand, and bring, as it were, the whole city under pay, so that she not only adorns, but supports herself as well from her own resources'...

The materials to be used were stone, bronze, ivory, gold, ebony, and cypress-wood; the arts which should elaborate and work up these materials were those of carpenter, molder, bronze-smith, stone-cutter, dyer, worker in gold and ivory, painter, embroiderer, embosser, to say nothing of the forwarders and furnishers of the material, such as factors, sailors and pilots by sea, and, by land, wagon-makers, trainers of yoked beasts, and drivers. There were also rope-makers, weavers, leather-workers, road-builders, and miners. And since each particular art, like a general with the army under his separate command, kept its own throng of unskilled and untrained laborers in compact array, to be as instrument unto player and as body unto soul in subordinate service, it came to pass that for every age, almost, and every capacity the city's great abundance was distributed and scattered abroad by such demands.

So then the works arose, no less towering in their grandeur than inimitable in the grace of their outlines, since the workmen eagerly strove to surpass themselves in the beauty of their handicraft. And yet the most wonderful thing about them was the speed with which they rose. Each one of them, men thought, would require many successive generations to complete it, but all of them were fully completed in the heyday of a single administration … And it is true that deftness and speed in working do not impart to the work an abiding weight of influence nor an exactness of beauty; whereas the time which is put out to loan in laboriously creating, pays a large and generous interest in the preservation of the creation. For this reason are the works of Pericles all the more to be wondered at; they were created in a short time for all time. Each one of them, in its beauty, was even then and at once antique; but in the freshness of its vigor it is, even to the present day, recent and newly wrought. Such is the bloom of perpetual newness, as it were, upon these works of his, which makes them ever to look untouched by time, as though the unfaltering breath of an ageless spirit had been infused into them.

24

On the so-called Elgin Marbles, from the report of the Select Committee of the House of Commons

Report from the Select Committee of the House of Commons on the Earl of Elgin's Collection of Sculptured Marbles; &c., London, 1816, pp. 1, 3, 8, 70–77, 87–88.

Available online at HathiTrust Digital Library

'Elgin Marbles' refers to the architectural sculptures removed by Lord Elgin from the buildings on the Athenian Acropolis in the nineteenth century and offered for sale to the British Museum in London. The following are excerpts from the commission reviewing the material and critiques by several contemporary experts as to the sculptures' cultural value. It is interesting to note that the experts compare the Athenian sculptures to what was considered the best in ancient art at the time: the Laocoön, the Belvedere torso, and the Belvedere Apollo (see Fig. 12 & 14). The canon has since changed; only the Laocoön is consistently included in introductory texts today.

In recent years, the government of Greece has requested that the sculptures be returned to Athens and even built a new Acropolis Museum designed to house and display them. While it seems unlikely that the British Museum will accede to this request in the immediate future, concerns regarding repatriation of cultural objects and trade in illicit antiquities has led to the enactment of such laws as the 1954 Hague Convention for the Protection of Cultural Property in the Event of Armed Conflict and the 1970 UNESCO Convention on the Means of Prohibiting and Preventing the Illicit Import, Export and Transfer of Ownership of Cultural Property.

The SELECT COMMITTEE appointed to inquire whether it be expedient that the Collection mentioned in the Earl of Elgin's Petition, presented to The House on the 15th day of February last, should be purchased on behalf of The Public, and if so, what Price it may be reasonable to allow for the same...

The success of the British arms in Egypt [i.e., liberation of Egypt from Napoleonic forces], and the expected restitution of that province to the Porte [i.e., Ottoman government], wrought a wonderful and instantaneous change in the disposition of all ranks and descriptions of people towards our Nation. Universal benevolence and goodwill appeared to take place of suspicion and aversion. Nothing was refused which was asked; and Lord Elgin, availing himself of this favorable and unexpected alteration, obtained, in the summer of 1801, access to the Acropolis for general purposes, with permission to draw, model, and remove; to which was added, a special license to excavate in a particular place. Lord Elgin mentions in his evidence, that he was obliged to send from Athens to Constantinople for leave to remove a house; at the same time remarking, that, in point of fact, all permissions issuing from the Porte to any distant provinces, are little better than authorities to make the best bargain that can be made with the local magistracies. The applications upon this subject, passed in verbal conversations; but the warrants or *fermauns* were granted in writing, addressed to the chief authorities resident at Athens, to whom they were delivered, and in whose hands they remained: so that your Committee had no opportunity of learning from Lord Elgin himself their exact tenor, or of ascertaining in what terms they noticed, or allowed the displacing, or carrying away of these Marble(s)...

The testimony of several of the most eminent Artists in this kingdom, who have been examined, rates these Marbles in the very first class of ancient art, some placing them a little above, and others but very little below the Apollo Belvidere [Fig. 14], the Laocoön, and the Torso of the Belvidere [Fig. 12]. They speak of them with admiration and enthusiasm...

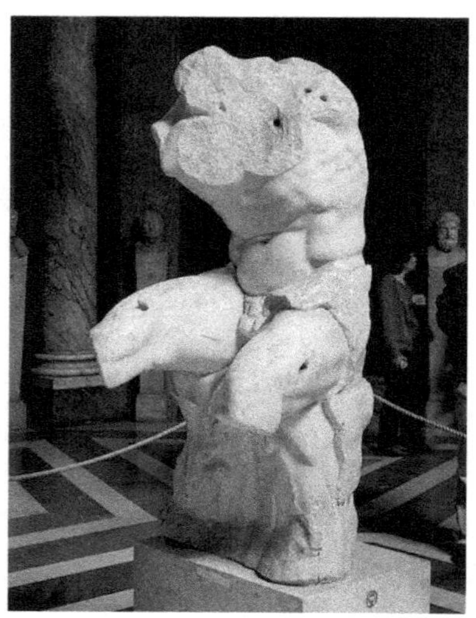

Fig. 12 Belvedere torso, 1st century BCE, Vatican Museum.

JOHN FLAXMAN, ESQUIRE, R. A. called in, and Examined

Are you well acquainted with the Elgin collection of marbles?—Yes, I have seen them frequently, and I have drawn from them; and I have made such enquiries as I thought necessary concerning them respecting my art.

In what class do you hold them, as compared with the first works of art which you have seen before?—The Elgin Marbles are mostly basso-relievos [Italian for bas relief or low relief], and the finest works of art I have seen. Those in the Pope's Museum, and the other galleries of Italy, were the Laocoön, the Apollo Belvidere; and the other most celebrated works of antiquity were groups and statues. These differ in the respect that they are chiefly basso-relievos, and fragments of statuary. With respect to their excellence, they are the most excellent of their kind that I have seen; and I have every reason to believe that they were executed by Pheidias, and those employed under him, or the general design of them given by him at the time the Temple was built; as we are informed he was the artist principally employed by Pericles and his principal scholars, mentioned by Pliny, Alcamenes, and about four others immediately under him; to which he adds a catalogue of seven or eight others, who followed in order; and he mentions their succeeding Pheidias, in the course of twenty years. I believe they are the works of those artists; and in this respect they are superior almost to any of the works of antiquity, excepting the Laocoön and Toro Farnese [=Farnese Bull], because they are known to have been executed by the artists whose names are recorded by the ancient authors. With respect to the beauty of the basso-relievos, they are as perfect nature as it is possible to put into the compass of the marble in which they are executed, and that of the most elegant kind. There is one statue also which is called a Hercules or Theseus [Fig. 13], of the first order of merit. The fragments are finely executed; but I do not, in my own estimation, think their merit is as great.

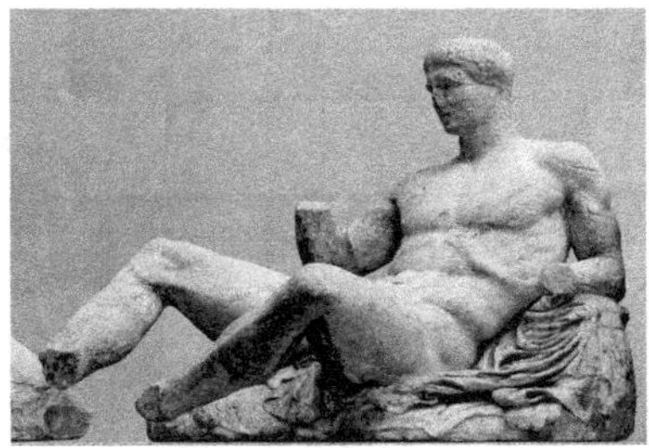

Fig. 13 Elgin marbles, East pediment Parthenon, reclining figure identified as Dionysos or Herakles or Theseus. British Museum, London.

What fragments do you speak of?—Several fragments of women; the groups without their heads.

You do not mean the metopes?—No, those statues which were in the east and west pediments originally.

In what estimation do you hold the Theseus [Fig. 13], as compared with the Apollo Belvidere [Fig. 14] and the Laocoön?—If you would permit me to compare it with a fragment I will mention, I should estimate it before the Torso Belvidere. [Fig. 12]

As compared with the Apollo Belvidere, in what rank do you hold the Theseus?—For two reasons, I cannot at this moment very correctly compare them in my own mind. In the first place, the Apollo Belvidere is a divinity of a higher order than the Hercules; and therefore I cannot so

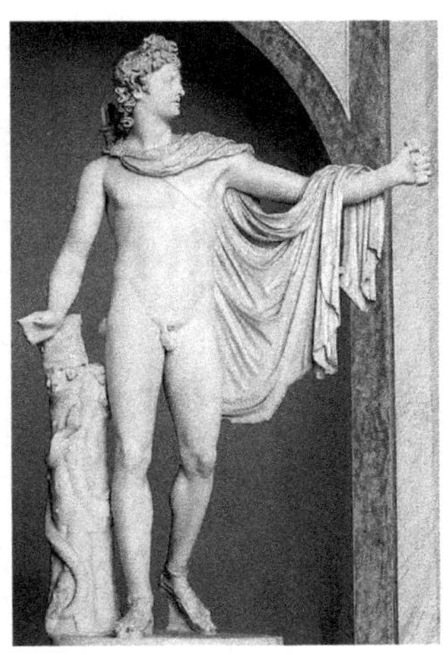

Fig. 14 Apollo Belvedere, Roman copy of 4th century BCE original, Vatican Museum.

well compare the two. I compared the Hercules with a Hercules before, to make the comparison more just. In the next place, the Theseus is not only on the surface corroded by the weather; but the head is in that impaired state that I can scarcely give an opinion upon it; and the limbs are mutilated. To answer the question, I should prefer the Apollo Belvidere certainly, though I believe it is only a copy.

Does the Apollo Belvidere partake more of ideal beauty than the Theseus?—In my mind it does decidedly; I have not the least question of it.

Do you think that increases its value?—Yes, very highly. The highest efforts of art in that class have always been the most difficult to succeed in, both among ancients and moderns, if they have succeeded in it.

Supposing the state of the Theseus to be perfect, would you value it more as a work of art than the Apollo?—No, I should value the Apollo for the ideal beauty before any male statue I know.

Although you think it is a copy?—I am sure it is a copy; the other is an original, and by a first rate artist.

The Committee is very anxious to know the reason you have for stating so decidedly your opinion that the Apollo is a copy?—There are many reasons; and I am afraid it would be troublesome to the Committee to go through them. The general appearance of the hair, and the mantle of the Apollo Belvidere, is in the style more of bronze than of marble...

Do you think it of great consequence to the progress of art in Britain, that this Collection should become the property of the Public?—Of the greatest importance, I think; and I always have thought so as an individual.

Do you conceive practically, that any improvement has taken place in the state of the arts in this country, since this Collection has been open to the Public?—Within these last twenty years, I think sculpture has improved in a very great degree, and I believe my opinion is not singular; but unless I was to take time to reflect upon the several causes, of which that has been the consequence, I cannot pretend to answer the question: I think works of such prime importance could not remain in the country without improving the public taste and the taste of the artists.

In what class do you hold the metopes as compared with the frieze?—I should think, from a parity of reasoning adopted between the metopes and the flat basso-relievos with that adopted between the Apollo Belvidere and the Theseus or Hercules, the metopes are preferable to the flat basso-relievos, inasmuch as the heroic style is preferable to that of common nature.

Should you have judged the metopes to be of very high antiquity if you had seen them, not knowing from what temple they were brought?—I should certainly have taken them to be of the age to which they are attributed, the age of Pheidias.

What characteristic marks do you observe of high antiquity, as compared with the other works of antiquity?—In the first place, I observe a particular classification of the parts of the body; and I have adverted to the medical writer of that age, Hippocrates, and find that the distinctions of the body, when they have been taken from the finest nature in the highest state of exercise, and in the best condition in all respects, which might be expected from those who possessed great personal beauty and cultivated habits of living, most likely to produce it, and who were accustomed to see it frequently in public exercises; this classification, which they appeared to prefer, is conformable to the distinctions in the statues... In a few words, the form of the body has a classification of a simple kind in a few parts, such as I find in the ancient anatomists, and such as are common in the outlines of the painted Greek vases: besides, as far as I can judge from our documents of antiquity, the painted Greek vases for example, those that come nearer to the time in which these Marbles are believed to be produced, are conceived in the same character, and drawn in the same manner.

Did not that classification continue much later than the time of Pericles?—Yes, it did continue later, but it became more complicated, and in some cases more geometrical.

Does the anatomy of these figures agree with the anatomy of the Laocoön or of the Toro Farnese?—They agree most with the Toro Farnese. I cannot judge very accurately of that at this time, for it was about to be removed from Rome at the time I was there, and it is very much broken. In respect to the Laocoön, I believe it to be a very posterior work, done after a time when considerable discoveries had been made in anatomy in the Alexandrian school; which I think had been communicated not only among physicians, but among artists all over Greece; and in the Laocoön the divisions are much more numerous.

Do you observe any considerable difference in the conformation of the horses, between the metopes and the procession [on the frieze]?—It is to be recollected, both in the metopes and the procession, that different hands have been employed upon them, so that it is difficult, unless I had them before me, to give a distinct opinion, particularly as the horses in the metopes have not horses heads; I do not think I can give a very decided opinion upon it, but in general the character appears to me very much the same.

Should you have judged the metopes and the frieze to be of the same age, if they had not come from the same temple?—Yes, undoubtedly I should.

Have you ever looked at this Collection, with a view to its value in money?—I never have; but I conceive that the value in money must be very considerable, judging only from the quantity of sculpture in it; the question never occurred to me before this morning, but it appears to me that there is a quantity of labor equal to three or four of the greatest public monuments that have lately been erected; and I think it is said either in Chandler's Inscriptions or in Stuart's Athens, that the temple cost a sum equal to £500,000...

CHARLES ROSS, ESQUIRE, R. A. called in, and Examined

Are you well acquainted with the Elgin Marbles?—Yes.

In what class of art do you reckon them?—The finest that I have ever seen.

Do you think any figures in Lord Elgin's Collection equal to the Apollo Belvidere and the Laocoön?—I think they are superior in my judgment.

Which do you consider as superior?—The Theseus and the River God, and the Torsos also; there are one or two of them, but they are very much mutilated.

In what class of art do you reckon the metopes?—The metopes I do not think so fine as the rest of the bas reliefs.

Do you think the metopes are of the same antiquity as the frieze and other parts?—Yes, I suppose they are.

Do you reckon the frieze of the Procession in the highest class of art?—Yes; they are in a superior style; I should say they were jewels.

In what class do you reckon the draped female figures?—One in particular is a very fine thing, I think.

Generally speaking, in what class do you place them?—In the very first.

Have you looked at this Collection, with a view to its money value?—Never.

Have you seen the Greek Marbles lately brought to the British Museum?—Yes.

In what class do you place them, as compared with the basso relievos of the frieze?—I consider them materially inferior to any of those of Lord Elgin's.

Do you think them of the same antiquity, or later or earlier?—I have never thought about that.

Do you think it of great consequence to the progress of art in this Country, that this Collection should become the property of the Public?—I think it is; it is the first Collection in the world, I think. I wrote a note to my friend Canova, at Paris, as an inducement for him to come over, saying, If he had not seen Lord Elgin's marbles, he had seen nothing yet; and when he saw them, he was satisfied they were as fine things as he had ever seen.

Image credits

25

Famous sculptors: Polykleitos, Lysippus, and Praxiteles, from Pliny the Elder's *Natural History*

K. Jex-Blake and E. Sellers, *The Elder Pliny's Chapters on the History of Art*, New York, Macmillan, 1896, revised reprinted Ares 1976, pp. 43, 45, 51, 53, 193, 195.

Available online at Internet Archive

Pliny the Elder, a Roman of the first century CE, is the author of a 37-volume encyclopedia called the Naturalis Historia. *Chapters 34–36 of this monumental work focus on famous Classical sculptors and painters and, as such, is our earliest history of Western art. His death from fumes inhaled while observing the eruption of Mt. Vesuvius is described in selection #40, a letter written by his nephew, Pliny the Younger.*

ON POLYKLEITOS, *NH* 34.55

Polykleitos of Sikyon was a pupil of Hagelaidas. He made an athlete binding the diadem about his head, which was famous for the sum of one hundred talents [circa £21,000 in 1976] which it realized. This *diadoumenos* has been described as 'a man, yet a boy', the *doryphoros* or spear-bearer as 'a boy, yet a man.' He also made the statue which sculptors call the 'canon,' referring to it as to a standard from which they can learn the first rules of their art. He is the only man who is held to have embodied the principles of his art in a single work ... He is considered to have brought the scientific knowledge of statuary to perfection, and to have systematized the art of which Pheidias had revealed the possibilities. It was his peculiar characteristic to represent his figures resting their weight on one leg.

ON LYSIPPUS, *NH* 34.65

His chief contributions to the art of sculpture are said to consist in his vivid rendering of the hair, in making the heads smaller than older artists had done, and the bodies slimmer and with less flesh, thus increasing the apparent height of his figures. There is no word in Latin for the canon of symmetry which he was so careful to preserve, bringing innovations which had never been thought of before into the square canon of the older artists, and he often said that the difference between himself and them was that they represented men as they were, and he as they appeared to be. His chief characteristic is extreme delicacy of execution even in the smallest details.

PRAXITELES AND THE APHRODITE OF KNIDOS, *NH* 36.20–21

Famous not only among the works of Praxiteles, but throughout the whole world, is the Aphrodite which multitudes have sailed to Knidos to look upon. He had offered two statues of Aphrodite for sale at the same time, the second being a draped figure, which for that reason was preferred by the people of Kos with whom lay the first choice; the price of the two figures was the same, but they flattered themselves they were giving proof of a severe modesty. The rejected statue, which was bought by the people of Knidos, enjoys an immeasurably greater reputation. King Nikomedes subsequently wished to buy it from them, offering to discharge the whole of their public debt, which was enormous. They, however, preferred to suffer the worst that could befall, and they showed their wisdom, for by this statue Praxiteles made Knidos illustrious. It stands in a small shrine, open all round so that the statue, which was made, as is believed, under the direct inspiration of the goddess, can be seen from every side, nor is there any point of view from which it is less admirable than from another.

26

The Amazon sculpture competition, from Pliny the Elder's *Natural History* (35.53)

K. Jex-Blake and E. Sellers, *The Elder Pliny's Chapters on the History of Art*, New York, Macmillan, 1896, revised reprinted Ares 1976, p. 41.

Available online at Internet Archive

This charming story about a sculptural competition in the late fifth century BCE has been equated with several Amazon statues that were much copied in antiquity (Fig. 15–17). While five artists are named, Kydon is probably a textual error for Kresilas of Kydonia, and the fifth artist Phradmon is essentially unattested elsewhere. The remaining three artists are each linked to a particular Amazon statue type: The Mattei type is usually ascribed to Pheidias (compare it to the Amazons on the Strangford shield), the Lansdowne to Polykleitos (compare it to his Spearbearer), and the Capitoline to Kresilas (compare it to his Perikles bust).

The most famous artists, although born at some distance of time from each other, still came into competition, since each had made a statue of an Amazon, to be dedicated in the temple of Artemis at Ephesus, when it was decided that the prize should be awarded to the one which the artists themselves, who were on the spot, declared to be the best. This proved to be the statue which each artist placed second to his own, namely that of Polykleitos; the statue of Pheidias was second, that of Kresilas third, Kydon's fourth, and Phradmon's fifth.

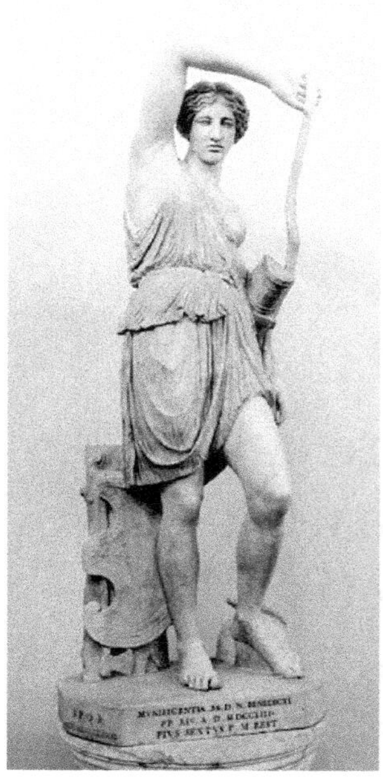

Fig. 15 Amazon, Mattei type (Pheidias?), Capitoline Museum, Rome

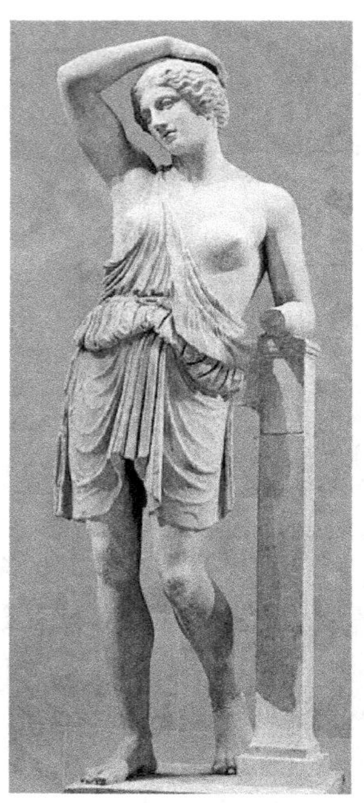

Fig. 16 Amazon, Lansdowne or Sciarra or Berlin type (Polykleitos?), Metropolitan Museum, New York.

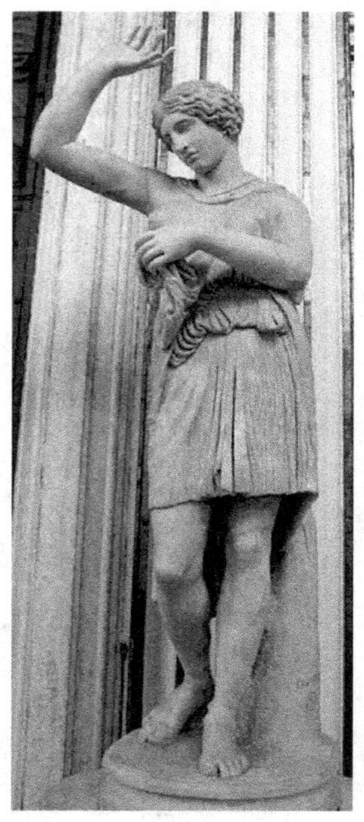

Fig. 17 Amazon, Capitoline or Sosikles type (Kresilas?), Capitoline Museum, Rome.

Image credits

Fig. 15: Copyright © Cåsver (CC BY-SA 2.0) at https://commons.wikimedia.org/wiki/File:Gladiatrix,_(Amazon),_Female_gladiator.jpg.

Fig. 16: Copyright © Maire-Lan Nguyen (CC BY-SA 2.5) at https://commons.wikimedia.org/wiki/File:Wounded_Amazon_Met_32.11.4_01.jpg.

Fig. 17: Copyright © Sailko (CC BY-SA 3.0) at https://commons.wikimedia.org/wiki/File:Statua_di_Amazzone_ferita_di_Sosikles,_da_policleto_(V_sec._ac.)_01.JPG.

27

The Mutilation of the Herms, from Thucydides' *History of the Peloponnesian War* (6.27–29, 53, 60)

Thucydides, with an English Translation by Charles Forster Smith, volume III, Loeb Classical Library, New York, Putnam Sons, 1921, pp. 231, 233, 235, 275, 277, 287, 289.

Available online at Google Books

Herms (in Greek herma, plural hermai or hermae), human-headed ithyphallic pillars, marked boundaries, roads, and passageways; they were particularly popular in Athens (Fig. 18). While the form originated in Greece, it was later adopted by the Romans, and revived in the Renaissance in the form of 'term' figures and Atlantes. In 415 BCE, just prior to launching the ambitious Sicilian expedition, Athenians awoke one morning to find that a large number of these Herms had been defaced overnight. Enemies of the expedition's leader, Alcibiades, used Athenian anger over the vandalism as a pretext to accuse him of other acts of impiety. What seems almost like a prank to us had far-reaching consequences including, indirectly, the trial in 399 BCE of Alcibiades' friend Socrates. He too was accused of impiety and corruption of the young and was eventually sentenced to death by hemlock. Thucydides, a contemporary of these events, details here what happened in the days immediately after the Herms were mutilated.

But in the meantime the stone statues of Hermes in the city of Athens— they are the pillars of square construction which according to local custom stand in great numbers both in the doorways of private houses and in sacred places—nearly all had their faces mutilated on the same night. No one knew the perpetrators, but great rewards were publicly offered for their detection;

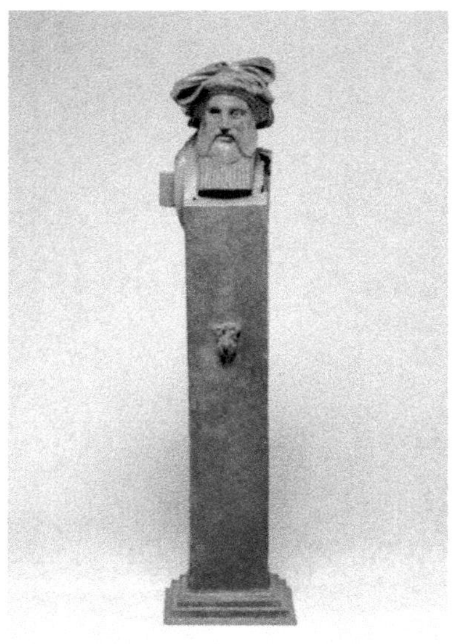

Fig. 18 Bronze and ivory herm of Dionysos, from Asia Minor, 2nd century BCE, Getty Villa Collection.

and it was voted, besides, that if anyone, citizen or stranger or slave, knew of any other profanation that had been done, whoever would, might fearlessly give information. The matter was taken very seriously; for it seemed to be ominous for the expedition and to have been done withal in furtherance of a conspiracy with a view to a revolution and the overthrow of the democracy.

Accordingly, information was given by certain metics [=resident aliens] and serving-men, not indeed about the statues of Hermes, but to the effect that before this there had been certain mutilations of other statues perpetrated by younger men in drunken sport, and also that the mysteries were being performed in private houses in mockery; and Alcibiades, among others, was implicated in the charges. They were taken up by those who were most jealous of him as an obstacle in the way of their secure preeminence among the people; and these men, thinking that if they could get rid of him they would have first place, magnified the matter and shouted that both the mockery of the mysteries and the mutilation of the Hermae had been committed with a view to the overthrow of the democracy, and that there was none of these things but had been done in collusion with him, citing as further proofs other instances of his undemocratic lawlessness of conduct.

He defended himself at the time against the informers' charges, and was ready before sailing—for already the preparations had been completed—to be tried on the question of his having done any of these things, and if he had been guilty of any of them to pay the penalty, but demanded that if he were acquitted he should keep his command. And he protested that they should not accept slanderous charges against him in his absence, but should put him to death at once if he were guilty, and that it was wiser not to send him at the head of so great an army, under such an imputation, until they had decided the question. But his enemies, fearing that the army might be favorable to him if he were brought to trial at once and that the populace might be lenient, inasmuch as it favored him because it was through his influence that the Argives and some of the Mantineans were taking part in the campaign, were eager to postpone the trial, suborning other orators who insisted that he should sail now and not delay the departure of the expedition, but that he should come back and be tried at an appointed time. Their purpose was to have a more slanderous charge—and this they would find it easier to procure in his absence—and then to have him recalled and brought home for trial. So it was determined that Alcibiades should sail.

[After some time, the Athenians sent a ship] for Alcibiades—to order him to come home and make his defense against the charges which the city was bringing—and for certain of the soldiers also, some of them having been denounced with him as guilty of profanation with regard to the mysteries, and some also with regard to the Hermae. For after the armament sailed, the Athenians had been pursuing with no less zeal than before their investigation of what had been done in the matter of the mysteries as well as the Hermae; and as they did not test the witnesses, but in their state of suspicion accepted everything, on the credit of bad men they arrested and threw into prison very excellent citizens, thinking it more expedient to sift the matter to the bottom and find out the truth, than that anybody, even one reputed to be good and accused only through the villainy of an informer, should escape without close investigation...

With these events in mind and recalling all that they knew of them by report, the Athenian people were in an ugly temper at this time and suspicious towards those who had incurred blame in the matter of the mysteries; and the whole thing seemed to them to have been done in connection with a conspiracy that aimed at an oligarchy or a tyranny. So when, in consequence of their anger on this account, many noteworthy men were already imprisoned and there seemed to be no end of the matter, but day by day they were growing more savage and still more men were being arrested, then at last one of the men in confinement, the one in fact who was regarded as the most guilty, was persuaded by one of his fellow-prisoners to make a confession, which may have been true or not; for there are conjectures both ways, but no one has been able, either then or afterwards, to tell the truth with reference to those who did the deed. At any rate, the other prisoner persuaded this man that, even if he had not done the deed, he ought, having first secured immunity, to save himself and free the state from the prevailing suspicion; for, he said, he had a surer chance of saving his life by confessing, with the promise of immunity, than by denying the charge and undergoing trial. Accordingly he informed against himself and others in the affair of the Hermae; and the people, delighted at getting the truth, as they thought, and already making much ado that they should not discover those who were plotting against the democracy, at once set free the informer and with him all the rest whom he had not denounced; but with regard to those who were accused they instituted trials and put to death all who had been arrested, while on those who had fled they passed sentence of death, offering a reward in money to anyone who killed them. And in all this it was uncertain whether those who suffered had not been punished unjustly; the city at large, however, at the time was clearly benefited.

Image credits

Fig. 18: J. Paul Getty Museum, "Herm of Dionysos," http://www.getty.edu/art/collection/ objects/8640/attributed-to-the-workshop-of-boethos-of-kalchedon-herm-of-dionysos-greek-about- 200-100-bc/.

28

A Poem inspired by the Sosibios Vase, John Keats' *Ode on a Grecian Urn*

"Ode on a Grecian Urn," written in 1819 and published in 1820, is a poem many of us read in high school. It describes figures on an ancient Greek vase, frozen in time and space, without season or sound. What is not commonly known is that the poet John Keats was inspired by actual ancient vases and we have his signed traced sketch of one in particular: a marble volute krater that once belonged to Louis XIV, king of France, and is now in the Louvre (Fig. 19–20). It was created around 50 BCE during the late Roman Republic and is signed by the Athenian artist Sosibios. The relief decoration shows Artemis and Hermes leading a Bacchic procession toward a burning altar.[1]

Thou still unravish'd bride of quietness!
Thou foster-child of Silence and slow Time,
Sylvan historian, who canst thus express
A flowery tale more sweetly than our rhyme:
What leaf-fringed legend haunts about thy shape
Of deities or mortals, or of both,
In Tempe or the dales of Arcady?
What men or gods are these? What maidens loath?
What mad pursuit? What struggle to escape?
What pipes and timbrels? What wild ecstasy?

---

1   See www.louvre.fr/en/oeuvre-notices/volute-krater

Heard melodies are sweet, but those unheard
Are sweeter; therefore, ye soft pipes, play on;
Not to the sensual ear, but, more endear'd,
Pipe to the spirit ditties of no tone:
Fair youth, beneath the trees, thou canst not leave
Thy song, nor ever can those trees be bare;
Bold Lover, never, never canst thou kiss,
Though winning near the goal—yet, do not grieve;
She cannot fade, though thou hast not thy bliss,
Forever wilt thou love, and she be fair!

Ah, happy, happy boughs! that cannot shed
Your leaves, nor ever bid the Spring adieu;
And, happy melodist, unwearied,
Forever piping songs forever new;
More happy love! more happy, happy love!
Forever warm and still to be enjoy'd,
Forever panting and forever young;
All breathing human passion far above,
That leaves a heart high sorrowful and cloy'd,
A burning forehead and a parching tongue.

Who are these coming to the sacrifice?
To what green altar, O mysterious priest,
Lead'st thou that heifer lowing at the skies,
And all her silken flanks with garlands drest?
What little town by river or sea-shore,
Or mountain-built with peaceful citadel,
Is emptied of its folk, this pious morn?
And, little town, thy streets for evermore
Will silent be; and not a soul to tell
Why thou art desolate, can e'er return.

O Attic shape! Fair attitude! with brede
Of marble men and maidens overwrought,
With forest branches and the trodden weed;
Thou, silent form! dost tease us out of thought
As doth eternity: Cold Pastoral!
When old age shall this generation waste,
Thou shalt remain, in midst of other woe
Than ours, a friend to man, to whom thou say'st,
"Beauty is truth, truth beauty,"—that is all
Ye know on earth, and all ye need to know.

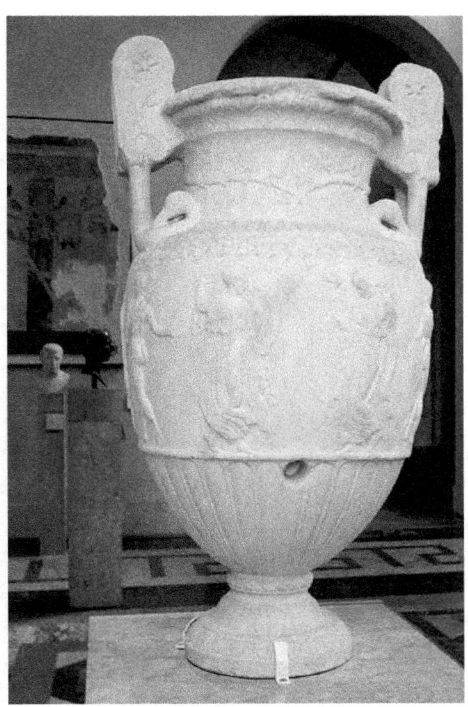

Fig. 19 The Sosibios vase, Louvre.

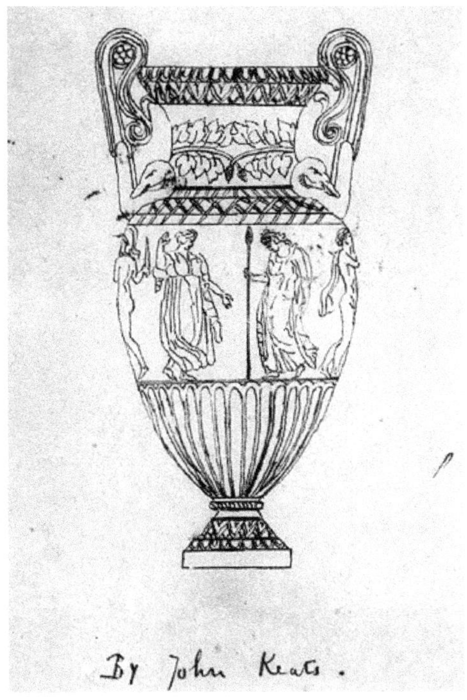

Fig. 20 A drawing traced by Keats from an engraving of the Sosibios vase, circa 1819, Louvre.

Image credits

29

The Mausoleum of Halikarnasos, from Pliny the Elder's *Natural History* (36.30)

K. Jex-Blake and E. Sellers, *The Elder Pliny's Chapters on the History of Art*, New York, Macmillan, 1896, revised reprinted Ares 1976, pp. 201, 203.

Available online at Internet Archive

Here, in another section from Pliny the Elder's chapters on the history of art (see also #25 and #26), is a description of the monumental tomb of Mausolaus. Mausolaus was a fourth century BCE Persian satrap or governor of the region around Halikarnasos, a town on the southwestern coast of present-day Turkey. Not only did several famous Greek sculptors work on the decoration of this tomb, but it was also listed among the Seven Wonders of the Ancient World and is the origin of the word "mausoleum," used to describe any fancy or elaborate place of burial.

Bryaxis, Tomotheos, and Leochares were rivals and contemporaries of Skopas, and must be mentioned with him, as they worked together on the Mausoleum. This is the tomb erected by Artemisia in honor of her husband Mausolos, prince of Karia, who died in the second year of the hundred and seventh Olympiad [351 BCE], and its place among the seven wonders of the world is largely due to these great sculptors. The length of the south and north sides is 163 feet; the two facades are shorter, and the whole perimeter is 440 feet; its height is 25 cubits [37.5 feet], and it has thirty-six columns. This colonnade is called a pteron. The sculptures of the eastern front are carved by Skopas, those on the north by Bryaxis, on the south by Timotheos, and on the west by Leochares. The queen died before the work was finished, but the artists carried it through to the end, deeming that it would be an abiding monument of their own glory and of the glory of art, and to this day they compete for the prize. A fifth sculptor also worked on the monument. Above the colonnade is a pyramid, of the same height as the lower structure, consisting of twenty-four retreating steps rising into a cone. On the apex stands a chariot and four horses in marble made by Pythis. Including this the height is 140 feet.

30

The stage scenery of Agatharchus, in Vitruvius' *On Architecture* (*De architectura* 7 praef 11)

In addition to cloth and objects made from precious or fragile materials, an entire array of visual language has been lost to us: any sort of performance, orations and speeches, public funerals (see #38), parades, and triumphs (see #47), to name just a few. Here, in another excerpt from Vitruvius (see #20), we read about stage scenery created by the fifth century BCE painter Agatharchus and what sounds remarkably like the beginnings of one-point perspective.

In the first place Agatharchus, in Athens, when Aeschylus was bringing out a tragedy, painted a scene, and left a commentary about it. This led Democritus and Anaxagoras to write on the same subject, showing how, given a center in a definite place, the lines should naturally correspond with due regard to the point of sight and the divergence of the visual rays, so that by this deception a faithful representation of the appearance of buildings might be given in painted scenery, and so that, though all is drawn on a vertical flat facade, some parts may seem to be withdrawing into the background, and others to be standing out in front.

31

A philosopher inspired by ancient Greek drama and mythology, Friedrich Nietzsche's *The Birth of Tragedy*

Friedrich Nietzsche, *The Birth of Tragedy*, translated with an Introduction and Notes by Douglas Smith, Oxford University Press, 2000, p. 19.

A different translation is available online at Internet Archive

Ancient Greek drama is utilized and reinterpreted to this day in Western culture. One example is The Birth of Tragedy, *the first treatise of the German philosopher Friedrich Nietzsche (published in 1872). In it he argues that the epitome of aesthetic creation was fifth century BCE Greek tragedy because it fused two elements: the Apollonian and the Dionysian. Reproduced below is the opening paragraph of the original publication where he starts to outline what these elements represented to him. Nietzsche's thinking impacted such later cultural commentators as Carl Jung, Michel Foucault, and artist Mark Rothko.*

We will have achieved much for the discipline of aesthetics when we have arrived not only at the logical insight but also at the immediate certainty of the view that the continuing development of art is tied to the duality of the *Apollonian* and the *Dionysian*; just as procreation depends on the duality of the sexes, which are engaged in a continual struggle interrupted only by temporary periods of reconciliation. These names are borrowed from the Greeks who revealed the profound secret doctrines of their view of art to the discerning mind precisely not in concepts but rather in the insistently clear forms of their pantheon. To both of their artistic deities, Apollo and Dionysus, is linked our knowledge that in the Greek world there existed a tremendous opposition in terms of origin and goals, between the Apollonian art of the sculptor and the imageless Dionysian art of music: these two very different drives run in parallel with one another, for the most part diverging openly with one another and continually stimulating each other to ever new and more powerful births, in order to perpetuate in themselves the struggle of that opposition only apparently bridged by the shared name of 'art'; until finally, through a metaphysical miracle of the Hellenic 'will', they appear coupled with one another and through this coupling at last give birth to a work of art which is as Dionysian as it is Apollonian – Attic tragedy.

32

The Death of Laocoön, from Virgil's *Aeneid* (2.40–56 and 2.195–233)

The Aeneid of Virgil, translated by Theodore C. Williams, Boston, Houghton Mifflin Co., 1938, pp. 39–40, 47–48.

Available online at Perseus Project

Credit: Virgil, "The Death of Laocoön," *The Aeneid of Virgil,* trans. Theodore C. Williams. Copyright in the Public Domain.

Virgil wrote the epic poem The Aeneid, *which describes the foundation of Rome by the Trojan hero Aeneas, between 30–19 BCE. The passage below relates the story of Laocoön who warned the Trojans not to bring the wooden horse left by the Greeks into the gates of Troy. The gods, however, had decided the war would end and sent snakes to kill and hence silence Laocoön. A highly influential statue of this subject was found during the Renaissance, with Michelangelo in attendance, near the ruins of Nero's Golden House in Rome (see #43).*

Then from the citadel, conspicuous,
Laocoön, with all his following choir,
hurried indignant down; and from afar
thus hailed the people: "O unhappy men!
What madness this? Who deems our foemen fled?
Think ye the gifts of Greece can lack for guile?
Have ye not known Ulysses? The Achaean
hides, caged in yonder beams; or this is reared
for enginery on our proud battlements,
to spy upon our roof-tops, or descend
in ruin on the city. 'Tis a snare.
Trust not this horse, O Troy, whate'er it bode!
I fear the Greeks, though gift on gift they bear."

So saying, he whirled with ponderous javelin
a sturdy stroke straight at the rounded side
of the great, jointed beast. A tremor struck
its towering form, and through the cavernous womb
rolled loud, reverberate rumbling, deep and long.
If heaven's decree, if our own wills, that hour,
had not been fixed on woe, his spear had brought
a bloody slaughter on our ambushed foe,
and Troy were standing on the earth this day!
O Priam's towers, ye were unfallen still...

But now a vaster spectacle of fear
burst over us, to vex our startled souls.
Laocoön, that day by cast of lot
priest unto Neptune, was in act to slay
a huge bull at the god's appointed fane.
Lo! o'er the tranquil deep from Tenedos
appeared a pair (I shudder as I tell)
of vastly coiling serpents, side by side,
stretching along the waves, and to the shore
taking swift course; their necks were lifted high,
their gory dragon-crests o'er topped the waves;
all else, half seen, trailed low along the sea;
while with loud cleavage of the foaming brine
their monstrous backs wound forward fold on fold.
Soon they made land; the furious bright eyes
glowed with ensanguined fire; their quivering tongues
lapped hungrily the hissing, gruesome jaws.
All terror-pale we fled. Unswerving then
the monsters to Laocoön made way.
First round the tender limbs of his two sons
each dragon coiled, and on the shrinking flesh
fixed fast and fed. Then seized they on the sire,
who flew to aid, a javelin in his hand,
embracing close in bondage serpentine
twice round the waist; and twice in scaly grasp
around his neck, and o'er him grimly peered
with lifted head and crest; he, all the while,
his holy fillet fouled with venomous blood,
tore at his fetters with a desperate hand,
and lifted up such agonizing voice,
as when a bull, death-wounded, seeks to flee
the sacrificial altar, and thrusts back
from his doomed head the ill-aimed, glancing blade.
then swiftly writhed the dragon-pair away
unto the templed height, and in the shrine
of cruel Pallas sure asylum found
beneath the goddess' feet and orbed shield.

Such trembling horror as we ne'er had known
seized now on every heart. "Of his vast guilt
Laocoön," they say, "receives reward;
for he with most abominable spear
did strike and violate that blessed wood.
Yon statue to the temple! Ask the grace
of glorious Pallas!" So the people cried
in general acclaim.

The Etruscans

33

On the behavior of Etruscan Women, from Timaeus and Theopompus (in Athenaeus' *Deipnosophistae* 12.14 or 517d-518a.G)

The Deipnosophists or Banquet of the Learned of Athenaeus, translated by C. D. Yonge, volume III, London, Henry G. Bohn, 1854, pp. 829–830.

Available online at Internet Archive

While reading this rather scurrilous account of the Etruscans, keep in mind that the authors are the product of a very different culture, one that strictly regulated access to women. Both Timaeus and Theopompus were Greeks of the fourth century BCE, although their comments on Etruscans are only known from Athenaeus, who lived almost five hundred years later in the third century CE. Imagine how such men might describe the behavior of present-day women.

And among the Tyrrhenians [=Etruscans], who carry their luxury to an extraordinary pitch, Timaeus, in his first book, relates that the female servants wait on the men in a state of nudity. And Theopompus, in the forty-third book of his History states, "that it is a law among the Tyrrhenians that all their women should be in common and that the women pay the greatest attention to their persons, and often practice gymnastic exercises, naked, among the men, and sometimes with one another; for it is not accounted shameful for them to be seen naked. And that they sup not with their own husbands, but with anyone who happens to be present; and they pledge [i.e., toast] whomever they please in their cups, and that they are wonderful women to drink, and very handsome. And that the Tyrrhenians bring up all the children that are born, no one knowing to what father each child belongs; and the children, too, live in the same manner as those who have brought them up, having feasts very frequently, and being intimate with all the women. Nor is it reckoned among the Tyrrhenians at all disgraceful either to do or suffer anything in the open air, or to be seen while it is going on; for it is quite the custom of their country and they are so far from thinking it disgraceful, that they even say, when the master of the house is indulging his appetites, and anyone asks for him, that he is doing so and so, using the coarsest possible words for his occupation. But when they are together in parties of companions or relations, they act in the following manner. First of all, when they have stopped drinking, and are about to go to sleep, while the lights are still burning, the servants introduce sometimes courtesans, and sometimes beautiful boys, and sometimes [their] women; and when they have enjoyed them, they proceed to acts of still grosser licentiousness; and they indulge their appetites, and make parties on purpose, sometimes keeping one another in sight, but more frequently making tents around the beds, which are made of plaited laths with cloths thrown over them. And the objects of their love are usually women; still they are not invariably as particular as they might be; and they are very beautiful, as is natural for people to be who live delicately, and who take great care of their persons." And all the barbarians who live towards the west smooth their bodies by rubbing them with pitch, and by shaving them; and among the Tyrrhenians there are many shops in which this trade is practiced, and many artists whose sole employment it is, just as there are barbers among us...

34

Touring Etruscan tombs, excerpts from D. H. Lawrence's *Etruscan Places*

D. H. Lawrence, *Etruscan Places*, London, Martin Secker, 1933, pp. 11–12, 23–24, 27–28, 67–70

Available online at Project Gutenberg Australia and Internet Archive

Although David Herbert Lawrence is perhaps best known for his novel Lady Chatterley's Lover *which was banned in the United States until 1959, he was a prolific British poet, novelist, playwright, and essayist. During the spring of 1927 he traveled with his friend Earl Brewster through the countryside of Tuscany and penned a series of essays. In these essays, a selection of which is reproduced here, he contrasts what he viewed as the exuberant world of the Etruscans with contemporary Italy under the dictatorship of Mussolini. His appreciation of the Etruscans is a welcome contrast to the opinions expressed in reading #33.*

CERVATERI. The Etruscans, as everyone knows, were the people who occupied the middle of Italy in early Roman days and whom the Romans, in their usual neighborly fashion, wiped out entirely in order to make room for Rome with a very big R. They couldn't have wiped them all out, there were too many of them. But they did wipe out the Etruscan existence as a nation and a people. However, this seems to be the inevitable result of expansion with a big E, which is the sole *raison d'étre* of people like the Romans. Now, we know nothing about the Etruscans except what we find in their tombs. There are references to them in Latin writers. But of first-hand knowledge we have nothing except what the tombs offer.

So to the tombs we must go: or to the museums containing the things that have been rifled from the tombs.

Myself, the first time I consciously saw Etruscan things, in the museum at Perugia, I was instinctively attracted to them. And it seems to be that way. Either there is instant sympathy, or instant contempt and indifference. Most people despise everything B.C. that isn't Greek, for the good reason that it ought to be Greek if it isn't. So Etruscan things are put down as a feeble Greco-Roman imitation...

There is a queer stillness and a curious peaceful repose about the Etruscan places I have been to, quite different from the weirdness of Celtic places, the slightly repellent feeling of Rome and the old Campagna, and the rather horrible feeling of the great pyramid places in Mexico, Teotihuacan and Cholula, and Mitla in the south; or the amiably idolatrous Buddha places in Ceylon. There is a stillness and a softness in these great grassy mounds with their ancient stone girdles, and down the central walk there lingers still a kind of homeliness and happiness. True, it was a still and sunny afternoon in April, and larks rose from the soft grass of the tombs. But there was a stillness and a soothingness in all the air, in that sunken place, and a feeling that it was good for one's soul to be there...

The tomb called the Grotta Bella is interesting because of the low-relief carvings and stucco reliefs on the pillars and the walls round the burial niches and above the stone death-bed that goes round the tomb. The things represented are mostly warriors' arms and insignia: shields, helmets, corselets, greaves for the legs, swords, spears, shoes, belts, the necklace of the noble: and then the sacred drinking bowl, the sceptre, the dog who is man's guardian even on the death journey, the two lions that stand by the gateway of life or death, the triton, or merman, and the goose, the bird that swims on the waters and thrusts its head deep into the flood of the Beginning and the End. All these are represented on the walls. And all these, no doubt, were laid, the actual objects, or figures to represent them, in this tomb. But now nothing is left. But when we remember the great store of treasure that every notable tomb must have contained: and that every large tumulus covered several tombs: and that in the necropolis of Cerveteri we can still discover hundreds of tombs: and that other tombs exist in great numbers on the other side of the old city, towards the sea; we can have an idea of the vast mass of wealth this city could afford to bury with its dead, in days when Rome had very little gold, and even bronze was precious.

The tombs seem so easy and friendly, cut out of rock underground. One does not feel oppressed, descending into them. It must be partly owing to the peculiar charm of natural proportion which is in all Etruscan things of the unspoilt, unromanized centuries. There is a simplicity, combined with a most peculiar, free-breasted naturalness and spontaneity, in the shapes and movements of the underworld walls and spaces, that at once reassures the spirit. The Greeks sought to make an impression, and Gothic still more seeks to impress the mind. The Etruscans, no. The things they did, in their easy centuries, are as natural and as easy as breathing. They leave the breast breathing freely and pleasantly, with a certain fullness of life. Even the tombs. And that is the true Etruscan quality: ease, naturalness, and an abundance of life, no need to force the mind or the soul in any direction.

And death, to the Etruscan, was a pleasant continuance of life, with jewels and wine and flutes playing for the dance. It was neither an ecstasy of bliss, a heaven, nor a purgatory of torment. It was just a natural continuance of the fullness of life. Everything was in terms of life, of living.

TARQUINIA. It is the Tomb of Hunting and Fishing, so called from the pictures on the walls, and it is supposed to date from the sixth century B.C. It is very badly damaged, pieces of the wall have fallen away, damp has eaten into the colors, nothing seems to be left. Yet in the dimness we perceive flights of birds flying through the haze, with the draught of life still in their wings. And as we take heart and look closer we see the little room is frescoed all round with hazy sky and sea, with birds flying and fishes leaping, and little men hunting, fishing, rowing in boats. The lower part of the wall is all a blue-green of sea with a silhouette surface that ripples all round the room. From the sea rises a tall rock, off which a naked man, shadowy but still distinct, is beautifully and cleanly diving into the sea, while a companion climbs up the rock after him, and on the water a boat waits with rested oars in it, three men watching the diver, the middle man standing up naked, holding out his arms. Meanwhile a great dolphin leaps behind the boat, a flight of birds soars upwards to pass the rock, in the clear air. Above all, from the bands of color that border the wall at the top hang the regular loops of garlands, garlands of flowers and leaves and buds and berries, garlands which belong to maidens and to women, and which represent the flowery circle of the female life and sex. The top border of the wall is formed of horizontal stripes or ribands of color that go all round the room, red and black and dull gold and blue and primrose, and these are the colors that occur invariably. Men are nearly always painted a darkish red, which is the color of many Italians when they go naked in the sun, as the Etruscans went. Women are colored paler, because women did not go naked in the sun.

At the end of the room, where there is a recess in the wall, is painted another rock rising from the sea, and on it a man with a sling is taking aim at the birds which rise scattering this way and that. A boat with a big paddle oar is holding off from the rock, a naked man amidships is giving a queer salute to the slinger, a man kneels over the bows with his back to the others, and is letting down .a net. The prow of the boat has a beautifully painted eye, so the vessel shall see where it is going. In Syracuse you will see many a two-eyed boat today come swimming in to quay. One dolphin is diving down into the sea, one is leaping out. The birds fly, and the garlands hang from the border.

It is all small and gay and quick with life, spontaneous as only young life can be. If only it were not so much damaged, one would be happy, because here is the real Etruscan liveliness and naturalness. It is not impressive or grand. But if you are content with just a sense of the quick ripple of life, then here it is.

The little tomb is empty, save for its shadowy paintings. It had no bed of rock around it: only a deep niche for holding vases, perhaps vases of precious things. The sarcophagus on the floor, perhaps under the slinger on the end wall. And it stood alone, for this is an individual tomb, for one person only, as is usual in the older tombs of this necropolis.

In the gable triangle of the end wall, above the slinger and the boat, the space is filled in with one of the frequent Etruscan banqueting scenes of the dead. The dead man, sadly obliterated, reclines upon his banqueting couch with his fiat wine-dish in his hand, resting on his elbow, and beside him, also half risen, reclines a handsome and jeweled lady in fine robes, apparently resting her left hand upon the naked breast of the man, and in her right holding up to him the garland—the garland of the female festive offering. Behind the man stands a naked slave-boy, perhaps with music, while another naked slave is just filling a wine-jug from a handsome amphora or wine-jar at the side. On the woman's side stands a maiden, apparently playing the flute: for a woman was supposed to play the flute at classic funerals; and beyond sit two maidens with garlands, one turning round to watch the banqueting pair, the other with her back to it all. Beyond the maidens in the corner are more garlands, and two birds, perhaps doves. On the wall behind the head of the banqueting lady is a problematic object, perhaps a bird-cage.

The scene is natural as life, and yet it has a heavy archaic fullness of meaning. It is the death-banquet; and at the same time it is the dead man banqueting in the underworld; for the underworld of the Etruscans was a gay place. While the living feasted out of doors, at the tomb of the dead, the dead himself feasted in like manner, with a lady to offer him garlands and slaves to bring him wine, away in the underworld. For the life on earth was so good, the life below could but be a continuance of it.

This profound belief in life, acceptance of life, seems characteristic of the Etruscans. It is still vivid in the painted tombs. There is a certain dance and glamour in all the movements, even in those of the naked slave men. They are by no means downtrodden menials, let later Romans say what they will. The slaves in the tombs are surging with full life.

35

The plan of Etruscan temples, from Vitruvius' *On Architecture* (*De architectura* 4.7.1–2)

Vitruvius, *The Ten Books on Architecture*, translated by Morris Hicky Morgan, Loeb Classical Library, Cambridge, Harvard University Press, 1914, reprinted Dover 1960, pp. 120, 122.

Available online at Perseus Project

Credit: Vitruvius, "The Plan of Etruscan Temples," *The Ten Books on Architecture*, trans. Morris Hicky Morgan. Copyright in the Public Domain.

The only Etruscan structures to survive in any quantity are tombs and city walls, yet the architecture of this culture was quite influential on Roman forms. The only significant written account of Etruscan building types is by Vitruvius (see also #20, #30, and #41), who wrote in the first century BCE, some two centuries after their absorption into the Roman world. In this passage Vitruvius describes the arrangement of a typical Etruscan-style temple.

The place where the temple is to be built having been divided on its length into six parts, deduct one and let the rest be given to its width. Then let the length be divided into two equal parts, of which let the inner be reserved as space for the cellae, and the part next the front left for the arrangement of the columns.

Next let the width be divided into ten parts. Of these, let three on the right and three on the left be given to the smaller cellae, or to the alae if there are to be alae, and the other four devoted to the middle of the temple. Let the space in front of the cellae, in the pronaos, be marked out for columns thus: the corner columns should be placed opposite the antae on the line of the outside walls; the two middle columns, set out on the line of the walls which are between the antae and the middle of the temple; and through the middle, between the antae and the front columns, a second row, arranged on the same lines. Let the thickness of the columns at the bottom be one seventh of their height, their height one third of the width of the temple, and the diminution of a column at the top, one fourth of its thickness at the bottom.

36

Rome under the Etruscans, from Livy's *History of Rome* (*Ab urbe condita* 1.55–56)

Livy, *History of Rome*, volume I, Books I and II, with an English translation by B. O. Foster, Loeb Classical Library, Cambridge, Harvard University Press, 1919, pp. 191, 193.

Available online at Perseus Project

Livy's History of Rome *begins with the earliest foundation legends of the city in the eighth century BCE and continues through the reign of Augustus. Rome was actually ruled by several Etruscan kings before their expulsion in 509 BCE and they left an indelible mark on the city. Livy describes here two of their most significant structural contributions: the primary temple of the Romans on the Capitoline Hill known as the Capitoleum and the main sewer of the city or Cloaca Maxima (Fig. 21).*

[Tarquinius Superbus] next turned his attention to affairs in the city. Here his first concern was to build a temple of Jupiter on the Tarpeian Mount [i.e., the Capitoline Hill] to stand as a memorial of his reign and of his name, testifying that of the two Tarquinii, both kings, the father had made the vow and the son had fulfilled it ... [Shortly after clearing the hilltop] there followed a prodigy foretelling the grandeur of their empire: a human head, its features intact, was found, so it is said, by the men who were digging for the foundations of the temple. This appearance plainly foreshowed that here was to be the citadel of the empire and the head of the world, and such was the interpretation of the soothsayers, both those who were in the City and those who were called in from Etruria to consider the matter. This made the king all the more ready to spend money on the work...

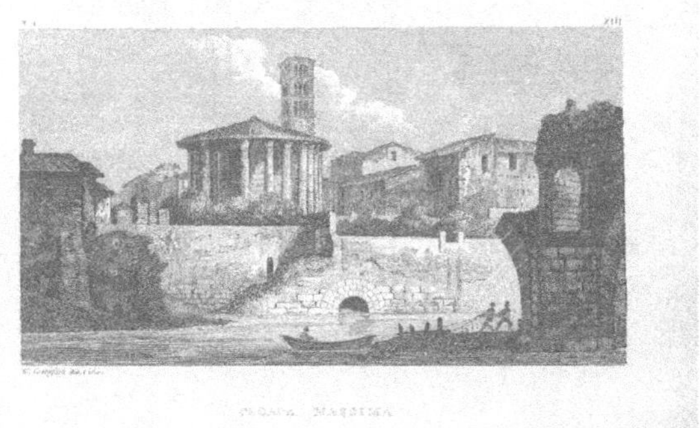

Fig. 21 The Cloaca Maxima or Great Sewer of Rome as it appeared in the 19th century. Temple of Hercules Victor above it. Ink drawing by G. Cottafavi.

Being intent upon completing the temple, the king called in workmen from every quarter of Etruria, and used for this purpose not only the state funds but laborers drawn from the commons. This work was far from light in itself, and was added to their military service. Yet the plebeians felt less abused at having to build with their own hands the temples of the gods, than they did when they came to be transferred to other tasks also, which, while less in show, were yet rather more laborious. I mean the erection of seats in the circus, and the construction underground of the Great Sewer, as a receptacle for all the offscourings of the City,—two works for which the new splendor of these days has scarcely been able to produce a match...

Image credits

37

Vulca of Veii and the decoration of the Capitoleum, from Pliny the Elder's *Natural History* (35.157–8)

K. Jex-Blake and E. Sellers, *The Elder Pliny's Chapters on the History of Art*, New York, Macmillan, 1896, revised reprinted Ares 1976, p. 181.

Available online at Internet Archive

The Capitoleum, an Etruscan-style temple dedicated to Jupiter, Juno and Minerva, was located on the Capitoline Hill in the center of ancient Rome. It was the locus of state sacrifices, where triumphal processions ended, and where the famous Capitoline She-wolf, another Etruscan creation, stood. Here Pliny describes how the temple was decorated, in what was an old way when he was writing, with Etruscan terracotta sculpture (Fig. 22).

The art of modeling, again, according to Varro, was developed in Italy, and more especially in Etruria, and Tarquin the Ancient summoned an artist called Vulca from Veii to make a statue of Jupiter for the Capitol. This statue was of clay and was therefore painted red; the four-horse chariots on the gables of the temple, which I have mentioned so often, were also of clay. Vulca further made the Hercules still known at Rome as 'the clay Hercules.' These were the most magnificent statues known in those days, and we have no reason to be ashamed of the men who worshipped deities of clay, and would not, even for their gods, change gold and silver into images. Effigies of clay still exist in different places, while gable ornaments in clay are still to be seen even at Rome as well as in provincial towns. The admirable execution of these figures, their artistic merits and their durability make them more worthy of honor than god, and they are at any rate more innocent.

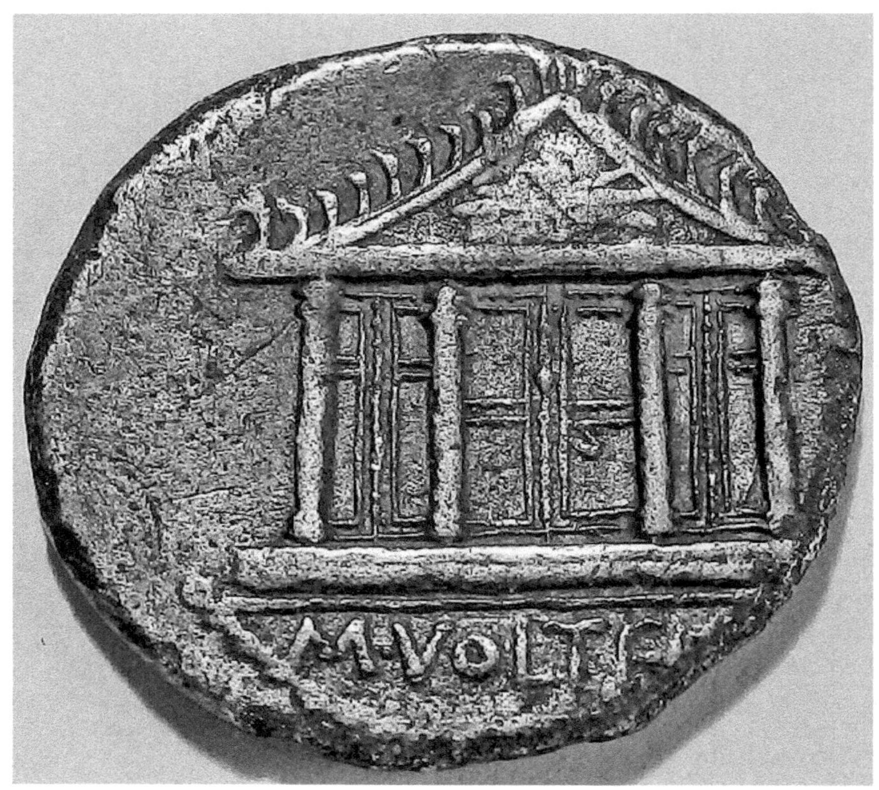

Fig. 22 Coin of 78 BCE showing the rebuilding of the Capitoleum after the original burned down in 83. It was rebuilt on the same plan but utilized more expensive material, including columns removed by Sulla from the temple of Zeus in Athens.

Image credits

Fig. 22: Copyright © Hermann Junghans (CC BY-SA 3.0 DE) at https://commons.wikimedia. org/wiki/File:Tempel_Jupiter_Optimus.JPG.

The Roman World

38

On early Roman Portraiture, from Polybius' *The Histories* (6.53)

The Histories of Polybius, translated from the text of F. Hultsch by Evelyn S. Shuckburgh, volume I, London, New York, Macmillan, 1889, reprinted Bloomington 1962, pp. 503–504.

Available online at Perseus Project

Credit: Polybius, "On Early Roman Portraiture," *The Histories of Polybius*, trans. Evelyn Shuckburgh. Copyright in the Public Domain.

Polybius, a Greek historian writing in the mid-second century BCE, is our earliest source for the Roman tradition of making ancestor portraits. How long it had been in existence before his time is unknown. The portraits themselves, as Pliny the Elder (see #25, #26, and #29) tells us in Natural History *35.2, were made of wax. Their display during public funeral processions paints quite a vivid picture.*

Whenever one of their illustrious men dies, in the course of his funeral, the body with all its paraphernalia is carried into the forum to the Rostra, as a raised platform there is called, and sometimes is propped upright upon it so as to be conspicuous, or, more rarely, is laid upon it. Then with all the people standing round, his son, if he has left one of full age and he is there, or, failing him, one of his relations, mounts the Rostra and delivers a speech concerning the virtues of the deceased, and the successful exploits performed by him in his lifetime.

By these means the people are reminded of what has been done, and made to see it with their own eyes,—not only such as were engaged in the actual transactions but those also who were not—and their sympathies are so deeply moved, that the loss appears not to be confined to the actual mourners, but to be a public one affecting the whole people. After the burial and all the usual ceremonies have been performed, they place the likeness of the deceased in the most conspicuous spot in his house, surmounted by a wooden canopy or shrine. This likeness consists of a mask made to represent the deceased with extraordinary fidelity both in shape and color. These likenesses they display at public sacrifices adorned with much care. And when any illustrious member of the family dies, they carry these masks to the funeral, putting them on men whom they thought as like the originals as possible in height and other personal peculiarities. And these substitutes assume clothes according to the rank of the person represented: if he was a consul or praetor, a toga with purple stripes; if a censor, whole purple if he had also celebrated a triumph or performed any exploit of that kind, a toga embroidered with gold.

These representatives also ride themselves in chariots, while the fasces and axes, and all the other customary insignia of the particular offices, lead the way, according to the dignity of the rank in the state enjoyed by the deceased in his lifetime; and on arriving at the Rostra they all take their seats on ivory chairs in their order.

There could not easily be a more inspiring spectacle than this for a young man of noble ambitions and virtuous aspirations. For can we conceive any one to be unmoved at the sight of all the likenesses collected together of the men who have earned glory, all as it were living and breathing? Or what could be a more glorious spectacle?

39

On the Roman craze for Greek art, from Plutarch's *Life of Marcellus* (21.1–5)

Plutarch's Lives, volume V, translated by Bernadotte Perrin, Loeb Classical Library, Cambridge, Harvard University Press, 1917, reprinted 1961, pp. 481, 493, 495.

Available online at Perseus Project

Another subject of one of Plutarch's biographies (see #23) is the third-century BCE Roman general Marcus Claudius Marcellus. Among his many military successes was the siege of the Greek city of Syracuse in Sicily. Here we are told how his plundering of the city started a craze for Greek art in Rome. Similar statements are also made by Livy (History of Rome 25.40.2–3 and 34.4.3–4, see #36). The cultural significance of this in terms of the history of Western art cannot be overemphasized, since it marked the beginning of Classical Greek influence on the Roman world and hence, in time, all of Europe.

When Marcellus was recalled by the Romans to the war in their home territories, he carried back with him the greater part and the most beautiful of the dedicatory offerings in Syracuse, that they might grace his triumph and adorn his city. For before this time Rome neither had nor knew about such elegant and exquisite productions, nor was there any love there for such graceful and subtle art; but filled full of barbaric arms and bloody spoils, and crowned roundabout with memorials and trophies of triumphs, she was not a gladdening or a reassuring sight, nor one for unwarlike and luxurious spectators ... Therefore with the common people Marcellus won more favor because he adorned the city with objects that had Hellenic grace and charm and fidelity; but with the elder citizens Fabius Maximus was more popular. For he neither disturbed nor brought away anything of this sort from Tarentum, when that city was taken, but while he carried off the money and the other valuables, he suffered the statues to remain in their places, adding the well-known saying: 'Let us leave these gods in their anger for the Tarentines.' And they blamed Marcellus, first, because he made the city odious, in that not only men, but even gods were led about in her triumphal processions like captives; and again, because, when the people was accustomed only to war or agriculture, and was inexperienced in luxury and ease, but, like the Heracles of Euripides, was "plain, unadorned, in a great crisis brave and true", he made them idle and full of glib talk about arts and artists, so that they spent a great part of the day in such clever disputation. Notwithstanding such censure, Marcellus spoke of this with pride even to the Greeks, declaring that he had taught the ignorant Romans to admire and honor the wonderful and beautiful productions of Greece.

40

On the eruption of Mount Vesuvius, from Pliny the Younger's *Letters* (6.16 & 6.20)

The Letters of the Younger Pliny, translated with an introduction by Betty Radice, London, Penguin Classics, 1969, pp.166–168, 170–173.

A different translation is available online at Project Gutenberg

The Younger Pliny (circa 61–113 CE) lost his father when he was quite young but was subsequently adopted by his uncle, the Elder Pliny and author of the Natural History *(see #25, #26, #29 and #37). When only eighteen years old, he witnessed and survived the eruption of Mount Vesuvius in 79 CE, but unfortunately his uncle did not. Here he gives a touching account of the death of his uncle and an eyewitness account of the eruption in two famous letters to the Roman historian Tacitus. For another of his letters, see #51.*

To Cornelius Tacitus

Thank you for asking me to send you a description of my uncle's death so that you can leave an accurate account of it for posterity; I know that immortal fame awaits him if his death is recorded by you. It is true that he perished in a catastrophe which destroyed the loveliest regions of the earth, a fate shared by whole cities and their people, and one so memorable that it is likely to make his name live forever: and he himself wrote a number of books of lasting value: but you write for all time and can still do much to perpetuate his memory. The fortunate man, in my opinion, is he to whom the gods have granted the power either to do something which is worth recording or to write what is worth reading, and most fortunate of all is the man who can do both. Such a man was my uncle, as his own books and yours will prove. So you set me a task I would choose for myself, and I am more than willing to start on it.

My uncle was stationed at Misenum, in active command of the fleet. On 24 August, in the early afternoon, my mother drew his attention to a cloud of unusual size and appearance. He had been out in the sun, had taken a cold bath, and lunched while lying down, and was then working at his books. He called for his shoes and climbed up to a place which would give him the best view of the phenomenon. It was not clear at that distance from which mountain the cloud was rising (it was afterwards known to be Vesuvius); its general appearance can best be expressed as being like an umbrella pine, for it rose to a great height on a sort of trunk and then split off into branches, I imagine because it was thrust upwards by the first blast and then left unsupported as the pressure subsided, or else it was borne down by its own weight so that it spread out and gradually dispersed. Sometimes it looked white, sometimes blotched and dirty, according to the amount of soil and ashes it carried with it. My uncle's scholarly acumen saw at once that it was important enough for a closer inspection, and he ordered a boat to be made ready, telling me I could come with him if I wished. I replied that I preferred to go on with my studies, and as it happened he had himself given me some writing to do.

As he was leaving the house he was handed a message from Rectina, wife of Tascius whose house was at the foot of the mountain, so that escape was impossible except by boat. She was terrified by the danger threatening her and implored him to rescue her from her fate. He changed his plans, and what he had begun in a spirit of inquiry he completed as a hero. He gave orders for the warships to be launched and went on board himself with the intention of bringing help to many more people besides Rectina, for this lovely stretch of coast was thickly populated. He hurried to the place which everyone else was hastily leaving, steering his course straight for the danger zone. He was entirely fearless, describing each new movement and phase of the portent to be noted down exactly as he observed them. Ashes were already falling, hotter and thicker as the ships drew near, followed by bits of pumice and blackened stones, charred and cracked by the flames: then suddenly they were in shallow water, and the shore was blocked by the debris from the mountain. For a moment my uncle wondered whether to turn back, but when the helmsman advised this he refused, telling him that Fortune stood by the courageous and they must make for Pomponianus at Stabiae. He was cut off there by the breadth of the bay (for the shore gradually curves round a basin filled by the sea) so that he was not as yet in danger, though it was clear that this would come nearer as it spread. Pomponianus had therefore already put his belongings on board ship, intending to escape if the contrary wind fell. This wind was of course full in my uncle's favor, and he was able to bring his ship in. He embraced his terrified friend, cheered and encouraged him, and thinking he could calm his fears by showing his own composure, gave orders that he was to be carried to the bathroom. After his bath he lay down and dined; he was quite cheerful, or at any rate he pretended he was, which was no less courageous.

Meanwhile on Mount Vesuvius broad sheets of fire and leaping flames blazed at several points, their bright glare emphasized by the darkness of night. My uncle tried to allay the fears of his companions by repeatedly declaring that these were nothing but bonfires left by the peasants in their terror, or else empty houses on fire in the districts they had abandoned. Then he went to rest and certainly slept, for as he was a stout man his breathing was rather loud and heavy and could be heard by people coming and going outside his door. By this time the courtyard giving access to his room was full of ashes mixed with pumice-stones, so that its level had risen, and if he had stayed in the room any longer he would never have got out. He was wakened, came out and joined Pomponianus and the rest of the household who had sat up all night. They debated whether to stay indoors or take their chance in the open, for the buildings were now shaking with violent shocks, and seemed to be swaying to and fro as if they were torn from their foundations. Outside on the other hand, there was the danger of falling pumice-stones, even though these were light and porous; however, after comparing the risks they chose the latter. In my uncle's case one reason outweighed the other, but for the others it was a choice of fears. As a protection against falling objects they put pillows on their heads tied down with cloths.

Elsewhere there was daylight by this time, but they were still in darkness, blacker and denser than any ordinary night, which they relieved by lighting torches and various kinds of lamp. My uncle decided to go down to the shore and investigate on the spot the possibility of any escape by sea, but he found the waves still wild and dangerous. A sheet was spread on the ground for him to lie down, and he repeatedly asked for cold water to drink. Then the flames and smell of sulfur which gave warning of the approaching fire drove the others to take flight and roused him to stand up. He stood leaning on two slaves and then suddenly collapsed, I imagine because the dense fumes choked his breathing by blocking his windpipe which was constitutionally weak and narrow and often inflamed. When daylight returned on the 26th—two days after the last day he had seen—his body was found intact and uninjured, still fully clothed and looking more like sleep than death.

Meanwhile my mother and I were at Misenum, but this is not of any historic interest, and you only wanted to hear about my uncle's death. I will say no more, except to add that I have described in detail every incident which I either witnessed myself or heard about immediately after the event, when reports were most likely to be accurate. It is for you to select what best suits your purpose, for there is a great difference between a letter to a friend and history written for all to read.

To Cornelius Tacitus

So the letter which you asked me to write on my uncle's death has made you eager to hear about the terrors and hazards I had to face when left at Misenum, for I broke off at the beginning of this part of my story. 'Though my mind shrinks from remembering ... I will begin' [paraphrase of *Aeneid* 11:12, see also #32]

After my uncle's departure I spent the rest of the day with my books as this was my reason for staying behind. Then I took a bath, dined and then dozed fitfully for a while. For several days past there had been earth tremors which were not particularly alarming because they are frequent in Campania: but that night the shocks were so violent that everything felt as if it were not only shaken but overturned. My mother hurried into my room and found me already getting up to wake her if she were still asleep. We sat down in the forecourt of the house, between the buildings and the sea close by. I don't know whether I should call this courage or folly on my part (I was only seventeen at the time) but I called for a volume of Livy [see #36] and went on reading as if I had nothing else to do. I even went on with the extracts I had been making. Up came a friend of my uncle's who had just come from Spain to join him. When he saw us sitting there and me actually reading, he scolded us both—me for my foolhardiness and my mother for allowing it. Nevertheless, I remained absorbed in my book.

By now it was dawn, but the light was still dim and faint. The buildings round us were already tottering, and the open space we were in was too small for us not to be in real and imminent danger if the house collapsed. This finally decided us to leave the town. We were followed by a panic-stricken mob of people wanting to act on someone else's decision in preference to their own (a point in which fear looks like prudence), who hurried us on our way by pressing hard behind in a dense crowd. Once beyond the buildings we stopped, and there we had some extraordinary experiences which thoroughly alarmed us. The carriages we had ordered to be brought out began to run in different directions though the ground was quite level, and would not remain stationary even when wedged with stones. We also saw the sea sucked away and apparently forced back by the earthquake: at any rate it receded from the shore so that quantities of sea creatures were left stranded on dry sand. On the landward side a fearful black cloud was rent by forked and quivering bursts of flame, and parted to reveal great tongues of fire, like flashes of lightning magnified in size.

At this point my uncle's friend from Spain spoke up still more urgently: 'If your brother, if your uncle is still alive, he will want you both to be saved; if he is dead, he would want you to survive him—why put off your escape?' We replied that we would not think of considering our own safety as long as we were uncertain of his. Without waiting any longer, our friend rushed off and hurried out of danger as fast as he could.

Soon afterwards the cloud sank down to earth and covered the sea; it had already blotted out Capri and hidden the promontory of Misenum from sight. Then my mother implored, entreated and commanded me to escape as best I could—a young man might escape, whereas she was old and slow and could die in peace as long as she had not been the cause of my death too. I refused to save myself without her, and grasping her hand forced her to quicken her pace. She gave in reluctantly, blaming herself for delaying me. Ashes were already falling, not as yet very thickly. I looked round: a dense black cloud was coming up behind us, spreading over the earth like a flood. 'Let us leave the road while we can still see,' I said, 'or we shall be knocked down and trampled underfoot in the dark by the crowd behind.' We had scarcely sat down to rest when darkness fell, not the dark of a moonless or cloudy night, but as if the lamp had been put out in a closed room. You could hear the shrieks of women, the wailing of infants, and the shouting of men; some were calling their parents, others their children or their wives, trying to recognize them by their voices. People bewailed their own fate or that of their relatives, and there were some who prayed for death in their terror of dying. Many besought the aid of the gods, but still more imagined there were no gods left, and that the universe was plunged into eternal darkness for evermore. There were people, too, who added to the real perils by inventing fictitious dangers: some reported that part of Misenum had collapsed or another part was on fire, and though their tales were false they found others to believe them. A gleam of light returned, but we took this to be a warning of the approaching flames rather than daylight. However, the flames remained some distance off; then darkness came on once more and ashes began to fall again, this time in heavy showers. We rose from time to time and shook them off, otherwise we should have been buried and crushed beneath their weight. I could boast that not a groan or cry of fear escaped me in these perils, had I not derived some poor consolation in my mortal lot from the belief that the whole world was dying with me and I with it.

At last the darkness thinned and dispersed into smoke or cloud; then there was genuine daylight, and the sun actually shone out, but yellowish as it is during an eclipse. We were terrified to see everything changed, buried deep in ashes like snowdrifts. We returned to Misenum where we attended to our physical needs as best we could, and then spent an anxious night alternating between hope and fear. Fear predominated, for the earthquakes went on, and several hysterical individuals made their won and other people's calamities seem ludicrous in comparison with their frightful predictions. But even then, in spite of the dangers we had been through and were still expecting, my mother and I had still no intention of leaving until we had news of my uncle.

Of course these details are not important enough for history, and you will read them without any idea of recording them; if they seem scarcely worth putting in a letter, you have only yourself to blame for asking for them. Farewell.

41

On Roman Wall Painting Styles, from Vitruvius' *On Architecture* (*De architectura* 7.5.1–4)

Vitruvius, *The Ten Books on Architecture*, translated by Morris Hicky Morgan, Cambridge, Harvard University Press, 1914, reprinted Dover 1960, pp. 210–212.

Available online at Perseus Project

In the following passage we can see that Vitruvius (see #20, #30, and #35) preferred the naturalistic traits of the First and Second Pompeiian wall-painting styles to the more ornamental and fantastic elements found in the Third and Fourth styles.

The ancients who introduced polished finishings began by representing different kinds of marble slabs in different positions, and then cornices and blocks of yellow ochre arranged in various ways.

Afterwards they made such progress as to represent the forms of buildings, and of columns, and projecting and overhanging pediments; in their open rooms, such as exedrae [base, bench or enclosure in the shape of a half circle], on account of the size, they depicted the facades of scenes in the tragic, comic, or satyric style; and their walks, on account of the great length, they decorated with a variety of landscapes, copying the characteristics of definite spots. In these paintings there are harbors, promontories, seashores, rivers, fountains, straits, fanes, groves, mountains, flocks, shepherds; in some places there are also pictures designed in the grand style, with figures of the gods or detailed mythological episodes, or the battles at Troy, or the wanderings of Ulysses, with landscape backgrounds, and other subjects reproduced on similar principles from real life.

But those subjects which were copied from actual realities are scorned in these days of bad taste. We now have fresco paintings of monstrosities, rather than truthful representations of definite things. For instance, reeds are put in the place of columns, fluted appendages with curly leaves and volutes, instead of pediments, candelabra supporting representations of shrines, and on top of their pediments numerous tender stalks and volutes growing up from the roots and having human figures senselessly seated upon them; sometimes stalks having only half-length figures, some with human heads, others with the heads of animals.

Such things do not exist and cannot exist and never have existed. Hence, it is the new taste that has caused bad judges of poor art to prevail over true artistic excellence. For how is it possible that a reed should really support a roof, or a candelabrum a pediment with its ornaments, or that such a slender, flexible thing as a stalk should support a figure perched upon it, or that roots and stalks should produce now flowers and now half-length figures? Yet when people see these frauds, they find no fault with them but on the contrary are delighted, and do not care whether any of them can exist or not. Their understanding is darkened by decadent critical principles, so that it is not capable of giving its approval authoritatively and on the principle of propriety to that which really can exist. The fact is that pictures which are unlike reality ought not to be approved, and even if they are technically fine, this is no reason why they should offhand be judged to be correct, if their subject is lacking in the principles of reality carried out with no violations.

42

Narcissus in Roman painting, from Philostratus' *Imagines* (*Eikones* 23)

Philostratus: Imagines, Callistratus: Descriptions with an English translation by Arthur Fairbanks, New York, Putnam Sons, 1931, pp. 89, 91, 93.

Available online at Internet Archive

Credit: Philostratus, "Myth of Narcissus in Roman Painting," *Philostratus Imagines, Callistratus Descriptions*, pp. 89, 91, 93, trans. Arthur Fairbanks. Copyright in the Public Domain.

*The story of Narcissus, a Greek youth who falls in love with, and dies pining after, a reflection of himself, is told most famously by the poet Ovid (*Metamorphoses *3.345–510). With its theme of reflections, objectification, spectatorship, and the gaze, it's understandable why the myth was such a popular subject among the frescoists at Pompeii (Fig. 23). Here Philostratus describes just such a painting, trying to illustrate it in words. Philostratus (like Callistratus in reading #13) was a late Roman writer of ekphrases, or descriptions of art, and a commentator on the Classical tradition of thinking about representation.*[1]

The pool paints Narcissus, and the painting represents both the pool and the whole story of Narcissus. A youth just returned from the hunt stands over a pool, drawing from within himself a kind of yearning and falling in love with his own beauty; and, as you see, he sheds a radiance into the water. The cave is sacred to Achelous and the Nymphs, and the scene is painted realistically. For the statues are of a crude art and made from a local stone; some of them are worn away by time, others have been mutilated by children of cowherds or shepherds while still young and unaware of the presence of the god. Nor

---

[1] John Elsner, "Naturalism and the Erotics of the Gaze, Intimations of Narcissus" in *Sexuality in Ancient Art*, Natalie Boymel Kampen editor, Cambridge, 1996, pp.247–261.

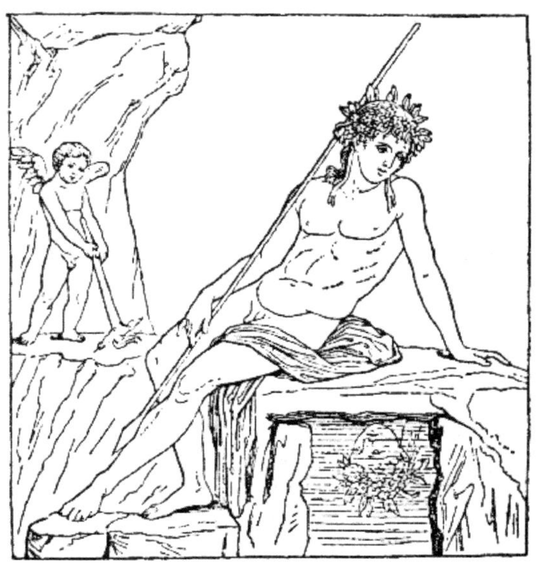

Fig. 23 Narcissus by a spring, after a fresco from Pompeii.

is the pool without some connection with the Bacchic rites of Dionysus, since he has made it known to the Nymphs of the wine-press; at any rate it is roofed over with vine and ivy and beautiful creeping plants, and it abounds in clusters of grapes and the trees that furnish the thyrsi, and tuneful birds disport themselves above it, each with its own note, and white flowers grow about the pool, not yet in blossom but just springing up in honor of the youth. The painting has such regard for realism that it even shows drops of dew dripping from the flowers and a bee settling on the flowers—whether a real bee has been deceived by the painted flowers or whether we are to be deceived into thinking that a painted bee is real I do not know. But let that pass. As for you, however, Narcissus, it is no painting that has deceived you, nor are you engrossed in a thing of pigments or wax; but you do not realize that the water represents you exactly as you are when you gaze upon it, nor do you see through the artifice of the pool, though to do so you have only to nod your head or change your expression or slightly move your hand, instead of standing in the same attitude; but acting as though you had met a companion, you wait for some move on his part. Do you then expect the pool to enter into conversation with you? Nay, this youth does not hear anything we say, but he is immersed, eyes and ears alike, in the water and we must interpret the painting for ourselves.

The youth, standing erect, is at rest; he has his legs crossed and supports one hand on the spear which is planted on his left, while his right hand is pressed against his hip so as to support his body and to produce the type of figure in which the buttocks are pushed out because of the inward bend of the left side. The arm shows an open space at the point where the elbow bends, a wrinkle where the wrist is twisted, and it casts a shadow as it ends in the palm of the hand, and the lines of the shadow are slanting because the fingers are bent in. Whether the panting of his breast remains from his hunting or is already the panting of love I do not know. The eye, surely, is that of a man deeply in love, for its natural brightness and intensity are softened by a longing that settles upon it, and he perhaps thinks that he is loved in return, since the reflection gazes at him in just the way that he looks at it. There would be much to say about the hair if we found him while hunting. For there are innumerable tossings of the hair in running, especially when it is blown by a wind; but even as it is the subject should not be passed over in silence. For it is very abundant and of a golden hue; and some of it clings to the neck, some is parted by the ears, some tumbles over the forehead, and some falls in ripples to the beard. Both the Narcissi are exactly alike in form and each repeats the traits of the other, except that one stands out in the open air while the other is immersed in the pool. For the youth stands over the youth who stands in the water, or rather who gazes intently at him and seems to be athirst for his beauty.

Image credits

43

Early emperors of Rome, from Suetonius' *The Twelve Caesars*

Suetonius, *The Lives of the Twelve Caesars*, translated by Alexander Thomson, revised and corrected by T. Forester. London, George Bell and Sons, 1890, pp. 91–92, 129–130, 217, 256–257, 300–302, 349–353, 359–360.

Available online at Perseus Project, Internet Archive, and Google Books

Suetonius, a Latin biographer writing during the time of Trajan and Hadrian, actually served on the staff of Pliny the Younger (see #40 and #51) when Pliny was governor of Bithynia and Pontus. His Lives of the Caesars *are biographies of the twelve Roman rulers from Julius Caesar to Domitian. What follows are excerpts from the lives of Augustus, Nero, Tiberius, Caligula, and Claudius.*

AUGUSTUS

29. The city, which was not built in a manner suitable to the grandeur of the empire, and was liable to inundations of the Tiber, as well as to fires, was so much improved under his administration, that he boasted, not without reason, that he "found it of brick, but left it of marble." He also rendered it secure for the time to come against such disasters, as far as could be effected by human foresight. A great number of public buildings were erected by him, the most considerable of which were a forum, containing the temple of Mars the Avenger, the temple of Apollo on the Palatine hill, and the temple of Jupiter Tonans in the capitol. The reason of his building a new forum was the vast increase in the population, and the number of causes to be tried in

the courts, for which, the two already existing not affording sufficient space, it was thought necessary to have a third.

79. In person he was handsome and graceful through every period of his life. But he was negligent in his dress; and so careless about dressing his hair, that he usually had it done in great haste, by several barbers at a time. His beard he sometimes clipped, and sometimes shaved; and either read or wrote during the operation. His countenance, either when discoursing or silent, was so calm and serene, that a Gaul of the first rank declared amongst his friends, that he was so softened by it, as to be restrained from throwing him down a precipice, in his passage over the Alps, when he had been admitted to approach him, under pretense of conferring with him. His eyes were bright and piercing; and he was willing it should be thought that there was something of a divine vigor in them. He was likewise not a little pleased to see people, upon his looking steadfastly at them, lower their countenances, as if the sun shone in their eyes. But in his old age, he saw very imperfectly with his left eye. His teeth were thin set, small and scaly, his hair a little curled, and inclining to a yellow color. His eye-brows met; his ears were small, and he had an aquiline nose. His complexion was betwixt brown and fair; his stature but low; though Julius Marathus, his freedman, says he was five feet and nine inches in height. This, however, was so much concealed by the just proportion of his limbs, that it was only perceivable upon comparison with some taller person standing by him.

ON NERO

20–23. Among the other liberal arts which he was taught in his youth, he was instructed in music ... Nor did he omit any of those expedients which artists in music adopt, for the preservation and improvement of their voices. He would lie upon his back with a sheet of lead upon his breast, clear his stomach and bowels by vomits and clysters, and forbear the eating of fruits, or food prejudicial to the voice. Encouraged by his proficiency, though his voice was neither loud nor clear, he was desirous of appearing upon the stage ... He played and sung in the same place several times, and for several days together; taking only now and then a little respite to refresh his voice ... During the time of his musical performance, nobody was allowed to stir out of the theatre upon any account, however necessary; insomuch, that it is said some women with child were delivered there. Many of the spectators being quite wearied with hearing and applauding him, because the town gates were shut, slipped privately over the walls; or counterfeiting themselves dead, were carried out for their funeral.

NERO AND THE DOMUS AUREA

31. In nothing was he more prodigal than in his buildings. He completed his palace by continuing it from the Palatine to the Esquiline hill, calling the building at first only "The Passage," but after it was burnt down and rebuilt, "The Golden House." Of its dimensions and furniture, it may be sufficient to say thus much: the porch was so high that there stood in it a colossal statue of himself a hundred and twenty feet in height; and the space included in it was so ample, that it had triple porticos a mile in length, and a lake like a sea, surrounded with buildings which had the appearance of a city. Within its area were corn fields, vineyards, pastures, and woods, containing a vast number of animals of various kinds, both wild and tame. In other parts it was entirely over-laid with gold, and adorned with jewels and mother of pearl. The supper rooms were vaulted, and compartments of the ceilings, inlaid with ivory, were made to revolve, and scatter flowers; while they contained pipes which shed unguents upon the guests. The chief banqueting room was circular, and revolved perpetually, night and day, in imitation of the motion of the celestial bodies. The baths were supplied with water from the sea and the Albula [Tiber River]. Upon the dedication of this magnificent house after it was finished, all he said in approval of it was, "that he had now a dwelling fit for a man."

TIBERIUS AND THE CAVE AT SPERLONGA

29. But after the loss of his two sons, of whom Germanicus died in Syria, and Drusus at Rome, he withdrew into Campania—from which, opinion and conversation were almost in agreement, he never would return, and would die soon. And both nearly turned out to be true. For indeed he nevermore came to Rome and narrowly escaped death a few days after leaving it, when at a villa of his called 'The Cave', near Terracina, during supper a great many huge stones fell from above and killed several of the guests and attendants.

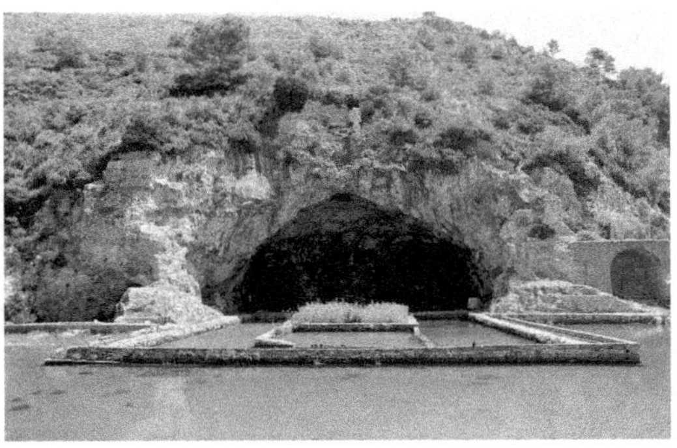

Fig. 24 The dining grotto at Tiberius' villa in Sperlonga. It was decorated with sculptural groups including the Blinding of Polyphemus (Fig. 10).

GAIUS (A.K.A. CALIGULA)

9. It was to the jokes of the soldiers in the camp that he owed the nickname of Caligula [i.e., little boots] he having been brought up among them in the dress of a common soldier. How much his education amongst them recommended him to their favor and affection, was quite apparent in the mutiny upon the death of Augustus, when the mere sight of him appeased their fury, though it had risen to a great height. For they persisted in it, until they observed that he was sent away to a neighboring city, to secure him against all danger. Then, at last, they began to relent, and, stopping the chariot in which he was conveyed, earnestly deprecated the odium to which such a proceeding would expose them.

10. ...He was then transferred to the family of his grandmother Antonia, and afterwards, in the twentieth year of his age, being called by Tiberius to Capri, he in one and the same day assumed the manly habit, and shaved his beard, but without receiving any of the honors which had been paid to his brothers on a similar occasion. While he remained in that island, many insidious artifices were practiced, to extort from him complaints against Tiberius, but by his circumspection he avoided falling into the snare. He affected to take no more notice of the ill treatment of his relations, than if nothing had befallen them. With regard to his own sufferings, he seemed utterly insensible of them, and behaved with such obsequiousness to his grandfather and all about him, that it was justly said of him, "There never was a better servant, nor a worse master."

11. But he could not even then conceal his natural disposition to cruelty and lewdness. He delighted in witnessing the inflictions of punishments, and frequented taverns and bawdy-houses in the nighttime, disguised in a periwig and a long coat; and was passionately addicted to the theatrical arts of singing and dancing. All these levities Tiberius readily connived at, in hopes that they might perhaps correct the roughness of his temper, which the sagacious old man so well understood, that he often said, "That Gaius was destined to be the ruin of himself and all mankind..."

CLAUDIUS

7. At last Gaius, his brother's son, upon his advancement to the empire, endeavoring to gain the affections of the public by all the arts of popularity, Claudius also was admitted to public offices, and held the consulship jointly with his nephew for two months ... He sometimes presided at the public spectacles, as the representative of Gaius; being always, on those occasions, complimented with the acclamations of the people, wishing him all happiness, sometimes under the title 'Emperor's Uncle", and sometimes under 'Germanicus' Brother'.

8. Still he was subjected to many slights. If at any time he came in late to supper, he was obliged to walk round the room some time before he could get a

place at table. When he indulged himself with sleep after eating, which was a common practice with him, the company used to throw olive-stones and dates at him. And the buffoons who attended would wake him, as if it were only in jest, with a cane or a whip. Sometimes they would put slippers upon his hands, as he lay snoring, that he might, upon awaking, rub his face with them.

10. Having spent the greater part of his life under these and the like circumstances, he came at last to the empire in the fiftieth year of his age, by a very surprising turn of fortune. Being, as well as the rest, prevented from approaching Gaius by the conspirators, who dispersed the crowd, under the pretext of his desiring to be private, he retired into an apartment called the Hermaeum; and soon afterwards, terrified by the report of Gaius being slain, he crept into an adjoining balcony, where he hid himself behind the hangings of the door. A common soldier, who happened to pass that way, spying his feet, and desirous to discover who he was, pulled him out; when immediately recognizing him, he threw himself in a great fright at his feet, and saluted him by the title of emperor.

Image credits

Fig. 24: Copyright © Carole Raddato (CC BY-SA 2.0) at https://commons.wikimedia.org/wiki/ File:Villa_of_Tiberius,_Sperlonga_(15134765456).jpg.

44

A Roman Dinner Party, from Petronius' *Satyrica* (49–53, 71)

Petronius, *Satyrica*, edited and translated by R. Bracht Branham and Daniel Kinney, Berkeley: University of California Press, 1996, pp. 44–48, 65–66.

A different translation is available online at Project Gutenberg

Petronius Arbiter was the "Arbiter of Elegance" at the court of Nero. What little is known of his life is recorded by the Roman historian Tacitus, who tells us in Annales *16.18–19 that Petronius, having been falsely accused by a member of Nero's court, committed suicide by making incisions in his veins and, as his life slowly drained away, continued to amuse his friends with lively banter. Petronius' masterpiece, the* Satyrica *(famous not least for its 1969 cinematic interpretation by Fellini) recounts the adventures of Encolpius and his lover Giton. The following excerpt describes an extravagant and absurd dinner party the two lovers and their friend Agamemnon attend at the home of the freedman Trimalchio. The other readings in this collection should give you enough background to judge just how ridiculous the character of Trimalchio is.*

---

49. Trimalchio was still chattering on like this when our table was covered by a tray with a huge pig on it. We were astonished by how speedily it had been prepared and swore you couldn't cook a run-of-the-mill rooster that fast, especially since the pig seemed much bigger than the boar that had been served a bit earlier. Then, looking intently at the pig, Trimalchio exclaimed, 'What is this? Has this pig been gutted? No, it hasn't, by god! Get that cook in here now!'

A contrite looking cook appeared in front of our table and admitted that he'd forgotten to gut the pig. 'What? Forgotten!' shouted Trimalchio. 'You'd think he'd forgotten to add the salt and pepper, the way he says it; off with his shirt!' In no time the poor man was stripped and flanked by two executioners. Everyone tried to get him off the hook saying: 'This happens all the time. Please, let him go. If it happens again, no one will speak up for him.'

Given my natural severity I couldn't resist turning to Agamemnon and whispering in his ear: 'This slave must be a perfect idiot: how could anyone forget to gut a pig? God knows, I wouldn't forgive him if he'd forgotten to clean a fish!'

Not so Trimalchio: his face relaxed into a hilarious grin as he said, 'O.K., since you've got such a bad memory, gut him right here in front of us.' The cook donned his tunic, again, grabbed his butcher knife, and sliced the pig's belly every which way with a quivering hand. The slits immediately gave way to the pressure from inside and roasted sausages and giblets gushed out of the wounds!

50. The slaves broke into applause for the trick and cheered in unison, 'Bravo Gaius!' The cook was honored with a drink and silver crown, and also received a drinking bowl served on a plate of Corinthian bronze. As Agamemnon eyed the plate rather closely, Trimalchio observed: 'I alone own genuine Corinthian.' I was waiting for him to boast as usual that his vases were imported directly from Corinth, but he did better than that: 'Perhaps you're wondering why I am unique in owning Corinthian plates? Because, of course, the dealer I buy it from is named "Corinthus". How could it be Corinthian unless you get it from Corinthus? I'm no ignoramus, ya know; I know very well how Corinthian bronze originated. When Troy was sacked, Hannibalz—a clever fellow and a real snake in the grass-piled all the bronze, gold and silver statues into a single heap and set them on fire; they melted into a single bronze alloy. From this amalgam craftsmen made little bowls, side dishes, and statuettes. Thus was Corinthian bronze born–neither this nor that, but one from all. If you don't mind my saying so, I actually prefer glass—it doesn't smell. If it didn't break, I'd prefer it to gold; as it is, the price is right.

51. 'But there once was a craftsman who made an unbreakable glass bowl. When he was given an audience with the emperor to present his invention... he had Caesar hand it back and then tossed it on the pavement. The emperor couldn't have been more alarmed! But this fellow picked the bowl up off the floor—it was dented like a bronze vase—pulled a hammer from his pocket, and smoothed it out very nicely. He thought he had Jupiter by the balls then, especially when the emperor asked, "Does anyone else know how to make glass like this?" 'But look what happened: he said "no" and the emperor had him beheaded! And no wonder! If an idea like that got out, our gold wouldn't be worth potter's clay!'

52. Of course, silver is my favorite. I have some enormous wine cups... showing how Cassandra killed her sons. The way the dead boys lie there—you'd think

they were alive!' I have a sacrificial bowl, which King Minos left my patron, that shows Daedalus shutting Niobe up in the Trojan horse. I even have the fights of the gladiators Hermeros and Petraites on my drinking cups—and, boy, are they heavy. You just can't put a price on that kind of thing.'

As he was talking, a slave dropped a drinking cup. Trimalchio glared at him and said, 'Quickly, off with your head, since you're good-for-nothing.' Instantly, the boy's face fell and he begged Trimalchio's pardon. 'Why do you ask me, as if I were your problem? I suggest you beg yourself not to be a good-for-nothing.' Finally, we prevailed on him to pardon the boy. As soon as he was off the hook, he danced about the table...

'Water for the outside, wine for the insides,' shouted Trimalchio, and we laughed approvingly at his jest, especially Agamemnon, who certainly knew how to get invited back to dinner. Feeling appreciated, Trimalchio drank happily and, when he was virtually drunk, said, 'Won't any of you ask my Fortunata to dance? Believe me, no one does the bump and grind better!'

He then held his hands up in front of his forehead and impersonated the actor Syrus, while the whole household chanted, 'Do it! Do it!' He would have taken the floor, if Fortunata hadn't whispered something in his ear. I imagine she told him that such clownery didn't become him. But nothing was so unpredictable: one moment he would cower before Fortunata, and the next, revert to his natural self.

53. The impulse to dance was checked by a clerk who read aloud as if from a government document:

'July 26th: on the estate at Cumae, which belongs to Trimalchio, there were born thirty male slaves, forty females; 500,000 pecks of wheat were transferred from the threshing floor to the barn; 500 oxen were broken in. On the same day, the slave Mithridates was crucified for speaking disrespectfully of the guardian spirit of our Gaius. On the same day, 10,000,000 in coin that could not be invested was returned to the strong-box. On the same day, there was a fire in the gardens at Pompeii that started in the house of Nasta the caretaker.'

'What's that? When did I buy gardens in Pompeii?' asked Trimalchio. 'Last year,' said the clerk. 'So they are not yet on the books.' Trimalchio was incensed: 'I forbid any property bought for me to be entered on the books unless I know of it within six months!'

Even the police reports were being read and the wills of some game-keepers, in which Trimalchio was disinherited in a codicil. The names of some caretakers followed and a divorce was announced—of a night watchman from a freedwoman: she had been caught *in flagrante* with a bath attendant. A porter had been exiled to Baiae; a steward was being prosecuted; and a law suit between some valets had been decided. But finally, the acrobats arrived...

71. Then turning to Habinnas he said, 'Tell me, old friend, are you building my tomb just as I told you to? Please be sure that you put my lap-dog at the foot of my statue along with plenty of wreathes and jars of perfume, and all the fights of Petraites so that, thanks to you, I may live on after my death. And please make my plot a hundred feet wide and two hundred feet deep. For I want every kind of fruit tree growing around my ashes and lots of vines. It makes no sense to decorate the house you live in now but not the one where you'll spend so much longer. That's why over everything else, I want this inscribed:

This Tomb Does NOT Go To My Heir!

But I'll make sure in my will that no one can wrong me when I'm dead; I'll appoint one of my freedmen to guard my tomb so that folks won't run up and take a crap on it!

And please put ships in full sail on the front and put me high on a ceremonial dais wearing my purple-striped toga and five golden rings as I pour money out of a sack in front of the whole town! .... On my right put a statue of Fortunata holding a dove, and let the puppy follow tied to her sash, and include my favorite boy, and some giant jars of wine properly sealed against leaks, and you can carve one urn broken and a boy weeping over it. And put a sundial in the middle so whoever checks the time will read my name, like it or not! Now listen to this epitaph and tell me if it sounds right:

Here lies C. Pompeius Trimalchio
Freedman of Maecenas
Elected Priest of Augustus
In Absentia:
He could have had any job in Rome –
But didn't.
Loyal, Brave, and True,
He started with a nickel in his pocket,
And left his heirs thirty million;
And he never once listened to a philosopher!
Farewell, Trimalchio
And you, too, traveler.

45

The inauguration of the Colosseum, from Dio Cassius' *Roman History* (66.25.1–9)

Dio's Roman History, volume VIII, translated by Earnest Cary, Loeb Classical Library, Cambridge, Harvard University Press, 1925, reprinted 1968, pp. 311, 313.

Available online at LacusCurtius

Dio Cassius was a Roman historian who wrote in Greek and published a history of Rome in eighty volumes in the early decades of the third century CE (see also #48). In this passage, he describes some of the events that took place during the inauguration of the Flavian amphitheater or Colosseum (now coliseum) by Titus in 80 CE.

In dedicating the hunting-theater [the Colosseum] and the baths that bear his name he [Titus] produced many remarkable spectacles. There was a battle between cranes and also between four elephants; animals both tame and wild were slain to the number of nine thousand; and women (not those of any prominence, however) took part in dispatching them. As for the men, several fought in single combat and several groups contended together both in infantry and naval battles. For Titus suddenly filled this same theatre with water and brought in horses and bulls and some other domesticated animals that had been taught to behave in the liquid element just as on land. He also brought in people on ships, who engaged in a sea-fight there, impersonating the Corcyreans and Corinthians; and others gave a similar exhibition outside the city in the grove of Gaius and Lucius, a place which Augustus had once excavated for this very purpose. There, too, on the first day there was a gladiatorial exhibition and wild-beast hunt, the lake in front of the images having first been covered over with a platform of planks and wooden stands erected around it. On the second day there was a horse-race, and on the third day a naval battle between three thousand men, followed by an infantry battle. The "Athenians" conquered the "Syracusans" (these were the names the combatants used), made a landing on the islet and assaulted and captured a wall that had been constructed around the monument. These were the spectacles that were offered, and they continued for a hundred days; but Titus also furnished some things that were of practical use to the people. He would throw down into the theater from aloft little wooden balls variously inscribed, one designating some article of food, another clothing, another a silver vessel or perhaps a gold one, or again horses, pack-animals, cattle or slaves. Those who seized them were to carry them to the dispensers of the bounty, from whom they would receive the article named.

46

A view on Gladiatorial Games, from Seneca's *Moral Epistles 7: Crowds*

Seneca in ten volumes, volume IV: Epistles 1–65, translated by Richard M. Gummere, Loeb Classical Library, Cambridge, Harvard University Press, 1917, reprinted 1996, pp. 31, 33.

Available online at The Stoics

Seneca was the tutor and later adviser to Nero. He retired in 62 CE, only to be accused three years later by Nero of involvement in a conspiracy. The emperor ordered Seneca to commit suicide, which he did with dignity. During the three years of his retirement, Seneca wrote a group of 124 letters called the Moral Epistles. Among them are his thoughts, presented below, on the gladiatorial games.

But nothing is so damaging to good character as the habit of lounging at the games; for then it is that vice steals subtly upon one through the avenue of pleasure. What do you think I mean? I mean that I come home more greedy, more ambitious, more voluptuous, and even more cruel and inhuman, because I have been among human beings. By chance I attended a mid-day exhibition, expecting some fun, wit, and relaxation,—an exhibition at which men's eyes have respite from the slaughter of their fellow-men. But it was quite the reverse. The previous combats were the essence of compassion; but now all the trifling is put aside and it is pure murder. The men have no defensive armor. They are exposed to blows at all points, and no one ever strikes in vain. Many persons prefer this program to the usual pairs and to the bouts "by request." Of course they do; there is no helmet or shield to deflect the weapon. What is the need of defensive armor, or of skill? All these mean delaying death. In the morning they throw men to the lions and the bears; at noon, they throw them to the spectators. The spectators demand that the slayer shall face the man who is to slay him in his turn; and they always reserve the latest conqueror for another butchering. The outcome of every fight is death, and the means are fire and sword. This sort of thing goes on while the arena is empty. You may retort: "But he was a highway robber; he killed a man!" And what of it? Granted that, as a murderer, he deserved this punishment, what crime have you committed, poor fellow, that you should deserve to sit and see this show? In the morning they cried "Kill him! Lash him! Burn him; Why does he meet the sword in so cowardly a way? Why does he strike so feebly? Why doesn't he die game? Whip him to meet his wounds! Let them receive blow for blow, with chests bare and exposed to the stroke!" And when the games stop for the intermission, they announce: "A little throat-cutting in the meantime, so that there may still be something going on!"

47

The Triumph of Titus, from Josephus' *The Jewish War* (7.121–157)

Josephus, volume III, with an English translation by H. St. J. Thackeray, Loeb Classical Library, Cambridge, Harvard University Press, 1928, pp. 541, 545, 547, 549.

Available online at Internet Archive

Credit: Flavius Josephus, "The Triumph of Titus," *Josephus*, volume III, pp. 541, 547, 549, trans. H. St. J. Thackeray. Copyright in the Public Domain.

After Judea revolted against the empire in 66 CE, both Vespasian and his son Titus campaigned to put down the rebellion. In 70 CE, Titus prevailed: Jerusalem was conquered, the city was destroyed, and the great Temple was burned. A description of these events was published in 78 CE by the Jewish historian Josephus. The passage reproduced below describes the triumphal procession voted by the Senate to honor Titus's victory. Note particularly his description of what seems to be pictorial parade floats. It serves as yet another reminder of how ephemeral so much of the visual arts are.

Before many days had elapsed [Vespasian and Titus] decided to celebrate their achievements by one triumph in common, though the senate had decreed a separate triumph to each. Previous notice having been given of the day on which the pageant of victory would take place, not a soul among that countless host in the city was left at home: all issued forth and occupied every position where it was but possible to stand, leaving only room for the necessary passage of those upon whom they were to gaze...

It is impossible to describe adequately the multitude of those spectacles and their magnificence under every conceivable aspect, whether in works of art or diversity of riches or natural rarities; for almost all the objects which men who have ever been blessed by fortune have acquired one by one—the wonderful and precious productions of various nations—by their collective exhibition on that day displayed the majesty of the Roman empire. Silver and gold and ivory in masses, wrought into all manner of forms, might be seen, not as if carried in procession, but flowing, so to speak, like a river; here were tapestries borne along, some of the rarest purple, others embroidered by Babylonian art with perfect portraiture; transparent gems, some set in golden crowns, some in other fashions, swept by in such profusion as to correct our erroneous supposition that any of them was rare. Then, too, there were carried images of their gods, of marvelous size and no mean craftsmanship, and of these not one but was of some rich material. Beasts of many species were led along all caparisoned with appropriate trappings. The numerous attendants conducting each group of animals were decked in garments of true purple dye, interwoven with gold; while those selected to take part in the pageant itself had about them choice ornaments of amazing richness. Moreover, even among the mob of captives, none was to be seen unadorned, the variety and beauty of their dresses concealing from view any unsightliness arising from bodily disfigurement.

But nothing in the procession excited so much astonishment as the structure of the moving pictorial stages; indeed, their massiveness afforded ground for alarm and misgiving as to their stability, many of them being three or four stories high, while the magnificence of the fabric was a source at once of delight and amazement. For many were enveloped in tapestries interwoven with gold, and all had a framework of gold and wrought ivory. The war was shown by numerous representations, in separate sections, affording a very vivid picture of its episodes. Here was to be seen a prosperous country devastated, there whole battalions of the enemy slaughtered; here a party in flight, there others led into captivity; walls of surpassing compass demolished by engines, strong fortresses overpowered, cities with well-manned defenses completely mastered and an army pouring within the ramparts, an area all deluged with blood, the hands of those incapable of resistance raised in supplication, temples set on fire, houses pulled down over their owners' heads, and, after general desolation and woe, rivers flowing, not over a cultivated land, nor supplying drink to man and beast, but across a country still on every side in flames. For to such sufferings were the Jews destined when they plunged into the war; and the art and magnificent workmanship of these structures now portrayed the incidents to those who had not witnessed them, as though they were happening before their eyes. On each of the stages was stationed the general of one of the captured cities in the attitude in which he was taken. A number of ships also followed.

The spoils in general were borne in promiscuous heaps; but conspicuous above all stood out those captured in the temple at Jerusalem. These consisted of a golden table, many talents in weight, and a lampstand, likewise made of gold, but constructed on a different pattern from those which we use in ordinary life. Affixed to a pedestal was a central shaft, from which there extended slender branches, arranged trident-fashion, a wrought lamp being attached to the extremity of each branch; of these there were seven, indicating the honor paid to that number among the Jews. After these, and last of all the spoils, was carried a copy of the Jewish Law. Then followed a large party carrying images of victory, all made of ivory and gold. Behind them drove Vespasian, followed by Titus; while Domitian rode beside them, in magnificent apparel and mounted on a steed that was itself a sight.

48

Hadrian and the architect Apollodorus of Damascus, from Dio Cassius' *Roman History* (69.4.1–5)

Dio's Roman History, volume VIII, translated by Earnest Cary, Loeb Classical Library, Cambridge, Harvard University Press, 1925, reprinted 1968, pp. 431, 433.

Available online at LacusCurtius

Apollodorus of Damascus was Trajan's architect who made the mistake of crossing the future emperor Hadrian. As we see in this passage from Dio Cassius (see also #45), it can certainly be dangerous to be an architect. Another famous example of the hazards of the profession is that of Postnik and Barma, the designers of the church of St Basil in Moscow. The tradition is that the Russian ruler, Ivan the Terrible, had them blinded so that they would never be able to reproduce the masterpiece they had created.

He [Hadrian] first banished and later put to death Apollodorus, the architect, who had built the various creations of Trajan in Rome—the forum, the odeum [music hall] and the gymnasium. The reason assigned was that he had been guilty of some misdemeanor; but the true reason was that once when Trajan was consulting him on some point about the buildings he had said to Hadrian, who had interrupted with some remark: "Be off, and draw your gourds. You don't understand any of these matters." (It chanced that Hadrian at the time was pluming himself upon some such drawing [probably a reference to the pumpkin-shaped segmented domes like those found at Hadrian's villa at Tivoli, see Fig 25]). When he became emperor, therefore, he remembered this slight and would not endure the man's freedom of speech. He sent him the plan of the temple of Venus and Roma by way of showing him that a great work could be

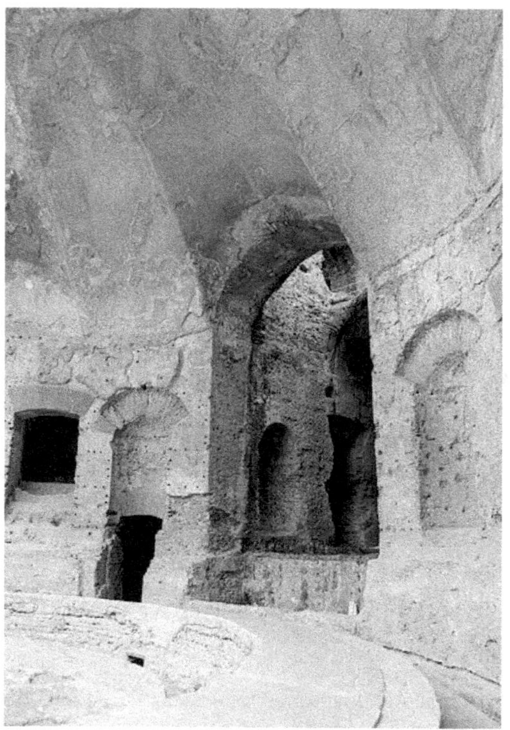

Fig. 25 An example of a segmented 'pumpkin' or 'gourd' dome, from the Serapeum at Hadrian's villa, Tivoli, Italy.

accomplished without his aid, and asked Apollodorus whether the proposed structure was satisfactory. The architect in his reply stated, first, in regard to the temple, that it ought to have been built on high ground and that the earth should have been excavated beneath it, so that it might have stood out more conspicuously on the Sacred Way from its higher position, and might also have accommodated the machines in its basement, so that they could be put together unobserved and brought into the theatre without anyone's being aware of them beforehand. Secondly, in regard to the statues, he said that they had been made too tall for the height of the cella. "For now," he said, "if the goddesses wish to get up and go out, they will be unable to do so." When he wrote this so bluntly to Hadrian, the emperor was both vexed and exceedingly grieved because he had fallen into a mistake that could not be righted, and he restrained neither his anger nor his grief, but slew the man.

Image credits

49

Roman Baths, from Lucian's *Hippias*

Lucian, *Works*, volume I, with an English translation by A. M. Harmon, Loeb Classical Library, Cambridge, Harvard University Press, 1913, pp. 39, 41, 43, 45.

Available online at Google Books

Lucian, a Greek satirist and early novelist of the second century CE, is probably best known for writing the first science fiction tale called A True Story *about a trip to the moon. In the less fantastic selection below, Lucian describes a bathing complex designed by the architect Hippias. It gives a real sense of the arrangement of these structures and some of their lavish decoration. Emperors like Titus, Trajan, Caracalla, and Diocletian (see Fig. 26) built baths in Rome on an incredibly impressive and crowd-pleasing scale.*

I shall not hesitate to speak of one of his achievements which I recently looked upon with wonder. Though the undertaking is a commonplace, and in our days a very frequent one, the construction of a bath, yet his thoughtfulness and intelligence even in this commonplace matter is marvelous.

The site was not flat, but quite sloping and steep; it was extremely low on one side when he took it in hand, but he made the whole level, not only constructing a firm basis for the entire work and laying foundations to ensure the safety of the superstructure, but strengthening the whole with buttresses, very sheer and, for security's sake, close together. The building suits the magnitude of the site, accords well with the correct proportions of such an establishment, and shows regard for the principles of lighting.

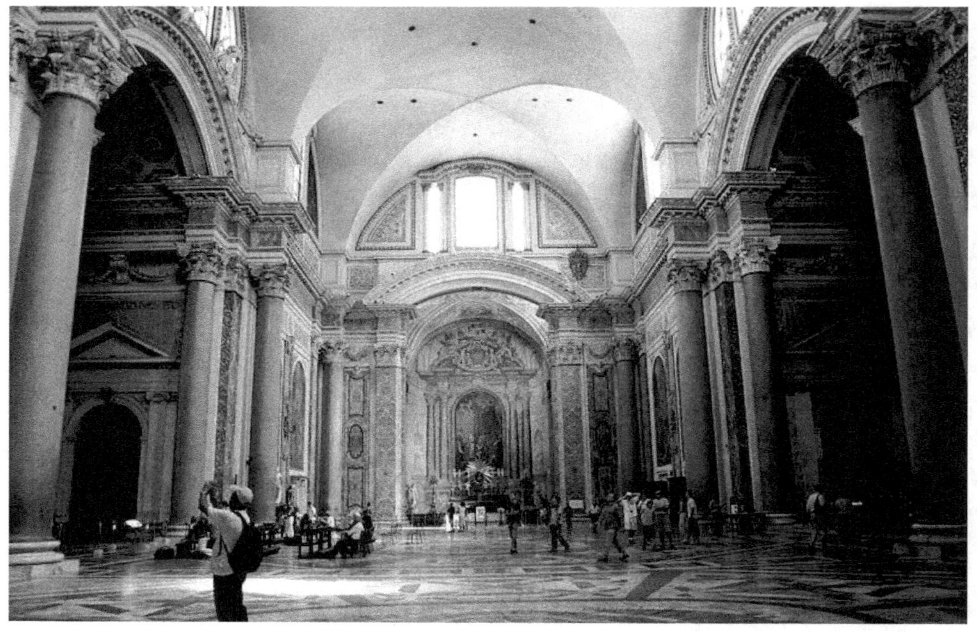

Fig. 26 Frigidarium of the Baths of Diocletian in Rome, now the church of Santa Maria degli Angeli.

The entrance is high, with a flight of broad steps of which the tread is greater than the pitch, to make them easy to ascend. On entering, one is received into a public hall of good size, with ample accommodations for servants and attendants. On the left are the lounging rooms, also of just the right sort for a bath, attractive, brightly lighted retreats. Then, beside them, a hall, larger than need be for the purposes of a bath, but necessary for the reception of the rich. Next, capacious locker-rooms to undress in, on each side, with a very high and brilliantly lighted hall between them, in which are three swimming-pools of cold water; it is finished in Laconian marble, and has two statues of white marble in the ancient technique, one of Hygieia, the other of Aesculapius.

On leaving this hall, you come into another which is slightly warmed instead of meeting you at once with fierce heat; it is oblong, and has a recess at each side. Next it, on the right, is a very bright hall, nicely fitted up for massage, which has on each side an entrance decorated with Phrygian marble, and receives those who come in from the exercising-floor. Then near this is another hall, the most beautiful in the world, in which one can sit or stand with comfort, linger without danger and stroll about with profit. It also is refulgent with Phrygian marble clear to the roof. Next comes the hot corridor, faced with Numidian marble. The hall beyond it is very beautiful, full of abundant light and aglow with color like that of purple hangings. It contains three hot tubs.

When you have bathed, you need not go back through the same rooms, but can go directly to the cold room through a slightly warmed apartment. Everywhere there is copious illumination and full indoor daylight. Furthermore, the height of each room is just, and the breadth proportionate to the length; and everywhere great beauty and loveliness prevail, for in the words of noble Pindar [Olympian Ode 6.3], "Your work should have a glorious countenance." This is probably due in the main to the light, the brightness and the windows. Hippias, being truly wise, built the room for cold baths to northward, though it does not lack a southern exposure; whereas he faced south, east, and west the rooms that require abundant heat. Why should I go on and tell you of the exercising-floors and of the cloakrooms, which have quick and direct communication with the hall containing the basin, so as to be convenient and to do away with all risk?

Let no one suppose that I have taken an insignificant achievement as my theme, and purpose to ennoble it by my eloquence. It requires more than a little wisdom, in my opinion, to invent new manifestations of beauty in commonplace things, as did our marvelous Hippias in producing this work. It has all the good points of a bath—usefulness, convenience, light, good proportions, fitness to its site, and the fact that it can be used without risk. Moreover, it is beautified with all other marks of thoughtfulness—with two toilets, many exits, and two devices for telling time, a water-clock that bellows like a bull, and a sundial.

For a man who has seen all this not to render the work its due of praise is not only foolish but ungrateful, even malignant, it seems to me. I for my part have done what I could to do justice both to the work and to the man who planned and built it. If Heaven ever grants you the privilege of bathing there, I know that I shall have many who will join me in my words of praise.

Image credits

50

The capture and death of an Emperor, from Lactantius' *On the Deaths of the Persecutors (De mortibus persecutorum 5)*

The Works of Lactantius. volume II, translated by William Fletcher, Edinburgh, 1871, pp. 167–168

Available online at Google Books

Valerian co-ruled with his son Gallienus from 253 until his capture in 260 CE by the Sassanian Persian ruler Shapur I. Valerian was also a persecutor of Christians. Since our author Lactantius was a Christian himself, it has been debated whether his description of the emperor's captivity and demise is reliable. Regardless, a relief from Naqsh-e Rustam, Iran, depicts Shapur I on horseback with Valerian kneeling and supplicating before him (Fig. 27). This 'horse-stomping' composition actually originated in earlier Roman imperial art: the Equestrian statue of Marcus Aurelius and the great Trajanic frieze on the arch of Constantine are just two examples. Ironically, Shapur usurps this image type to depict his own victory.

And presently Valerian also, in a mood alike frantic, lifted up his impious hands to assault God, and, although his time was short, shed much righteous blood. But God punished him in a new and extraordinary manner, that it might be a lesson to future ages that the adversaries of Heaven always receive the just recompense of their iniquities. He, having been made prisoner by the Persians, lost not only that power which he had exercised without moderation, but also the liberty of which be had deprived others; and he wasted the remainder of his days in the vilest condition of slavery: for Sapores [=Shapur I], the king of the Persians, who had made him prisoner, whenever he chose to

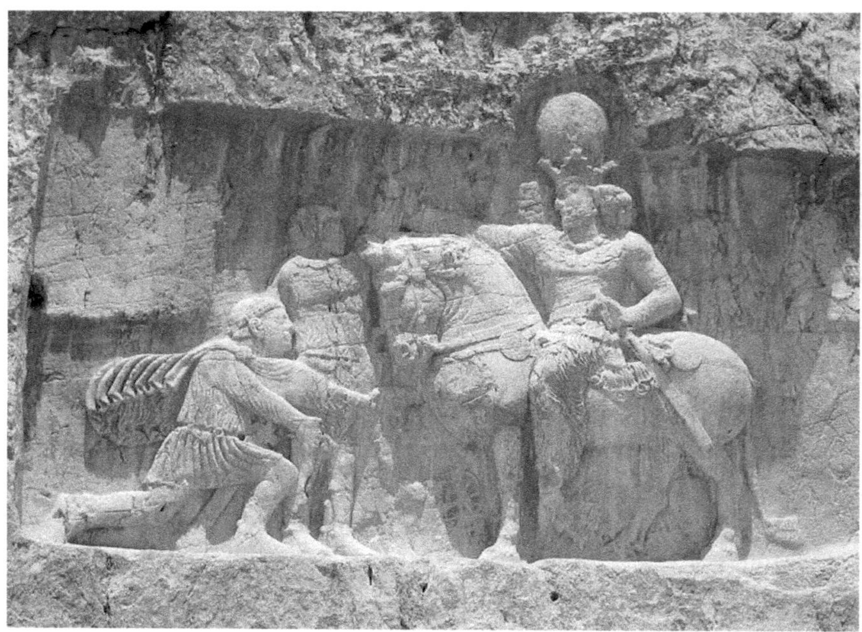

Fig. 27 Triumph of Sassanian ruler Shapur I over the Roman Emperor Valerian, Naqsh-e Rustam, Iran.

get into his carriage or to mount on horseback, commanded the Roman to stoop and present his back; then, setting his foot on the shoulders of Valerian, he said, with a smile of reproach, "This is true, and not what the Romans delineate on board or plaster." Valerian lived for a considerable time under the well-merited insults of his conqueror; so that the Roman name remained long the scoff and derision of the barbarians: and this also was added to the severity of his punishment, that although he had an emperor for his son, he found no one to revenge his captivity and most abject and servile state; neither indeed was he ever demanded back. Afterward, when he had finished this shameful life under so great dishonor, he was flayed, and his skin, stripped from the flesh, was dyed with vermilion, and placed in the temple of the gods of the barbarians, that the remembrance of a triumph so signal might be perpetuated, and that this spectacle might always be exhibited to our ambassadors, as an admonition to the Romans, that, beholding the spoils of their captive emperor in a Persian temple, they should not place too great confidence in their own strength.

Image credits

Early Christianity

51

Persecution of Christians, from Pliny the Younger's *Letters* (10.96 & 10.97)

Persecution of Christians began in the first century CE and continued, off and on, until the early 4th century. The following letter, written by the younger Pliny (see also #40) while acting as the Emperor's representative in the province of Bithynia and Pontus (northern Asia Minor or modern day Turkey) in 110–112 CE, illustrates some of the thinking of the time. Trajan's response follows.

Pliny to the Emperor Trajan

It is my custom to refer all my difficulties to you, Sir, for no one is better able to resolve my doubts and to inform my ignorance:

I have never been present at an examination of Christians. Consequently, I do not know the nature of the extent of the punishments usually meted out to them, nor the grounds for starting an investigation and how far it should be pressed. Nor am I at all sure whether any distinction should be made between them on the grounds of age, or if young people and adults should be treated alike; whether a pardon ought to be granted to anyone retracting his beliefs, or if he has once professed Christianity, he shall gain nothing by renouncing it; and whether it is the mere name of Christian which is punishable, even if innocent of crime, or rather the crimes associated with the name.

For the moment this is the line I have taken with all persons brought before me on the charge of being Christians. I have asked them in person if they are Christians, and if they admit it, I repeat the question a second and third time, with a warning of the punishment awaiting them. If they persist, I order them to be led away for execution; for, whatever the nature of their admission, I am convinced that their stubbornness and unshakable obstinacy ought not to go unpunished. There have been others similarly fanatical who are Roman citizens. I have entered them on the list of persons to be sent to Rome for trial.

Now that I have begun to deal with this problem, as so often happens, the charges are becoming more widespread and increasing in variety. An anonymous pamphlet has been circulated which contains the names of a number of accused persons. Amongst these I considered that I should dismiss any who denied that they were or ever had been Christians when they had repeated after me a formula of invocation to the gods and had made offerings of wine and incense to your statue (which I had ordered to be brought into court for this purpose along with the images of the gods), and furthermore had reviled the name of Christ: none of which things, I understand, any genuine Christian can be induced to do.

Others, whose names were given to me by an informer, first admitted the charge and then denied it; they said that they had ceased to be Christians two or more years previously, and some of them even twenty years ago. They all did reverence to your statue and the images of the gods in the same way as the others, and reviled the name of Christ. They also declared that the sum total of their guilt or error amounted to no more than this: they had met regularly more dawn on a fixed day to teat verses alternately amongst themselves in honor of Christ as if to a god, and also to bind themselves by oath, not for any criminal purpose, but to abstain from theft, robbery, and adultery, to commit no breach of trust and not to deny a deposit when called upon to restore it. After this ceremony it had been their custom to disperse and reassemble later to take food of an ordinary, harmless kind; but they had in fact given up this practice since my edict, issued on your instructions, which banned all political societies. This made me decide it was all the more necessary to extract the truth by torture from two slave-women, whom they call deaconesses. I found nothing but a degenerate sort of cult carried to extravagant lengths.

I have therefore postponed any further examination and hastened to consult you. The question seems to me to be worthy of your consideration, especially in view of the number of persons endangered; for a great many individuals of every age and class, both men and women, are being brought to trial, and this is likely to continue. It is not only the towns, but villages and rural districts too which are infected through contact with this wretched cult. I think though that it is still possible for it to be checked and directed to better ends, for there is no doubt that people have begun to throng the temples which had been almost entirely deserted for a long time; the sacred rites which had been allowed to lapse are being performed again, and flesh of sacrificial victims is on sale everywhere, though up till recently scarcely anyone could be found to buy it. It is easy to infer from this that a great many people could be reformed if they were given an opportunity to repent.

Trajan to Pliny

You have followed the right course of procedure, my dear Pliny, in your examination of the cases of persons charged with being Christians, for it is impossible to lay down a general rule to a fixed formula. These people must not be hunted out; if they are brought before you and the charge against them is proved, they must be punished, but in the case of anyone who denies that he is a Christian, and makes it clear that he is not by offering prayers to our gods, he is to be pardoned as a result of his repentance however suspect his past conduct may be. But pamphlets circulated anonymously must play no part in any accusation. They create the worst sort of precedent and are quite out of keeping with the spirit of our age.

52

The Vision of Constantine, from Eusebius' *The Life of Constantine* (1.27–31)

Eusebius, *The Life of the Blessed Emperor Constantine*, originally published by Samuel Bagster and Sons in 1845, revised translation with prolegomena and notes by Ernest Cushing Richardson, New York, 1890, pp. 489–491.

Available online at Internet Medieval Sourcebook

The Life of Constantine is attributed to the Christian historian Eusebius, bishop of Caesaria in Palestine (260's-330's CE). The following selection recounts Contantine's vision, and subsequent conversion to Christianity, during his campaign against Maxentius in 312.

Being convinced, however, that he needed some more powerful aid than his military forces could afford him, on account of the wicked and magical enchantments which were so diligently practiced by the tyrant, he sought Divine assistance ... Accordingly he called on him with earnest prayer and supplications that he would reveal to him who he was, and stretch forth his right hand to help him in his present difficulties. And while he was thus praying with fervent entreaty, a most marvelous sign appeared to him from heaven, the account of which it might have been hard to believe had it been related by any other person. But since the victorious emperor himself long afterwards declared it to the writer of this history, when he was honored with his acquaintance and society, and confirmed his statement by an oath, who could hesitate to accredit the relation, especially since the testimony of after-time has established its truth? He said that about noon, when the day was already beginning to decline, he saw with his own eyes the trophy of a cross of light in the heavens, above the sun, and bearing the inscription, CONQUER

BY THIS. At this sight he himself was struck with amazement, and his whole army also, which followed him on this expedition, and witnessed the miracle.

He said, moreover, that he doubted within himself what the import of this apparition could be. And while he continued to ponder and reason on its meaning, night suddenly came on; then in his sleep the Christ of God appeared to him with the same sign which he had seen in the heavens, and commanded him to make a likeness of that sign which he had seen in the heavens, and to use it as a safeguard in all engagements with his enemies.

At dawn of day he arose, and communicated the marvel to his friends: and then, calling together the workers in gold and precious stones, he sat in the midst of them, and described to them the figure of the sign he had seen, bidding them represent it in gold and precious stones. And this representation I myself have had an opportunity of seeing.

Now it was made in the following manner. A long spear, overlaid with gold, formed the figure of the cross by means of a transverse bar laid over it. On the top of the whole was fixed a wreath of gold and precious stones; and within this, the symbol of the Savior's name, two letters indicating the name of Christ by means of its initial characters, the letter P being intersected by X in its center, and these letters the emperor was in the habit of wearing on his helmet at a later period. From the cross-bar of the spear was suspended a cloth, a royal piece, covered with a profuse embroidery of most brilliant precious stones; and which, being also richly interlaced with gold, presented an indescribable degree of beauty to the beholder. This banner was of a square form, and the upright staff, whose lower section was of great length, bore a golden half-length portrait of the pious emperor and his children on its upper part, beneath the trophy of the cross, and immediately above the embroidered banner.

The emperor constantly made use of this sign of salvation as a safeguard against every adverse and hostile power, and commanded that others similar to it should be carried at the head of all his armies.

53

Constantine's gifts to Old St. Peters, from "The Life of Pope Sylvester I", *The Book of the Popes* (*Liber Pontificalis*, chapter 34)

The Book of the Popes (Liber Pontificalis), volume I, translated with an introduction by Louise Ropes Loomis, New York, Columbia University Press, 1916, pp. 53–5.

Available online at Internet Archive

Credit: "Constantine's Gifts to Old St. Peters," *The Book of the Popes*, vol. 1, trans. Louise Ropes Loomis. Copyright in the Public Domain.

The Liber Pontificalis *is a series of papal biographies, compiled by multiple authors, that begins with Saint Peter in the first century CE. The following is a list of gifts given by the emperor Constantine to Old St. Peter's in the time of Pope Sylvester* I *(314–335 CE). Imagine the stunning visual effect so much gold and silver and jewels had on visitors to these early churches.*

Constantine Augustus built the basilica of blessed Peter, the apostle... and laid there the coffin with the body of the holy Peter; the coffin itself he enclosed on all sides with bronze... Above he set porphyry columns for adornment and other spiral columns which he brought from Greece. He made also a vaulted roof in the basilica, gleaming with polished gold, and over the body of the blessed Peter, above the bronze which enclosed it, he set a cross of purest gold weighing 150 lbs., ... He gave also 4 brass candlesticks, 10 feet in height, overlaid with silver, with figures in silver of the acts of the apostles weighing each 300 lbs., ... 3 golden chalices ... 2 silver jars ... 20 silver chalices ... 2 golden pitchers ... 5 silver pitchers ... a golden paten with a turret of purest gold and a dove ... a golden crown before the body, that is a chandelier, with 50 dolphins ... 32 silver lamps in the body of the basilica, with dolphins ... for the right of the basilica 30 silver lamps ... the altar itself of silver overlaid with gold, adorned on every side with gems, 400 in number ... a censer of purest gold adorned on every side with jewels 60 in number.

The Byzantine World

54

Theodora, a depraved woman, from Procopius' *The Secret History* (9–10)

Procopius, *Secret History*, translated by Richard Atwater, Chicago, P. Covici, 1927, reprinted Ann Arbor, University of Michigan Press, 1961, pp. 45–54.

Available online at Internet Medieval Sourcebook

The historian Procopius of Caesaria (sixth century CE) wrote The Wars of Justinian *and* The Buildings of Justinian *(see #55). He wrote* The Secret History *as a supplement in which he launched vicious attacks against the imperial court, especially against the empress Theodora. Some of Procopius' revelations about Theodora's life prior to her marriage to Justinian, such as presented in the passage below, are remarkably titillating but appear to be at least partially based in fact.*

Acacius was the keeper of wild beasts used in the amphitheater in Constantinople; he belonged to the Green faction and was nicknamed the Bear keeper. This man, during the rule of Anastasius, fell sick and died, leaving three daughters named Comito, Theodora and Anastasia: of whom the eldest was not yet seven years old. His widow took a second husband, who with her undertook to keep up Acacius's family and profession...

When these children reached the age of girlhood, their mother put them on the local stage, for they were fair to look upon; she sent them forth, however, not all at the same time, but as each one seemed to her to have reached a suitable age... Now Theodora was still too young to know the normal relation of man with maid, but consented to the unnatural violence of villainous slaves who, following their masters to the theater, employed their leisure in this infamous manner. And for some time in a brothel she suffered such misuse.

But as soon as she arrived at the age of youth, and was now ready for the world, her mother put her on the stage. Forthwith, she became a courtesan, and such as the ancient Greeks used to call a common one, at that: for she was not a flute or harp player, nor was she even trained to dance, but only gave her youth to anyone she met, in utter abandonment. Her general favors included, of course, the actors in the theater; and in their productions she took part in the low comedy scenes. For she was very funny and a good mimic and immediately became popular in this art. There was no shame in the girl, and no one ever saw her dismayed: no role was too scandalous for her to, accept without a blush.

She was the kind of comedienne who delights the audience by letting herself be cuffed and slapped on the cheeks, and makes them guffaw by raising her skirts to reveal to the spectators those feminine secrets here and there which custom veils from the eyes of the opposite sex. With pretended laziness she mocked her lovers, and coquettishly adopting ever new ways of embracing, was able to keep in a constant turmoil the hearts of the sophisticated. And she did not wait to be asked by anyone she met, but on the contrary, with inviting jests and a comic flaunting of her skirts herself tempted all men who passed by, especially those who were adolescent.

On the field of pleasure she was never defeated. Often she would go picnicking with ten young men or more, in the flower of their strength and virility, and dallied with them all, the whole night through. When they wearied of the sport, she would approach their servants, perhaps thirty in number, and fight a duel with each of these; and even thus found no allayment of her craving...

Often, even in the theater, in the sight of all the people, she removed her costume and stood nude in their midst, except for a girdle about the groin: not that she was abashed at revealing that, too, to the audience, but because there was a law against appearing altogether naked on the stage, without at least this much of a fig-leaf. Covered thus with a ribbon, she would sink down to the stage floor and recline on her back. Slaves to whom the duty was entrusted would then scatter grains of barley from above into the calyx of this passion flower, whence geese, trained for the purpose, would next pick the grains one by one with their bills and eat. When she rose, it was not with a blush, but she seemed rather to glory in the performance. For she was not only impudent herself, but endeavored to make everybody else as audacious. Often when she was alone with other actors she would undress in their midst and arch her back provocatively, advertising like a peacock both to those who had experience of her and to those who had not yet had that privilege her trained suppleness...

Later, she followed Hecebolus, a Tyrian who had been made governor of Pentapolis, serving him in the basest of ways; but finally she quarreled with him and was sent summarily away. Consequently, she found herself destitute of the means of life, which she proceeded to earn by prostitution, as she had done before this adventure. She came thus to Alexandria, and then traversing all the East, worked her way to Constantinople; in every city plying a trade (which it is safer, I fancy, in the sight of God not to name too clearly) as if the Devil were determined there be no land on earth that should not know the sins of Theodora.

Thus was this woman born and bred, and her name was a byword beyond that of other common wenches on the tongues of all men.

But when she came back to Constantinople, Justinian fell violently in love with her. At first he kept her only as a mistress, though he raised her to patrician rank. Through him Theodora was able immediately to acquire an unholy power and exceedingly great riches. She seemed to him the sweetest thing in the world, and like all lovers, he desired to please his charmer with every possible favor and requite her with all his wealth. The extravagance added fuel to the flames of passion. With her now to help spend his money he plundered the people more than ever, not only in the capital, but throughout the Roman Empire...

Thus it was that Theodora, though born and brought up as I have related, rose to royal dignity over all obstacles. For no thought of shame came to Justinian in marrying her, though he might have taken his pick of the noblest born, most highly educated, most modest, carefully nurtured, virtuous and beautiful virgins of all the ladies in the whole Roman Empire: a maiden, as they say, with upstanding breasts. Instead, he preferred to make his own what had been common to all men, alike, careless of all her revealed history, took in wedlock a woman who was not only guilty of every other contamination but boasted of her many abortions...

Now Theodora was fair of face and of a very graceful, though small, person; her complexion was moderately colorful, if somewhat pale; and her eyes were dazzling and vivacious. All eternity would not be long enough to allow one to tell her escapades while she was on the stage, but the few details I have mentioned above should be sufficient to demonstrate the woman's character to future generations.

55

The Hagia Sophia, from Procopius' *Buildings* (1.1.23–49)

Procopius in seven volumes, volume VII: *On Buildings*, translated by H. B. Dewing. Loeb Classical Library. Cambridge, Harvard University Press, 1940, reprinted 2002, pp.11, 13, 17, 19, 21, 23.

Available online at LacusCurtius

Credit: Procopius, "The Hagia Sophia," *Procopius in Seven Volumes*, vol. 7, trans. H.B. Dewing. Copyright in the Public Domain.

Procopius was a historian during the reign of Emperor Justinian (see #54). He wrote an entire book about the fortifications, aqueducts, churches, and other public buildings constructed by Justinian throughout the Byzantine Empire. The book begins with the greatest of these, the Hagia Sophia or church of Holy Wisdom in Constantinople, now Istanbul.

The Emperor, disregarding all questions of expense, eagerly pressed on to begin the work of construction, and began to gather all the artisans from the whole world. And Anthemius of Tralles, the most learned man in the skilled craft which is known as the art of building... ministered to the Emperor's enthusiasm, duly regulating the tasks of the various artisans, and preparing in advance designs of the future construction; and associated with him with another master-builder, Isidorus by name, a Milesian by birth...

So the church has become a spectacle of marvelous beauty, overwhelming to those who see it, but to those who know it by hearsay altogether incredible. For it soars to a height to match the sky, and as if surging up from amongst the other buildings it stands on high and looks down upon the remainder of the city... Both its breadth and its length have been so carefully proportioned, that it may not improperly be said to be exceedingly long and at the same time unusually broad. And it exults in an indescribable beauty.

For it proudly reveals its mass and the harmony of its proportions, having neither excess nor deficiency, since it is both more pretentious than the buildings to which we are accustomed, and considerably more noble than those which are merely huge, and it abounds exceedingly in sunlight and in the reflection of the sun's rays from the marble. Indeed one might say that its interior is not illuminated from without by the sun, but that the radiance comes into being within it, such an abundance of light bathes this shrine...

And in the center of the church stand four man-made eminences, which they call piers, two on the north side and two on the south, opposite and equal to each other, each pair having between them just four columns. The piers are composed of huge stones joined together, carefully selected and skillfully fitted to one another by the masons, and rising to a great height. One might suppose that they were sheer mountain-peaks. From these spring four arches which rise over the four sides of a square...Upon the crowns of the arches rests a circular structure, cylindrical in shape; it is through this that the light of day always first smiles... And since the arches where they are joined together are so constructed as to form a four-cornered plan, the stonework between the arches produces four triangles [i.e., pendentives]... And upon this circle rests the huge spherical dome which makes the structure exceptionally beautiful. Yet it seems not to rest upon solid masonry, but to cover the space suspended from Heaven by a golden chain. All these details, fitted together with incredible skill in mid-air and floating off from each other and resting only on the parts next to them, produce a single and most extraordinary harmony in the work, and yet do not permit the spectator to linger much over the study of any one of them, but each detail attracts the eye and draws it on irresistibly to itself. So the vision constantly shifts suddenly, for the beholder is utterly unable to select which particular detail he should admire more than all the others. But even so, though they turn their attention to every side and look with contracted brows upon every detail, observers are still unable to understand the skillful craftsmanship, but they always depart from there overwhelmed by the bewildering sight. So much, then, for this.

56

The church of S. Apollinare Nuovo, from "The Life of Bishop Agnellus" in Andreas Agnellus' *Book of the Pontiffs of the Church of Ravenna (De Agnello 28.86 & 88)*

The Book of Pontiffs of the Church of Ravenna, translated with an introduction and notes by Deborah Mauskopf Deliyannis, Washington, Catholic University of America Press, 2004, pp. 200–202

Andreas Agnellus of Ravenna was a 9th century historian and author of the Liber Pontificalis Ecclesiae Ravennatis (LPR). Modeled after the Liber Pontificalis (see #53), the LPR recounts the deeds of the first 48 bishops of Ravenna and is a rich source of information concerning the buildings and inscriptions in that city. Here Andreas Agnellus describes how the 28th bishop, also named Agnellus (circa 557–570), made some changes to a church originally built by the Ostrogoth ruler Theodoric (see Fig. 28). Because Theodoric was a heretical Arian, the church's dedication was changed from Christ the Redeemer to St. Martin, a well-known foe of Arianism. Later, in 856, the basilica was re-consecrated again to St. Apollinaris when that saint's relics were moved there from his church in Ravenna's port city of Classe.

Therefore this most blessed one [Bishop Agnellus] reconciled all the churches of the Goths, which were built in the times of the Goths or of King Theodoric, which were held by Arian Falsehood and the sect, doctrine and credulity of the heretics...

Therefore the most blessed Bishop Agnellus reconciled the church of St. Martin the Confessor [now S. Apollinare Nuovo] in this city, which King

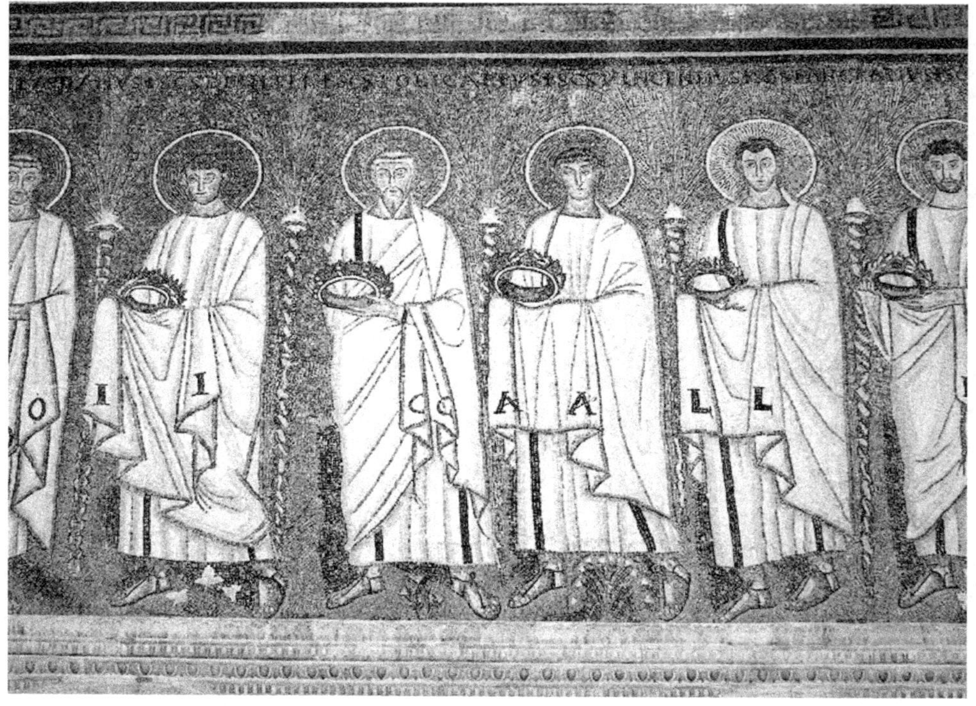

Fig. 28 Detail of the procession of the martyrs mosaic inside S. Apollinare Nuovo in Ravenna.

Theodoric founded, which is called the Golden Heaven; he decorated the apse and both side walls with images in mosaic of processions of martyrs and virgins; indeed he laid over this stucco covered with gold, he stuck multi-colored stones to the side walls and composed a pavement of wonderful cut marble pieces. If you look on its façade on the inside you will find the image of Emperor Justinian and Bishop Agnellus decorated with gold mosaics. No church or house is similar to this one in beams and coffers of its ceiling. And after he consecrated it, he feasted in the episcopal palace of that confessor. Indeed in the apse, if you look closely, you will find the following written above the windows in stone letters: "King Theodoric made this church from its foundations in the name of our Lord Jesus Christ."

…You can see this on the wall: there, as I said, two cities were made. From Ravenna the martyrs lead forth, on the men's [south] side, going to Christ; from Classe the virgins proceed, proceeding to the holy Virgin of virgins, and the Magi going before them, offering gifts.

But why are they depicted in different clothing and not all wearing the same garment? Because the artist followed divine Scripture. For Caspar offered gold in a reddish garment, and in this garment signifies marriage. Balthasar offered frankincense in a yellow garment, and in this garment signifies virginity. Melchior offered myrrh in a multicolored costume, and in this costume signifies penitence.

He who went first, wearing a purple mantle, through it signifies the King who was born and suffered. He who offered his gift to the Newborn in a multicolored mantle signifies through this that Christ cares for all the weary, and was whipped by the various injuries and blows of the Jews... He who offered his gift in white signifies that He exists in divine clarity after the resurrection.

For likewise the three precious gifts contain divine mysteries in them, that is, by gold is meant regal wealth, by frankincense the figure of the priest, by myrrh death, thus through all these things they show him to be the one who undertook the iniquities of men, that is, Christ; and thus in their mantles, as we said, these three gifts are contained.

Why did not four, not six, not two, but only these three come from the east? So that they might entirely signify the perfect plenitude of the Trinity, for the love of whom that most blessed Agnellus decorated part of the fine linen altar cloth, as we made mention above, which his predecessor Maximian had not finished, decorated it perfectly with the story of the Magi, and his image was inserted with embroidery.

Image credits

Fig. 28: Georges Jansoone, "Mosaic detail from S. Apollinare Nuovo," https://commons.wikime-dia.org/wiki/File:Sant%27.Apollinare.Nuovo04.jpg. Copyright in the Public Domain.

57

The healing power of an image of Saints Cosmos and Damian, from the records of The Second Church Council at Nicaea

The Seventh Great Council, the second of Nicaea, held A.D. 787 in which the worship of images was established: with copious notes from the 'Caroline Books', translated by John Mendham, London, William Edward Painter, 1850, pp.194–95.

Available online at Google Books

The text quoted below is one of many miraculous image stories presented at the second Council of Nicaea in 787. This was used as a form of proof that such images were sanctioned by heaven and should not, therefore, be destroyed. Indeed, this council ended the period of Iconoclasm in the Byzantine Empire. Saints Cosmos and Damian were twin physicians martyred during the reign of Diocletian in the third century CE. Here, a woman is healed by actually ingesting the painted plaster from a frescoed image of them. What icons of saints were to the Byzantine east, the physical remains or relics of saints were to the Western Church. Compare this to the power of the sacred relics of St. Giles from the Pilgrim's Guide to Santiago de Compostela *(#79).*

A believing woman... was not content with having these great and wonderful Saints, Cosmas and Damian, every day in her mind, but she must have their pictures painted on every wall in her house, as if she could never be satisfied with gazing upon them. From this, her superabundant affection, the following event took place; and let no one deem it unworthy of belief, for want of faith is everywhere to be condemned as injurious to the interests of the soul. It happened that this woman was afflicted with an internal disease and was confined to her house with unmitigated pains; and she rolled in her bed in incessant agonies, nor had she a moment's rest from her pangs. On one occasion she found herself for a short time alone; and, as she reflected on her danger, she contrived to drag herself along and to descend from the bed. And making towards that part of the wall where the images—these all-wise Saints–had been painted, using her faith as a crutch, she raised herself up; and, having scratched off a little of the paint with her nails and cast it into water she drank up the mixture, and immediately she was made whole—her internal pains ceasing at once on the entering in of the Saints!

58

Resurrecting images in the Hagia Sophia, from Photios' *Homilies* (17)

The Homilies of Photios Patriarch of Constantinople, English translation, introduction and commentary by Cyril Mango, Cambridge, Harvard University Press, 1958, pp. 291–3.

Credit: Photios, "Resurrecting Images in the Hagia Sophia," *The Homilies of Photius, Patriarch of Constantinople (#17)*, pp. 291-293, trans. Cyril Mango. Copyright in the Public Domain.

Photios was the Patriarch of Constantinople during the second half of the ninth century. Here he dedicates an image of the Virgin and Child on March 29, 867 and celebrates the Eastern Orthodox Church's victory over Iconoclasm. The image is probably the mosaic still visible in the apse of the Hagia Sophia today (Fig. 29). It was originally surrounded by a text, now only partially preserved, that read: "The images which the impostors had cast down here pious emperors have again set up."

Of the Same Most-Blessed Photios, Patriarch of Constantinople, Homily Delivered from the Ambo of the Great Church, on Holy Saturday, in the Presence of the Christ-Loving Emperors, when the Form of the Theotokos had been Depicted and Uncovered.

...And so, as the eye of the universe, this celebrated and sacred church, looked sad with its visual mysteries scraped off, as it were (for it had not yet received the privilege of pictorial restoration), it shed but faint rays from its face to visitors, and in this respect the countenance of Orthodoxy appeared gloomy. Now, casting off this sadness also, and beautifying herself with all her own conspicuous ornaments, and displaying her rich dowry, gladly and joyously she hearkens to the Bridegroom's voice, Who cries out saying, "All fair is my companion, and there is no spot in her. Fair is my companion."

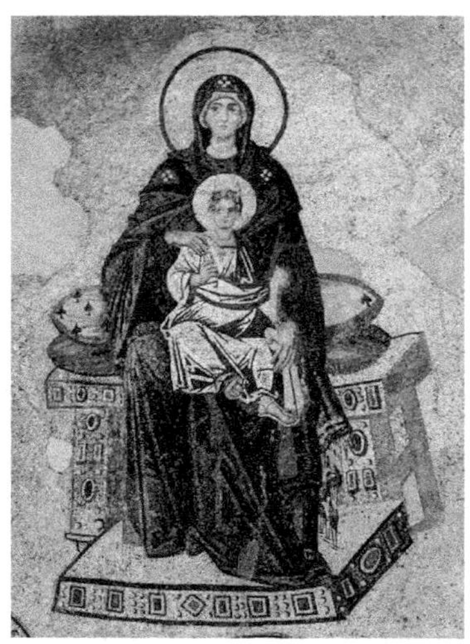

Fig. 29 Mosaic of the Virgin and Child, apse of the Hagia Sophia, Istanbul.

For, having mingled the bloom of colors with religious truth, and by means of both having in holy manner fashioned unto herself a holy beauty, and bearing, so to speak, a complete and perfect image of piety, she is seen not only to be fair in beauty surpassing the sons of men, but elevated to an inexpressible fairness of dignity beyond any comparison beside. All fair is my companion. She has escaped the blows, has been freed of her wounds, has wiped off all blemish, has cast down her detractors into Hell, has raised up those who sang her praises. And there is no spot in her. She has overcome the blemishes wherewith a foul foreign hand had aimed and spotted her whole body. She has wiped off all those stains, and taking up again her former bridal raiment, she has put it on…

We too, with gladness and joy in our souls, join the choir of this festival, and sharing today in the celebration of this restoration, we exclaim those prophetic words, saying, "Rejoice greatly, O daughter of Sion; cry aloud, O daughter of Jerusalem. The Lord has taken away thine injuries; He has delivered thee from the hand of thine enemies. Lift up thine eyes round about, and see thy children gathered. For behold, all thy sons have come from far, yea and thy daughters, bearing unto thee not gold and frankincense and stones, all begotten of the earth and by human custom adorning what is precious, but purer than all gold, and more precious than all stones, the ancestral faith unadulterated. Rejoice and delight thyself with all thine heart, for behold, the Lord is coming, and He shall fix His tabernacle in thy midst." What could be more agreeable than this day? What could be more explicit than this feast to give expression to gladness and joy? This is another shaft being driven today right through the heart of Death, not as the Savior is engulfed by the tomb of mortality for the common resurrection of our kind, but as the image of the Mother rises up from the very depths of oblivion, and raises along with herself the likenesses of the saints. Christ came to us in the flesh, and was borne in the arms of His Mother. This is seen and confirmed and proclaimed in pictures, the teaching made manifest by means of personal eyewitness, and impelling the spectators to unhesitating assent…

Image credits

59

Image of the Pantocrator, from Nicholas Mesarites' *Description of the Church of the Holy Apostles*

Glanville Downey, "Nikolaos Mesarites: Description of the Church of the Holy Apostles at Constantinople" *Transactions of the American Philosophical Society*, 47, 1957, pp. 869–870.

Available online at JStor

The Church of the Holy Apostles in Constantinople, destroyed in the fifteenth century, was decorated with mosaics by the artist Eulalios in the twelfth century. As at the church of the Dormition at Daphne, the central dome displayed an image of the Pantocrator. In this text a contemporary author, Nicholas Mesarites, offers an interpretation of this figure of Christ in the dome.

This dome shows in pictured form the God-man Christ, leaning and gazing out as though from the rim of heaven, at the point where the dome begins toward the floor of the Church and everything in it, but not with His whole body or in His whole form. This I think was very wisely done by the artist as he turned the matter over in his mind and revealed the very clever conclusion of his intelligence through his art to those who do not observe superficially, because for one thing, I believe, we now know in part as though in a riddle and in a glass, the things concerning Christ and in accord with Christ; and for another thing the God-Man will appear to us from heaven at the time of His second sojourn [i.e., Second Coming] on earth, though the space of time until that coming has never yet been wholly measured, and because He himself dwells in heaven in the bosom of His Father and together with His own

Father will return to men on earth according to that saying the "I and my Father will come and make our abode with him." Wherefore one can see Him, to use the words of the Song [Canticle 2:9], looking forth at the windows, leaning out as far as His navel through the lattice at the summit of the dome like an earnest and vehement lover. His head is of the same size as the body which is depicted as far as the navel; His eyes, to those who have achieved a clean understanding, are gentle and friendly... to those, however, who are condemned by their own judgment they are scornful and hostile and boding of ill; the face is wrathful, terrifying, stern and filled with hardness, for the face of the Lord is of this fashion for evildoers. The right hand blesses those who are straight in their paths and warns those who are not straight and so to speak sends them back and turns them from their disorderly way. The left hand, spreading its fingers as far as possible from each other, supports the Gospel of Him who holds it, and grasps it closely and as it were rests it on the left side of the breast, and by the resting of it there procures no small relief from the burden.

60

Concerning the Statues of Constantinople destroyed by the Crusaders, from Nicetas Choniates' *Historia*

Michaud's History of the Crusades, volume III, translated from the French by W. Robson, London, George Routledge and Co., 1852, pp. 435–437.

Available online at Internet Archive

Nicetas of Chonae, a Byzantine historian, was an eyewitness to the capture of Constantinople by the Fourth Crusade in 1204. In this short treatise he describes the plundering of graves and churches by the Crusaders. He also describes how a number of ancient bronze statues that were still standing in the public places of the city at the time were melted down for the value of their metal. Indeed, most of the great sculptors of antiquity worked in bronze and plunder is the reason why we have so few original bronze statues from the antiquity to study.

The Latins manifested that love of gold which characterizes their nation, by thinking of a new species of plunder, till that time unknown to all the former spoilers of this city of cities. After opening the coffins of the emperors which are in the Heroon, erected near the magnificent Church of the disciples of Jesus Christ, they pillaged them all during the night; and, in violation of the laws of equity, they took away all the ornaments in gold, pearls, and precious transparent stones, which had so long remained untouched in that sacred place. Having found, likewise, the body of the Emperor Justinian, still perfect and undecomposed, after the lapse of so many years, this spectacle struck them with admiration; but they paid no more respect, on that account, to the ornaments with which the body had been buried.

It may be affirmed that the Westerners spared neither the living nor the dead, and beginning with God and his servants, they made all, indifferently, sensible to the effects of their impiety. A short time after, they bore away from the great church [Haghia Sophia] that veil which was valued at many thousand silver minae, and which was ornamented with thick golden embroidery. But as even all these riches could not satisfy the boundless cupidity of these barbarians, they cast their eyes upon the bronze statues, and consigned them to the flames The Juno of bronze, which stood in the Square of Constantine, was taken to pieces and sent to the melting house, to be transformed into staters [coins]; so large was this statue that the head was as much as four pairs of oxen could draw to the palace.

After the Juno, they took down from its base a group of Paris and Venus; the shepherd offering the goddess the golden apple of discord... This work, of admirable beauty, was likewise melted, as was a colossal statue, which stood in the place of Taurus, and represented a man on horseback in heroic costume... There was an ancient tradition, which was preserved to our times, and known to everybody, that under the left forefoot of this horse, was concealed the figure of a man, representing, according to some a Venetian, and according to others, some other enemy from the West, bearing a Roman name, or else it was a Bulgarian. Efforts had often been made to render this foot so firm and so solid that it might not be possible to discover what was said to be hidden beneath it. When this horse and his rider were taken to pieces to be melted, the figure was really found concealed under the foot of the horse; it was clothed in a mantle, much in appearance like one of wool; but the Latins, troubling themselves very little about the predictions concerning it, cast it also into the fire. Many other statues and admirable works, standing in the Hippodrome, shared the same fate, and were destroyed by these barbarians, who, incapable of admiration for the beautiful, converted all these master-pieces into coin, and annihilated monuments which had cost so much, for the sake of such an inconsiderable amount of money.

The Art of Islam

61

Description of Paradise, from *The Koran*

For Muslims, the Koran (or Qur'an, meaning 'The Recital') is the word of God as revealed to the Prophet Mohammed (circa 570–632). Hence, the speaker throughout the Koran, with very few exceptions, is God or Allah. The text is divided into chapters or surahs and arranged not in chronological order but generally in order of length. What follows below is one of the latter shorter surahs ('The Merciful') which includes one of the fuller descriptions of paradise—which the grounds of the Taj Mahal mausoleum, built by the Mughal emperor Shah Jahan for his wife Mumtaz Mahal, attempt to embody.

...But for those that fear the majesty of their Lord there are two gardens (which of you Lord's blessings would you deny?) planted with shady trees. Which of your Lord's blessings would you deny?

Each is watered by a flowing spring. Which of your Lord's blessings would you deny?

Each bears every kind of fruit in pairs. Which of your Lord's blessings would you deny?

They shall recline on couches lined with thick brocade and within reach will hang the fruits of both gardens. Which of your Lord's blessings would you deny?

Therein are bashful virgins whom neither man nor jinee will have touched before. Which of your Lord's blessings would you deny?

Virgins as fair as corals and rubies. Which of your Lord's blessings would you deny?

Shall the reward of goodness be anything but goo? Which of your Lord's blessings would you deny?

And beside these there shall be two other gardens (which of your Lord's blessings would you deny?) of darkest green. Which of your Lord's blessings would you deny?

A gushing fountain shall flow in each. Which of your Lord's blessings would you deny?

Each planted with fruit-trees, the palm and the pomegranate. Which of your Lord's blessings would you deny?

In each there shall be virgins chaste and fair. Which of your Lord's blessings would you deny?

Dark-eyed virgins sheltered in their tents (which of your Lord's blessings would you deny?) whom neither man nor jinnee will have touched before. Which of your Lord's blessings would you deny?

They shall recline on green cushions and fine carpets. Which of your Lord's blessings would you deny?

Blessed be the name of your Lord, the Lord of majesty and glory!

62

The importance of Calligraphy, excerpt from the 2nd Dervish story in *A Thousand and One Arabian Nights*

The Arabian Nights, edited by Muhsin Mahdi, translated by Husain Haddawy, New York, W. W. Norton & Company, 1990, pp. 127–129.

The speaker here is a prince who has been turned into an ape by a jinnee. He proves his humanity in a distant land by demonstrating his ability to write verse in six cursive calligraphic scripts. The highly esteemed art form of calligraphy, the earliest of which is called Kufic, can be found on all sorts of surfaces in the Islamic world including buildings, textiles, ceramics, and glass. Its decorative use was even imitated in Medieval and Renaissance European art (see Fig. 30). The tales collected in the Arabian Nights *have their roots in Arabic, Mesopotamian, Persian, Indian, Jewish, and Egyptian folklore and are often imbedded in larger frame stories. For example, the second Dervish story (Central Asian possibly) is imbedded within the tale of the Porter and the Three Ladies of Baghdad (Mesopotamian), and that within the larger narrative of Shahrazad (Persian). As such, the* Arabian Nights *reflects the vast area of the Islamic world, and its complex interweaving of themes from far-flung regions is perhaps the one universal element in all early Islamic art.*

For fifty days the ship sailed on before a fair wind until we came to a great city, vast and teeming with countless people. No sooner had we entered the port and cast anchor then we were visited by messengers from the king of that city. They boarded the ship and said, "Merchants, our king congratulates you on

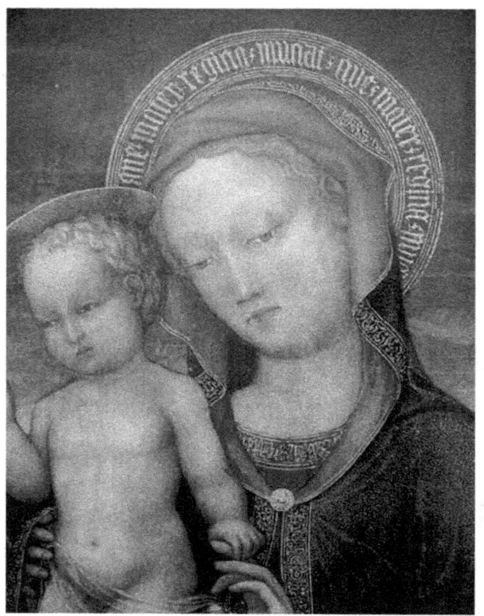

Fig. 30 Imitation Arabic calligraphy (called pseudo-kufic) on the edge of the Virgin's robes; the halo, however, is in Roman script. Detail of Jacopo Billini's The Madonna of Humility adored by a prince of the House of Este, 1440.

your safe arrival, sends you this roll of paper, and bids each of you write one line on it. For the king's vizier, a man learned in state affairs and a skilled calligrapher, has died, and the king has sworn a solemn oath that he will appoint none in his place, save one who can write as well as he could." Then they handed the merchants a roll of paper, ten cubits long and one cubit wide, and each of the merchants who knew how to write wrote a line. When they came to the end, I snatched the scroll out of their hands, and they screamed and scolded me, fearing that I would throw it into the sea or tear it to pieces, but as I signed to them that I wanted to write on it, and they were exceedingly amazed, saying, "We have never yet seen an ape write." the captain said to them, "Let him write what he likes, and if he merely scribbles, I will beat him and chase him away, but if he writes well, I will adopt him as my son, for I have never seen a more intelligent or better-behaved ape. I wish that my son had this ape's understanding and good manners."

Then I held the pen, dipped it in the inkpot, and in Ruqa' script wrote the following lines:

> Time's record of the favors of the great
> Has been effaced by your greater favor.
> Of you your children God will not deprive,
> You, being to grace both mother and father.

Then under these, in Muhaqqiq script I wrote the following lines:

> His pen has showered bounty everywhere
> And without favor favored every land.
> Yet even the Nile, which destroys the earth,
> Cannot its ink use with such mighty hand.

And in Raihani script I wrote the following lines:

> I wore, whoever uses me to write,
> By the One, Peerless, Everlasting God,
> That he would never any man deny

With one of the pen's strokes his livelihood.

Then in Naskhi script I wrote the following lines:

> There is no writer who from death will flee,
> But what his hand has written time will keep.
> Commit to paper nothing then, except
> What you would like on Judgment Day to see.

Then in Thuluth script I wrote the following lines:

> When the events of life our love condemned
> And painful separation was our end,
> We turned to the inkwell's mouth to complain,
> And voiced with the pen's tongue our parting's pain.

Then in Tumar script I wrote the following lines:

> When you open the inkwell of your boon
> And fame, let the ink be munificence and grace.
> Write good and generous deeds while write you can;
> Both pen and sword such noble deeds will praise.

Then I handed them the scroll, and they took it back in amazement... The messengers took the scroll and returned with it to the king, and when he looked at it, my writing pleased him and he said, "Take this robe of honor and this she-mule to the master of these seven [sic, there are six] scripts." The men smiled, and seeing that their smiling had made the kin angry, they said, "O King of the age and sovereign of the world, the writer of these lines is an ape." The king asked, "Is this true what you say?" They replied, "Yes, by your bounty, the writer is an ape." The king was greatly amazed and said, "I wish to see this ape."

Image credits

Fig. 30: World Imaging, "Pseudo-Kufic on Billini's Madonna of Humility," https://commons. wikimedia.org/wiki/File:Jacopo_Bellini_La_Vierge_d_humilite_adoree_par_un_prince_de_la_ maison_d_Estee_1440_detail.jpg. Copyright in the Public Domain.

63

The battle of Poitiers, from the *Chronicle of St. Denis*

William Stearns Davis, editor, *Readings in Ancient History: Illustrative Extracts from the Sources*, Vol. II: *Rome and the West*, Boston, Allyn and Bacon, 1912–13, pp. 362–364.

Available online at Internet Medieval Sourcebook and Google Books

The Franks, led by Charles Martel or "the Hammer", defeated the Arabs at Tours (more properly the road between Poitiers and Tours) in 732. The Frankish victory is considered by many a turning point in the history of Europe. If the Muslims had seized southern Gaul, they would have been poised to conquer Italy and Rome itself, and the Western world, and its art, would have evolved in a very different way.

The Muslims planned to go to Tours to destroy the Church of St. Martin, the city, and the whole country. Then came against them the glorious Prince Charles, at the head of his whole force. He drew up his host, and he fought as fiercely as the hungry wolf falls upon the stag. By the grace of Our Lord, he wrought a great slaughter upon the enemies of Christian faith, so that—as history bears witness—he slew in that battle 300,000 men, likewise their king by name Abderrahman [=Abdul Rahman al Ghafiqi]. Then was he first called "Martel," for as a hammer of iron, of steel, and of every other metal, even so he dashed and smote in the battle all his enemies. And what was the greatest marvel of all, he only lost in that battle 1500 men. The tents and harness [of the enemy] were taken; and whatever else they possessed became a prey to him and his followers. Eudes, Duke of Aquitaine, being now reconciled with Prince Charles Martel, later slew as many of the Saracens as he could find who had escaped from the battle.

64

The battle of Poitiers, an
Arab perspective

Sir Edward Creasy, *Fifteen Decisive Battles of the World*, Everyman's Library, edited by Ernest Rhys, New York, E. P. Dutton and Co., 1908, reprinted 1910, p. 169.

Available online at Project Gutenberg and HathiTrust Digital Library

The author, Edward Creasy, says the following about the source for this anonymous text: "The Arabian chronicles were compiled and translated into Spanish by Don Jose Antonio Conde, in his Historia de la Dominacion de los Arabos an Espana, *published at Madrid in 1820." While neither account of the battle (#63 and #64) may be terribly accurate or reliable, it is rare to have a description of a battle from the perspective of both the victor and the vanquished.*

Near the river Owar, [probably the Loire] the two great hosts of the two languages and the two creeds were set in array against each other. The hearts of Abderrahman, his captains, and his men were filled with wrath and pride, and they were the first to begin the fight. The Muslim horseman dashed fierce and frequent forward against the battalions of the Franks, who resisted manfully, and many fell dead on either side, until the going down of the sun. Night parted the two armies: but in the grey of the morning the Muslims returned to the battle. Their cavaliers had soon hewn their way into the center of the Christian host. But many of the Muslims were fearful for the safety of the spoil which they had stored in their tents, and a false cry arose in their ranks that some of the enemy were plundering the camp; whereupon several squadrons of the Muslim horseman rode off to protect their tents. But it seemed as if they fled; and all the host was troubled. And while Abderrahman strove to check their tumult, and to lead them back to battle, the warriors of the Franks came around him, and he was pierced through with many spears, so that he died. Then all the host fled before the enemy, and many died in the flight. This deadly defeat of the Muslims, and the loss of the great leader and good cavalier Abderrahman, took place in the hundred and fifteenth year.

65

Dome of the Rock, from Al-Muqaddasi's *Best Divisions for Knowledge of the Regions*

Palestine under the Moslems: A description of Syria and the Holy Land from A.D. 650 to 1500, translated from the works of the mediaeval Arab geographers by Guy Le Strange, London, 1890, pp. 5–6, 117–118, 123–124.

Available online at HathiTrust Digital Library

Credit: Al-Muqaddasi, "Dome of the Rock," *Palestine under the Moslems: A description of Syria and the Holy Land from A.D. 650 to 1500*, pp. 117-118, 123-124, trans. Guy Le Strange. Copyright in the Public Domain.

Muhammad ibn Ahmad Shams al-Din al-Muqaddasi was a notable early Arab geographer from Al-Quds (Jerusalem). He is best known for his treatise entitled Ahsan at-Taqasim fi Ma'arifat al-Aqalim *(The Best Classification/ Divisions for the Knowledge of the Climes/Regions) written in 985 CE. Here he relates why Caliph al Walid (705–715) and his father Caliph al Malik built the first Islamic monumental structures and describes the appearance of the Dome of the Rock in his day.*

Now one day I said, speaking to my father's brother, 'O my uncle, verily it was not well of the Khalif [=Caliph] al Walid to expend so much of the wealth of the Muslims on the Mosque at Damascus. Had he expended the same on making roads, or for caravanserais, or in the restoration of the Frontier Fortresses, it would have been more fitting and more excellent of him.' But my uncle said to me in answer, 'O my little son, thou hast not understanding! Verily Al Walid was right, and he was prompted to a worthy work. For he beheld Syria to be a country that had long been occupied by the Christians, and he noted herein the beautiful churches still belonging to them, so enchantingly fair, and so renowned for their splendor, even as are the Kumamah [the Church of the Holy Sepulcher at Jerusalem], and the churches of Lydda and Edessa.

So he sought to build for the Muslims a mosque that should prevent their regarding these, and that should be unique and a wonder to the world. And in like manner is it not evident how the Khalif 'Abd al Malik, noting the greatness of the Dome of the Kumamah and its magnificence, was moved lest it should dazzle the minds of the Muslims, and hence erected above the Rock, the Dome which now is seen there?'…

The Court [of the Haram Area in Jerusalem] is paved in all parts; in its center rises a Platform, like that in the Mosque at Al Medina, to which, from all four sides, ascend broad flights of steps. On this Platform stand four Domes. Of these, the Dome of the Chain, the Dome of the Ascension, and the Dome of the Prophet are of small size. Their domes are covered with sheet lead, and are supported on marble pillars, being without walls.

In the center of the Platform is the Dome of the Rock, which rises above an octagonal building having four gates, one opposite to each of the flights of steps leading up from the Court. These four are the *Kiblah* [or southern] Gate; the Gate of [the Angel] *Israfil* [to the east]; the Gate *As Sur* [or of the Trumpet], to the north; and the Women's Gate [*Bab an Nisa*], which last opens towards the west. All these are adorned with gold, and closing each of them is a beautiful door of cedar-wood finely worked in patterns. These last were sent hither by command of the mother of the Khalif Al Muktadir-billah. Over each of the gates is a porch of marble, wrought with cedar-wood, with brass work without; and in this porch, likewise, are doors, but these are unornamented.

Within the building are three concentric colonnades, with columns of the most beautiful marble, polished, that can be seen, and above is a low vaulting. Inside these [colonnades] is the central hall over the Rock; it is circular, not octagonal, and is surrounded by columns of polished marble supporting circular arches. Built above these, and rising high into the air, is the drum, in which are large windows; and over the drum is the Dome. The Dome, from the floor up to the pinnacle, which rises into the air, is in height 100 ells. From afar off you may perceive on the summit of the Dome the beautiful pinnacle [set thereon], the size of which is a fathom and a span. The Dome, externally, is completely covered with brass plates gilt, while the building itself, its floor, and its walls, and the drum, both within and with out, are ornamented with marble and mosaics, after the manner that we shall describe when speaking of the Mosque of Damascus. The Cupola of the Dome is built in three sections; the inner is of ornamental panels. Next come iron beams interlaced, set in free, so that the wind may not cause the Cupola to shift; and the third casing is of wood, on which are fixed the outer plates. Up through the middle of the Cupola goes a passageway, by which a workman may ascend to the pinnacle for aught that may be wanting, or in order to repair the structure. At the dawn, when the light of the sun first strikes on the Cupola, and the Drum reflects his rays, then is this edifice a marvelous sight to behold, and one such that in all Islam I have never seen the equal; neither have I heard tell of aught built in pagan times that could rival in grace this Dome of the Rock.

66

Damascus and the Great Mosque, from Al-Muqaddasi's *Best Divisions for Knowledge of the Regions*

Palestine under the Moslems: A description of Syria and the Holy Land from A.D. 650 to 1500, translated from the works of the mediaeval Arab geographers by Guy Le Strange, London, 1890, pp. 225, 227–228.

Available online at HathiTrust Digital Library

In this section of Al Muqaddasi's geography he describes both the city of Damascus and the Great Mosque referenced above in #65.

Damascus is the chief town of Syria, and was the capital of the sovereigns of the House of Omayyah [=Ummayad Dynasty]. Here were their palaces and their monuments, their edifices in wood and in brick. The rampart round the city, which I saw when I was there, is built of mud-bricks. Most of the markets are roofed in, but there is one among them, a fine one, which is open, running the whole length of the town. Damascus is a city intersected by streams and begirt with trees. Here prices are moderate, fruits and snow abound, and the products of both hot and cold climes are found. Nowhere else will be seen such magnificent hot baths, nor such beautiful fountains, nor people more worthy of consideration.

The city is in itself a very pleasant place, but of its disadvantages are, that the climate is scorching and the inhabitants are turbulent. Fruit here is insipid, and meat hard; also the houses are small, and the streets somber. Finally, the bread there is bad, and a livelihood is difficult to make. Around the city, for the distance of half a league in every direction, there, stretches the level Plain...

The Mosque of Damascus is the fairest of any that the Muslims now hold, and nowhere is there collected together greater magnificence. Its outer walls are built of squared stones, accurately set, and of large size; and crowning the walls are splendid battlements. The columns supporting the roof of the Mosque consist of black polished pillars in a triple row, and set widely apart. In the center of the building, over the space fronting the Mihrab is a great dome. Round the court are lofty colonnades, above which are arched windows, and the whole area is paved with white marble. The [inner] walls of the Mosque, for twice the height of a man, are faced with variegated marbles; and, above this, even to the very ceiling, are mosaics of various colors and in gold, showing figures of trees and towns and beautiful inscriptions, all most exquisitely and finely worked. And rare are the trees, and few the well-known towns that will not be found figured on these walls! The capitals of the columns are covered with gold, and the vaulting above the arcades is everywhere ornamented in mosaic. The columns round the court are all of white marble, while the walls that enclose it, the vaulted arcades, and the arched windows above, are adorned in mosaic with arabesque designs. The roofs are everywhere overlaid with plates of lead, and the battlements on both sides are faced with the mosaic work.

On the right [or western] side of the court is the treasure house [*Bait Mal*] raised on eight columns, finely ornamented, and the walls are covered with mosaic. Both within the Mihrab, and around it, are set cut-agates and turquoises of the size of the finest stones that are used in rings. Beside the [great] Mihrab, and to the left [east] of it, there is another, which is for the special use of the Sultan. It was formerly much dilapidated; but I hear now that he has expended thereon five hundred Dinars to restore the same to its former condition. On the summit of the Dome of the Mosque is an orange, and above it a pomegranate, both in gold. But of the most wonderful of the sights here worthy of remark is verily the setting of the various colored marbles, and how the veining in each follows from that of its neighbor; and it is such that, should an artist come daily during a whole year and stand before these mosaics, he might always discover some new pattern and some fresh design. It is said that the Khalif al Walid, in order to construct these mosaics, brought skilled workmen from Persia, India, Western Africa, and Byzantium, spending thereon the whole revenues of Syria for seven years, as well as eighteen shiploads of gold and silver, which came from Cyprus. And this does not include what the Emperor of Byzantium and the Emirs of the Muslims gave to him in the matter of precious stones and other materials for the mosaics...

The Omayyad Khalif 'Omar ibn 'Abd al Aziz, it is said, wished at one time to demolish the Mosque, and make use of its materials in the public works of the Muslims, but he was at last persuaded to abandon the design. I have read in some book that there was expended on this Mosque the value of eighteen mule-loads of gold.

67

A Jewish traveler's description of Baghdad, from *The Itinerary of Benjamin of Tudela*

The Itinerary of Benjamin of Tudela, critical text, translation and commentary by Marcus Nathan Adler, London, Oxford University Press, 1907, pp. 35–39, 42.

Available online at Internet Archives

Benjamin of the Spanish city Tudela was an early Jewish traveler to the Near East during the twelfth century, a hundred years before Marco Polo. His book emphasizes the Jewish communities in the regions he visits. He lists population and structures, names leaders, and makes observations on living conditions—the direst of which were in Constantinople. In contrast, the Jewish population in Baghdad under the Abbasid Emir al Muminin enjoyed prominence and respect.

Thence it is two days to Baghdad, the great city and the royal residence of the Caliph Emir al Muminin al Abbasi of the family of Mohammed. He is at the head of the Mohammedan religion, and all the kings of Islam obey him; he occupies a similar position to that held by the Pope over the Christians. He has a palace in Baghdad three miles in extent, wherein is a great park with all varieties of trees, fruit-bearing and otherwise, and all manner of animals. The whole is surrounded by a wall, and in the park there is a lake whose waters are fed by the river Hiddekel. Whenever the king desires to indulge in recreation and to rejoice and feast, his servants catch all manner of birds, game and fish, and he goes to his palace with his counselors and princes. There the great king, Al Abbasi the Caliph holds his court, and he is kind unto Israel, and many belonging to the people of Israel are his attendants; he knows all languages, and is well versed in the law of Israel. He reads and writes the holy language [Hebrew]. He will not partake of anything unless he has earned it by the work of his own hands. He makes coverlets to which he attaches his seal; his courtiers sell them in the market, and the great ones of the land purchase them, and the proceeds thereof provide his sustenance. He is truthful and trusty, speaking peace to all men. The men of Islam see him but once in the year. The pilgrims that come from distant lands to go unto Mecca which is in the land El-Yemen, are anxious to see his face, and they assemble before the palace exclaiming 'Our Lord, light of Islam and glory of our Law, show us the effulgence of thy countenance," but he pays no regard to their words. Then the princes who minister unto him say to him, "Our Lord, spread forth thy peace unto the men that have come from distant lands, who crave to abide under the shadow of thy graciousness," and thereupon he arises and lets down the hem of his robe from the window, and the pilgrims come and kiss it, and a prince says unto them " Go forth in peace, for our Master the Lord of Islam granteth peace to you." He is regarded by them as Mohammed and they go to their houses rejoicing at the salutation which the prince has vouchsafed unto them, and glad at heart that they have kissed his robe.

Each of his brothers and the members of his family has an abode in his palace, but they are all fettered in chains of iron, and guards are placed over each of their houses so that they may not rise against the great Caliph. For once it happened to a predecessor that his brothers rose up against him and proclaimed one of themselves as Caliph; then it was decreed that all the members of his family should be bound, that they might not rise up against the ruling Caliph. Each one of them resides in his palace in great splendor, and they own villages and towns, and their stewards bring them the tribute thereof, and they eat and drink and rejoice all the days of their life. Within the domains of the palace of the Caliph there are great buildings of marble and columns of silver and gold, and carvings upon rare stones are fixed in the walls. In the Caliph's palace are great riches and towers filled with gold, silken garments and all precious stones. He does not issue forth from his palace save once in the year, at the feast which the Mohammedans call El-id-bed Ramadan, and they come from distant lands that day to see him. He rides on a mule and is attired in the royal robes of gold and silver and fine linen; on his head is a turban adorned with precious stones of priceless value, and over the turban is a black shawl as a sign of his modesty, implying that all this glory will be covered by darkness on the day of death. He is accompanied by all the nobles of Islam dressed in fine garments and riding on horses, the princes of Arabia, the princes of Togarma and Daylam [Gilan] and the princes of Persia, Media and Ghuzz, and the princes of the land of Tibet, which is three months' journey distant, and westward of which lies the land of Samarkand. He proceeds from his palace to the great mosque of Islam which is by the Basrah Gate. Along the road the walls are adorned with silk and purple, and the inhabitants receive him with all kinds of song and exultation, and they dance before the great king who is styled the Caliph. They salute him with a loud voice and say, " Peace unto thee, our Lord the King and Light of Islam!" He kisses his robe, and stretching forth the hem thereof he salutes them. Then he proceeds to the court of the mosque, mounts a wooden pulpit and expounds to them their Law. Then the learned ones of Islam arise and pray for him and extol his greatness and his graciousness, to which they all respond. Afterwards he gives them his blessing, and they bring before him a camel which he slays, and this is their Passover sacrifice. He gives thereof unto the princes and they distribute it to all, so that they may taste of the sacrifice brought by their sacred king; and they all rejoice. Afterwards he leaves the mosque and returns alone to his palace by way of the river Hiddekel, and the grandees of Islam accompany him in ships on the river until he enters his palace. He does not return the way he came; and the road which he takes along the riverside is watched all the year through, so that no man shall tread in his footsteps. He does not leave the palace again for a whole year. He is a benevolent man.

He built, on the other side of the river, on the banks of an arm of the Euphrates which there borders the city, a hospital consisting of blocks of houses and hospices for the sick poor who come to be healed. Here there are about sixty physicians' stores which are provided from the Caliph's house with drugs and whatever else may be required. Every sick man who comes is maintained at the Caliph's expense and is medically treated. Here is a building which is called Dar-al-Maristan, where they keep charge of the demented people who have become insane in the towns through the great heat in the summer, and they chain each of them in iron chains until their reason becomes restored to them in the winter-time. Whilst they abide there, they are provided with food from the house of the Caliph, and when their reason is restored they are dismissed and each one of them goes to his house and his home. Money is given to those that have stayed in the hospices on their return to their homes. Every month the officers of the Caliph inquire and investigate whether they have regained their reason, in which case they are discharged. All this the Caliph does out of charity to those that come to the city of Baghdad, whether they be sick or insane. The Caliph is a righteous man, and all his actions are for good.

In Baghdad there are about 40,000 Jews, and they dwell in security, prosperity and honor under the great Caliph, and amongst them are great sages, the heads of Academies engaged in the study of the law... And at the head of them all is Daniel the son of Hisdai, who is styled "Our Lord the Head of the Captivity of all Israel"... and the Mohammedans call him " Saidna ben Daoud," and he has been invested with authority over all the congregations of Israel at the hands of the Emir al Muminin, the Lord of Islam...

In Baghdad there are twenty-eight Jewish Synagogues, situated either in the city itself or in Al-Karkh on the other side of the Tigris; for the river divides the metropolis into two parts. The great synagogue of the Head of the Captivity has columns of marble of various colors overlaid with silver and gold, and on these columns are sentences of the Psalms in golden letters. And in front of the ark are about ten steps of marble; on the topmost step are the seats of the Head of the Captivity and of the Princes of the House of David. The city of Baghdad is twenty miles in circumference, situated in a land of palms, gardens and plantations, the like of which is not to be found in the whole land of Shinar. People come thither with merchandise from all lands. Wise men live there, philosophers who know all manner of wisdom, and magicians expert in all manner of witchcraft.

68

A festival of tents in Samarkand, from the *Narrative of the embassy of Ruy Gonzalez de Clavijo to the court of Timour at Samarcand*

Narrative of the embassy of Ruy Gonzalez de Clavijo to the court of Timour at Samarcand, A.D. 1403–6, translated for the first time, with notes, a preface, and an introductory life of Timour Beg, by Clements R. Markham, London, 1849; facsimile reprinted 2001 in New Delhi for Asian Educational Services, pp. 142–3.

Available online at HathiTrust Digital Library

Samarkand is a city in modern-day Uzbekistan made prosperous by its location on the Silk Road. It became the capital of the empire of Timur (Tamerlane) in the fourteenth century. Tents, although rarely considered in terms of display, played an important role in court life and were counted as precious objects (for a Mughal India example, see Fig. 31). They could be enormous and lavish. For instance, one royal tent took a hundred camels to transport, another was nicknamed the 'Slayer' because at least two people were killed every time it was pitched. Ruy Gonzalez de Clavijo traveled from Spain to the court of Timur at Samarkand as part of an embassy and describes here an outdoor tent city pitched for a lavish open-air feast.[1]

On Monday, the 6th of October, the lord ordered a great feast to be given, at the place where his horde was encamped on the plain, and he ordered that his relations and women, all his sons and grandsons who were near, his councilors, and all the people who were scattered round, should assemble at this place. On this day the ambassadors were brought to the plain, and, when they arrived,

---

1   Robert Irwin, *Islamic At in Context*, Harry N. Abrams Inc., New York, 1997, p. 119.

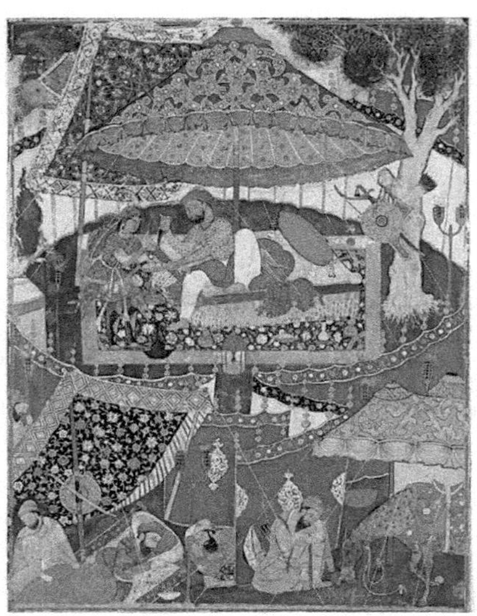

Fig. 31 A lavish royal tent from Mughal India, from a 16th century Hamzanama manuscript.

they found many handsome tents pitched, most of them on the banks of the river, close together, and it was a very beautiful sight. The ambassadors went through some streets of tents, where they sold all that was required by this great host; and, when they were near the tents of the lord, they were placed under an awning, made of white linen cloth, ornamented with cloths of various colors, and it was long, and secured above by cords, to two poles, and there were many awnings of this kind on the plain, and they make them long and high, that the sun may be screened off, and that air may enter freely. Near these awnings, there was a great and lofty pavilion, which was like a tent, only square, and three lances high. It was a hundred paces broad, and had four corners, and the ceiling was round, like a vault. It was pitched against twelve poles, each as large round as a man, measured round the chest.

They were painted gold and blue, and other colors, and from corner to corner there were poles, three fastened together, and making one. When they pitched the tents, they used wheels, like those of a cart, which were turned by men, and they have ropes fixed in various directions, to assist them. From the vault of the ceiling of the pavilion silken cloths descended, between each of the poles, which were fastened to them, and when they were fastened, they made an arch from one side to the other. Outside this square pavilion, there were porticoes, joined above to the pavilion, and supported by twenty-four poles, not so large as the central ones, so that the whole pavilion was supported by thirty-six poles. From this pavilion at least five hundred red cords were extended, and inside there was a crimson carpet, beautifully ornamented with silken cloths of many colors, and embroidered with gold threads. In the center of the ceiling there was the richest work of all; and in the four corners were the figures of four eagles, with their wings closed. The outside of the pavilion was lined with silk cloths, in black, white, and yellow stripes. At each corner there was a high pole, with a copper ball, and the figure of a crescent on the top and in the center, there was another tall pole, with a much larger copper ball and crescent; and, on the top of the pavilion, between these poles, there was a tower of silken cloths, with turrets, and an entrance door; and when the wind blew the pavilion about, or made the poles unsteady, men went on the top, and secured anything that was loose. This pavilion was so large and high that, from a distance, it looked like a castle; and it was a very wonderful thing to see, and possessed more beauty than it is possible to describe.

Image credits

*Fig. 31: DcoetzeeBot, "A Mughal royal tent, a page of the Dastan-I Amir Hamza (Hamzanama),"
https://commons.wikimedia.org/wiki/File:Mughal_-_A_page_of_the_Dastan-i_Amir_Hamza_
(Hamzanama)_-_Google_Art_Project.jpg. Copyright in the Public Domain.*

Early Medieval Europe

69

A Viking Ship Burial, from Ahmed Ibn Fadlan's *Account of a Traveler*

Albert Stanburrough Cook, "Ibn Fadlan's Account of Scandinavian Merchants on the Volga in 922", *Journal of English and Germanic Philology*, 22, 1923, pp. 54–63.

Available online at JStor

The caliph of Baghdad sent Ibn Fadlan as an ambassador to the king of Bulgaria. In route, in 922, he encountered a tribe of armed merchants on the Volga River whom he called Northmen or Rus. Most scholars identify the tribe as Swedish Vikings settled in Russia. Here Ibn Fadlan gives an eyewitness account of one of their funerals.

I saw how the Northmen had arrived with their wares, and pitched their camp beside the Volga. Never did I see people so gigantic; they are tall as palm trees, and florid and ruddy of complexion ... From the tip of the fingernails to the neck, each man of them is tattooed with pictures of trees, living beings and other things ... I was told that the least of what they do for their chiefs when they die, is to consume them with fire. When I was finally informed of the death of one of their magnates, I sought to witness what befell. First they laid him in his grave—over which a roof was erected—for the space of ten days, until they had completed the cutting and sewing of his clothes. In the case of a poor man, however, they merely build for him a boat, in which they place him, and consume it with fire ... When one of their chiefs dies, his family asks his girls and pages: "Which one of you will die with him?" One of them answered, "I." She was then committed to two girls, who were to keep watch over her, accompany her wherever she went, and even, on occasion, wash her feet … When the day was now come that the dead man and the girl were to be committed to the flames, I went to the river in which his ship lay, but found that it had already been drawn ashore …

They carried [the dead man] into a tent placed in the ship, seated him on the wadded and quilted covering, supported him with the pillows, and bringing strong drink, fruits, and basil, placed them all beside him. Then they brought a dog, which they cut in two, and threw into the ship; laid all his weapons beside him; and led up two horses which they chased until they were dripping with seat, whereupon they cut them in pieces with their swords, and threw the flesh into the ship. Two oxen were then brought forward, cut in pieces, and flung into the ship. Finally they brought a cock and a hen, killed them, and threw them in also.

The girl who had devoted herself to death meanwhile walked to and fro, entering one after another of the tents which they had there. The occupant of each tent lay with her, saying, "Tell your master, 'I did this only for love of you'" … Then they led her away to the ship.

Here she took off her two bracelets, and gave them to the old woman who was called the angel of death, and who was to murder her, She also drew off her two anklets, and passed them to the two serving-maids, who were the daughters of the so-called angel of death. Then they lifted her into the ship, but did not yet admit her to the tent. Now men came up with shields and staves, and handed her a cup of strong drink. This she took, sang over it, and emptied it. "With this," so the interpreter told me, "she is taking leave of those who are dear to her." Then another cup was handed her, which she also took, and began a lengthy song. The crone admonished her to drain the cup without lingering, and to enter the tent where her master lay. By this time, as it seemed to me, the girl had become dazed; she made as though she would enter the tent, and had brought her head forward between the tent and the ship, when the hag seized her by the head, and dragged her in. At this moment the men began to beat upon their shields with the staves, in order to drown the noise of her outcries, which might have terrified the other girls, and deterred them from seeking death with their masters in the future. Then six men followed into the tent, and each and every one had carnal companionship with her. Then they laid her down by her master's side, while two of the men seized her by the feet, and two by the hands. The old woman known as the angel of death now knotted a rope around her neck, and handed the ends to two of the men to pull. Then with a broad-bladed dagger she smote her between the ribs, and drew the blade forth, while the two men strangled her with the rope till she died.

The next of kin to the dead man now drew near, and, taking a piece of wood, lighted it, and walked backwards toward the ship, holding the stick in one hand, with the other placed upon his buttocks (he being naked), until the wood which had been piled under the ship was ignited. Then the others came up with staves and firewood, each one carrying a stick already lighted at the upper end, and threw it all on the pyre. The pile was soon aflame, then the ship, finally the tent, the man, and the girl, and everything else in the ship...

Thereupon, they heaped over the place where the ship had stood something like a rounded hill, and, erecting on the center of it a large birchen post, wrote on it the name of the deceased, along with that of the king of the Northmen. Having done this, they left the spot.

70

On the conversion of the Anglo-Saxons, from Bede's *Ecclesiastical History of the English People* (1.30)

James Harvey Robinson, *Readings in European History*, volume I, Boston: Ginn and Co., 1905, pp. 100–101.

Available online at Internet Archive

Credit: Venerable Bede, "On the Conversion of the Anglo-Saxons," *Readings in European History*, vol. 1, ed. James Harvey Robinson. Copyright in the Public Domain.

The conversion of the Anglo-Saxons was chronicled by the Venerable Bede, a monk in northern England. His Ecclesiastical History of the English People *was written around 731 and was based on historical records from churches in England and on documents from Rome. The selection reproduced here is a letter of 601 from Pope Gregory the Great to Abbot Mellitus, an English missionary. In it Gregory urges the churchman to incorporate pagan elements into Christian practices as a way to win converts.*

When Almighty God shall bring you to the most reverend Bishop Augustine, our brother, tell him what I have, after mature deliberation on the affairs of the English, determined upon, namely, that the temples of the idols in that nation ought not to be destroyed, but let the idols that are in them be destroyed; let holy water be made and sprinkled in the said temples—let altars be erected, and relics placed. For if those temples are well built, it is requisite that the be converted from the worship of devils to the service of the true God; that the nation, seeing that their temples are not destroyed, may remove error from their hearts and, knowing and adoring the true God, may the more familiarly resort to the places to which they have been accustomed.

And because they have been used to slaughter many oxen in the sacrifices to devils, some solemnity must be substituted for them on this account, as, for instance, that on the day of the dedication, or of the nativities of the holy martyrs whose relics are there deposited, they may build themselves huts of the boughs of trees about those churches which have been turned to that use from temples, and celebrate the solemnity with religious feasting, no more offering beasts to the devil, but killing cattle to the praise of God in their eating, and returning thanks to the Giver of all things for their sustenance; to the end that, whilst some outward gratifications are permitted them, they may the more easily consent to thee inward consolations of the grace of God.

For there is no doubt that it is impossible to efface everything at once from their obdurate minds, because he who endeavors to ascend to the highest place rises by degrees or steps and not by leaps. This the Lord made himself known to the people of Israel in Egypt: and yet he allowed them to use the sacrifices which they were wont to offer to the devil in his own worship, commanding them in his sacrifice to kill beasts to the end that, changing their hearts they mad lay aside one part of the sacrifice whilst retained another: that while they offered the same beasts which they were wont to offer, they should offer them to God, and not to idols, and thus they would no longer be the same sacrifices.

71

On the Destruction of Images, from a letter of Pope Gregory I to Bishop Serenus of Marseilles

Translated by James Barmby, *A Select Library of the Nicene and Post-Nicene Fathers*, Second Series, edited by Philip Schaff and Henry Wace, Grand Rapids, Wm. B. Eerdmans Publishing Co., 1961, volume 13: Part II Gregory the Great. Ephraim Syrus. Aphrahat. 1898, p. 86.

Available online at Documenta Catholica Omnia

In another letter of Pope Gregory the Great (see #70), this one dated to around 600, he reprimands the Bishop of Marseilles for destroying images of the saints. This was a much-debated issue as the early church considered what was idolatrous; in the eastern empire it resulted in a long period of Iconoclasm (Fig. 32). Gregory points out here that images serve to teach those who cannot read. This remained the standard defense for representational art in the Western church throughout the Middle Ages.

It has been reported to us that, inflamed with inconsiderate zeal, you have broken images of saints, as though under the plea that they ought not to be adored. And indeed in that you forbade them to be adored, we altogether praise you; but we blame you for having broken them. Say, brother, what priest has ever been heard of as doing what you have done? If nothing else, should not even this thought have restrained you, so as not to despise other brethren, supposing yourself alone to be holy and wise? For to adore a picture is one thing, but to learn through the story of a picture what is to be adored is another. For what writing presents to readers, this picture presents to the

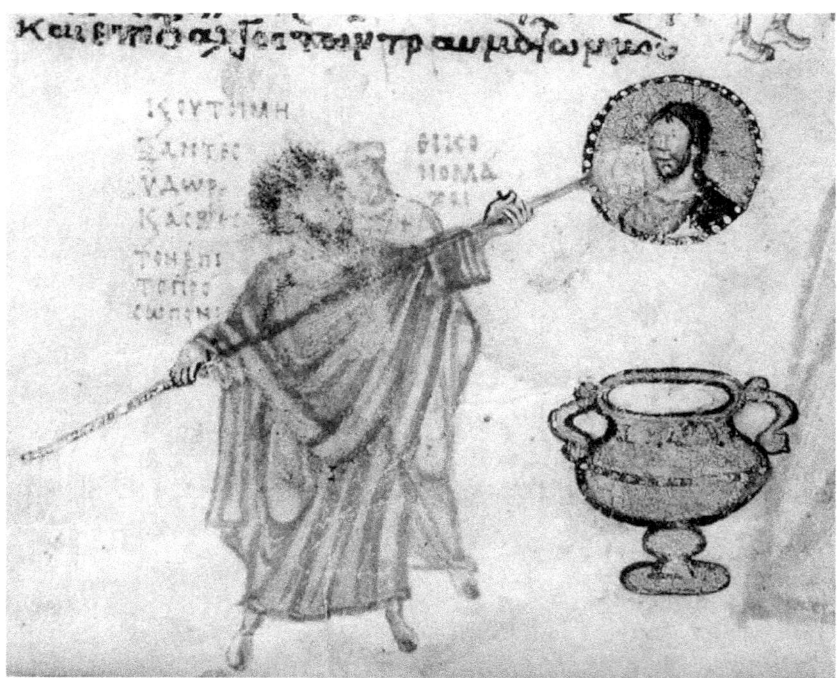

Fig. 32 An image of Christ is destroyed by vinegar during the period of Iconoclasm in the Byzantine world, detail from the Khludov Psalter, 9th century, State Historical Museum, Moscow.

unlearned who behold it, since in it even the ignorant see what they ought to follow.

Image credits

72

The Synod of Whitby, from Bede's *Ecclesiastical History of the English People* (3.25)

Bede, *The Ecclesiastical History of the English Nation*, introduction by Vida D. Scudder, New York, E.P. Dutton, 1910, pp. 146–152.

Available online at Internet Archive and Internet Medieval Sourcebook

The Synod of Whitby was a meeting and debate held at a monastery later called Whitby Abbey in 664 CE. It resulted in the Anglo-Saxon Northumbrian king deciding to follow the customs of the church in Rome rather than those of the Celtic church of the Irish, Britons, and Scots. It was an important step in the unification of the Christian church and a pivotal moment in the evolution of the Insular artistic style. Insular art, or the post-Roman art found on the islands of Hibernia (Latin name for Ireland) and Britain, is sometimes called Hiberno-Saxon to reflect this interaction.

HOW THE CONTROVERSY AROSE ABOUT THE DUE TIME OF KEEPING EASTER, WITH THOSE THAT CAME OUT OF SCOTLAND. [652 CE.]

In the meantime, Bishop Aidan being dead, Finan, who was ordained and sent by the Scots, succeeded him in the bishopric, and built a church in the Isle of Lindisfarne, the episcopal see; nevertheless, after the manner of the Scots, he made it, not of stone, hut of hewn oak, and covered it with reeds; and the same was afterwards dedicated in honor of St. Peter the Apostle, by the reverend Archbishop Theodore. Eadbert, also bishop of that place, took off the thatch, and covered it, both roof and walls, with plates of lead.

At this time, a great and frequent controversy happened about the observance of Easter; those that came from Kent or France affirming, that the Scots kept Easter Sunday contrary to the custom of the universal church. Among them was a most zealous defender of the true Easter, whose name was Ronan, a Scot by nation, but instructed in ecclesiastical truth, either in France or Italy, who, disputing with Finan, convinced many, or at least induced them to make a more strict inquiry after the truth; yet he could not prevail upon Finan, but, on the contrary, made him the more inveterate by reproof, and a professed opposer of the truth, being of a hot and violent temper. James, formerly the deacon of the venerable Archbishop Paulinus, as has been said above, kept the true and Catholic Easter, with all those that he could persuade to adopt the right way. Queen Eanfleda and her followers also observed the same as she had seen practiced in Kent, having with her a Kentish priest that followed the Catholic mode, whose name was Romanus. Thus it is said to have happened in those times that Easter was twice kept in one year; and that when the king having ended the time of fasting, kept his Easter, the queen and her followers were still fasting, and celebrating Palm Sunday. This difference about the observance of Easter, whilst Aidan lived, was patiently tolerated by all men, as being sensible, that though he could not keep Easter contrary to the custom of those who had sent him, yet he industriously labored to practice all works of faith, piety, and love, according to the custom of all holy men; for which reason he was deservedly beloved by all; even by those who differed in opinion concerning Easter, and was held in veneration, not only by indifferent persons, but even by the bishops, Hononus of Canterbury, and Felix of the East Angles.

But after the death of Finan, who succeeded him, when Colman, who was also sent out of Scotland, came to be bishop, a greater controversy arose about the observance of Easter, and the rules of ecclesiastical life. Whereupon this dispute began naturally to influence the thoughts and hearts of many, who feared, lest having received the name of Christians, they might happen to run, or to have run, in vain. This reached the ears of King Oswy and his son Alfrid; for Oswy, having been instructed and baptized by the Scots, and being very perfectly skilled in their language, thought nothing better than what they taught. But Alfrid, having been instructed in Christianity by Wilfrid, a most learned man, who had first gone to Rome to learn the ecclesiastical doctrine, and spent much time at Lyons with Dalfin, archbishop of France, from whom also he had received the ecclesiastical tonsure, rightly thought this man's doctrine ought to be preferred before all the traditions of the Scots. For this reason he had also given him a monastery of forty families, at a place called Rhypum; which place, not long before, he had given to those that followed the system of the Scots for a monastery; but forasmuch as they afterwards, being left to their choice, prepared to quit the place rather than alter their opinion, he gave the place to him, whose life and doctrine were worthy of it.

Agilbert, bishop of the West Saxons, above-mentioned, a friend to King Alfrid and to Abbot Wufrid, had at that time come into the province of the Northumbrians, and was making some stay among them; at the request of Alfrid, made Wilfrid a priest in his monastery. He had in his company a priest, whose name was Agatho. The controversy being there started, concerning Easter, or the tonsure, or other ecclesiastical affairs, it was agreed, that a **synod** should be held in the monastery of Streaneshaich, which signifies the Bay of the Lighthouse, where the Abbess Hilda, a woman devoted to God, then presided; and that there this controversy should be decided. The kings, both father and son, came thither, Bishop Colman with his Scottish clerks, and Agilbert with the priests Agatho and Wilfrid, James and Romanus were on their side; but the Abbess Hilda and her followers were for the Scots, as was also the venerable Bishop Cedd, long before ordained by the Scots, as has been said above, and he was in that council a most careful interpreter for both parties.

King Oswy first observed, that it behooved those who served one God to observe the same rule of life; and as they all expected the same kingdom in heaven, so they ought not to differ in the celebration of the Divine mysteries; but rather to inquire which was the truest tradition, that the same might be followed by all; he then commanded his bishop, Colman, first to declare what the custom was which he observed, and whence it derived its origin. Then Colman said, "The Easter which I keep, I received from my elders, who sent me bishop hither; all our forefathers, men beloved of God, are known to have kept it after the same manner; and that the same may not seem to any contemptible or worthy to be rejected, it is the same which St. John the Evangelist, the disciple beloved of our Lord, with all the churches over which he presided, is recorded to have observed." Having said thus much, and more to the like effect, the king commanded Agilbert to show whence his custom of keeping Easter was derived, or on what authority it was grounded. Agilbert answered, "I desire that my disciple, the priest Wufrid, may speak in my stead; because we both concur with the other followers of the ecclesiastical tradition that are here present, and he can better explain our opinion in the English language, than I can by an interpreter."

Then Wilfrid, being ordered by the king to speak, delivered himself thus: "The Easter which we observe, we saw celebrated by all at Rome, where the blessed apostles, Peter and Paul, lived, taught, suffered, and were buried; we saw the same done in Italy and in France, when we traveled through those countries for pilgrimage and prayer. We found the same practiced in Africa, Asia, Egypt, Greece, and all the world, wherever the church of Christ is spread abroad, through several nations and tongues, at one and the same time; except only these and their accomplices in obstinacy, I mean the Picts and the Britons, who foolishly, in these two remote islands of the world, and only in part even of them, oppose all the rest of the universe..."

To this Colman rejoined: "Did Anatolius, a holy man, and much commended in church history, act contrary to the law and the Gospel, when he wrote, that Easter was to be celebrated from the fourteenth to the twentieth? Is it to be believed that our most reverend Father Columba and his successors, men beloved by God, who kept Easter after the same manner, thought or acted contrary to the Divine writings? Whereas there were many among them, whose sanctity is testified by heavenly signs and the working of miracles, whose life, customs, and discipline I never cease to follow, not questioning their being saints in heaven."

"It is evident," said Wufrid, "that Anatolius was a most holy, learned, and commendable man; but what have you to do with him, since you do not observe his decrees? For he, following the rule of truth in his Easter, appointed a revolution of nineteen years, which either you are ignorant of, or if you know it, though it is kept by the whole church of Christ, yet you despise it... Concerning your Father Columba and his followers, whose sanctity you say you imitate, and whose rules and precepts you observe, which have been confirmed by signs from heaven, I may answer, that... I do not deny those to have been God's servants, and beloved by Him, who with rustic simplicity, but pious intentions, have themselves loved Him. Nor do I think that such keeping of Easter was very prejudicial to them, as long as none came to show them a more perfect rule; and yet I do believe that they, if any catholic adviser had come among them, would have as readily followed his admonitions, as they are known to have kept those commandments of God, which they had learned and knew.

"But as for you and your companions, you certainly sin, if, having heard the decrees of the Apostolic See, and of the universal church, and that the same is confirmed by holy writ, you refuse to follow them; for, though your fathers were holy, do you think that their small number, in a corner of the remotest island, is to be preferred before the universal church of Christ throughout the world? And if that Columba of yours (and, I may say, ours also, if he was Christ's servant), was a holy man and powerful in miracles, yet could he be preferred before the most blessed prince of the apostles, to whom our Lord said, 'Thou art Peter, and upon this rock I will build my church, and the gates of hell shall not prevail against it, and to thee I will give the keys of the kingdom of heaven?'"

When Wufrid had spoken thus, the king said, "Is it true, Colman, that these words were spoken to Peter by our Lord?" He answered, "It is true, O king" Then says he, "Can you show any such power given to your Columba?" Colman answered, "None." Then added the king, "Do you both agree that these words were principally directed to Peter, and that the keys of heaven were given to him by our Lord?" They both answered, "We do." Then the king concluded, "And I also say unto you, that he is the door-keeper, whom I will not contradict, but will, as far as I know and am able, in all things obey his decrees, lest, when I come to the gates of the kingdom of heaven, there should be none to open them, he being my adversary who is proved to have the keys." The king having said this, all present, both great and small, gave their assent, and renouncing the more imperfect institution, resolved to conform to that which they found to be of better.

73

A medieval view of distant lands, from Isidore of Seville's *Etymologies* (*Etymologiae* 11.3.12–25)

Stephen Barney, W. J. Lewis, J. A. Beach Oliver Berghof, *The Etymologies of Isidore of Seville*, Cambridge University Press, 2006, pp. 244–245.

Just as the thriving Irish culture would be disrupted by Viking raids in the late eighth and ninth centuries, so the flourishing Visigothic Kingdom in Spain would be stymied by the Arab invasion in 711. Prior to this Isidore, as Bishop of Seville for three decades (died 636), promoted both a form of representational government and Classical education. He is most known for his Etymologies, *an encyclopedia of world knowledge. It consists largely of excerpts and paraphrases from numerous earlier writers including many found in this collection (e.g., #25 Pliny the Elder, #43 Suetonius, #47 Josephus, and #52 Eusebius). For this monumental, if often fanciful, work Isidore is sometimes considered the last scholar of antiquity. The section reproduced here describes fantastic peoples of distant lands. If you look at the edges of the tympanum at the later Romanesque church at Vezelay (Fig. 33), for instance, you can catch a glimpse of some of them.*

Just as, in individual nations, there are instances of monstrous people, so in the whole of humankind there are certain monstrous races, like the Giants, the Cynocephali, the Cyclopes, and others... The Cynocephali are so called because they have dogs' heads, and their barking indeed reveals that they are rather beasts than humans. These originate in India... People believe that the Blemmyans in Libya are born as trunks without heads, and having their

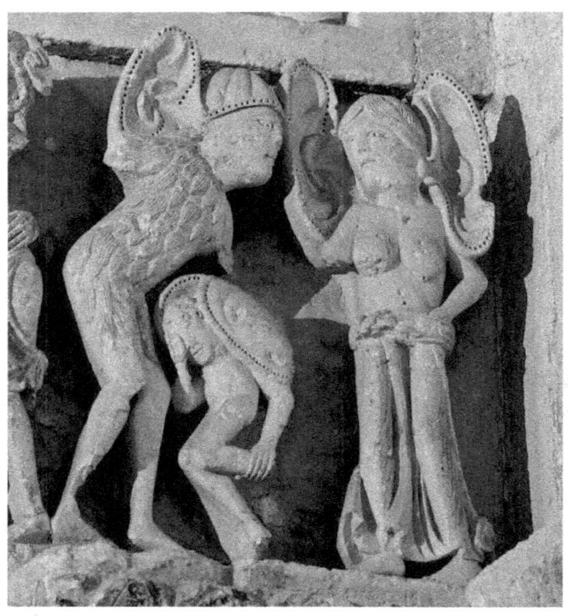

Fig. 33 Big-eared 'Paniotians of Scythia', Church of La Madeleine, Vezelay, France

mouth and eyes in their chest, and that another race is born without necks and having their eyes in their shoulders. Moreover, people write about the monstrous faces of nations in the far East: some with no noses, having completely flat faces and a shapeless countenance; some with a lower lip so protruding that when they are sleeping it protects the whole face from the heat of the sun; some with mouths grown shut, taking in nourishment only through a small opening by means of hollow straws. Some are said to have no tongues, using nods or gestures in place of words. They tell of the Panotians of Scythia, who have such huge ears that they cover all the body... The Artabatitans of Ethiopia are said to walk on all fours, like cattle; none passes the age of forty... The race of Sciopodes are said to live in Ethiopia; they have only one leg and are wonderfully speedy. The Greeks call them *skiopodes* [i.e., shade footed] because when it is hot they lie on their backs on the ground and are shaded by the great size of their feet. The Antipodes in Libya have the soles of their feet twisted behind their legs, and eight toes on each foot. The Hippopodes are in Scythia, and have a human form and horses' hooves.

Image credits

Fig. 33: Copyright © Han van Hagen (CC BY-SA 2.5) at https://commons.wikimedia.org/wiki/File:Panoteanen.jpg.

74

The Palatine Chapel at Aachen, from Notker the Stammerer's *Regarding Carolus Magnus (De Carolo Magno 28)*

Early Lives of Charlemagne by Eginhard and the Monk of St. Gall, translated by A. J. Grant, London, Chatto and Windus, 1926, pp. 93–94.

Available online at Internet Medieval Sourcebook

Regarding Carolus Magnus (i.e., Charles the Great or Charlemagne) was written by a monk at the monastery of St. Gall in Switzerland usually identified as one Notker the Stammerer (died 912). Here he describes an episode that occurred during the building of the palace chapel at Aachen.

When the most energetic Emperor Charlemagne could rest awhile he sought not sluggish ease, but labored in the service of God. He desired therefore to build upon his native soil a cathedral finer even than the works of the Romans, and soon his purpose was realized. For the building thereof he summoned architects and skilled workmen from all lands beyond the seas; and above all he placed a certain knavish abbot whose competence for the execution of such tasks he knew, though he knew not his character. When the emperor had gone on a certain journey, this abbot allowed anyone to depart home who would pay sufficient money; those who could not purchase their discharge, or were not allowed to return by their masters, he burdened with unending labors, as the Egyptians once afflicted the people of God. By such knavish tricks he gathered together a great mass of gold and silver and silken robes; and exhibiting in his chamber only the least precious articles, he concealed in boxes and chests all the richest treasures. Well, one day there was brought to him suddenly the news that his house was on fire. He ran, in great excitement, and pushed his way through the bursting flames into the strong room where his boxes, stuffed with gold, were kept; he was not satisfied to take one away, but would only leave after he had loaded his servants with a box apiece. And as he was going out a huge beam, dislodged by the fire, fell on the top of him; and then his body was burnt by temporal and his soul by eternal flames. Thus did the judgment of God keep watch for the most religious Emperor Charlemagne, when his attention was withdrawn by the business of his kingdom.

75

The monastic life, from St. Benedict's *The Rule*

Select Historical Documents of the Middle Ages, translated and edited by Ernest Henderson, London, G. Bell and Sons LTD., 1912, pp. 274–311.

Available online at Internet Archive

Credit: "The Monastic Life," *Select Historical Documents of the Middle Ages*, trans. Ernest Henderson. Copyright in the Public Domain.

Monastic communities generally had a rule, or set of regulations, prescribing the discipline of their members' daily life. The 73 rules written by St. Benedict (circa 480–550) for his community at Montecassino in southern Italy was admired by Pope Gregory the Great and by Charlemagne, who obtained an exact copy of it. The plan of an ideal monastery found at the abbey of St. Gall reflects this Carolingian effort for monastic reform.

CHAPTER 1: Concerning the kinds of monks

It is manifest that there are four kinds of monks. The cenobites are the first kind; that is, those living in a monastery, serving under a rule or an abbot. Then the second kind is that of the anchorites; that is, the hermits... A third very bad kind of monks are the sarabaites, approved by no rule... being shut up by twos or threes, or, indeed alone, without a shepherd, not in the Lord's but in their own sheep-folds,—their law is the satisfaction of their own desires... The fourth kind of monks is the kind which is called gyratory. During their whole life they are guests, for three or four days at a time, in the cells of the different monasteries... always wandering and never stationary, given over to the service of their own pleasures and the joys of the palate and in every way worse than the sarabaites... These things therefore being omitted, let us proceed, with the aid of God, to treat of the best kind, the cenobites.

CHAPTER 3: Calling the brothers to council

As often as anything special is to be done in the monastery, the abbot shall call together the whole congregation, and shall himself explain the question at issue. And, having heard the advice of the brethren, he shall think it over by himself, and shall do what he considers most advantageous.

CHAPTER 16: The Day Office

As the prophet says: "Seven times in the day do I praise Thee" [Psalms 119:164]. This sacred number of seven will thus be fulfilled by us if, at matins, at the first, third, sixth, ninth hours, at vespers time, and at compline we perform the duties of our service

CHAPTER 22: How the monks shall sleep

They shall sleep separately in separate beds. They shall receive positions for their beds [i.e., bedding] after the manner of their characters according to the dispensation of their abbot. If it can be done, they shall all sleep in one place. If, however, their number does not permit it, they shall rest by tens or twenties, with elders who will concern themselves about them. A candle shall always be burning in that same cell until early in the morning. They shall sleep clothed, and girt with belts or with ropes; and they shall not have their knives at their sides while they sleep, lest perchance in a dream they should wound the sleepers. And let the monks always be on the alert; and when the signal is given, rising without delay, let them hasten to mutually prepare themselves for the service of God, with all gravity and modesty. The younger brothers shall not have beds by themselves, but interspersed among those of the elder ones. And when they rise for the service of God, they shall exhort each other mutually with moderation, on account of the excuses that those who are sleepy are inclined to make.

CHAPTER 33: Whether the monks should have anything of their own

He should have absolutely nothing: neither a book, nor tablets, nor a pen— nothing at all. For indeed it is not allowed to the monks to have their own bodies or wills in their own power. But all things necessary they must expect from the abbot.

CHAPTER 40: Concerning the amount of drink

Each one has his own gift from God, the one in this way, the other in that. Therefore it is with some hesitation that the amount of daily sustenance for others is fixed by us. Nevertheless, in view of the weakness of the infirm we believe that a hemina [around ½ liter] of wine a day is enough for each one.

CHAPTER 48: Concerning the daily manual labor

Idleness is the enemy of the soul. And therefore, at fixed times, the brothers ought to be occupied in manual labor; and again, at fixed times, in sacred reading... They shall receive separate books from the library which they shall read entirely through in order. These books are to be given out on the first day of Lent. Above all there shall certainly be appointed one or two elders who shall go round the monastery at the hours in which the brothers are engaged in reading, and see to it that no troublesome brother chance to be found who is open to idleness and trifling, and is not intent on his reading, being not only of no use to himself, but also stirring up others.

CHAPTER 53: The reception of guests

All guests who come shall be received as though they were Christ for He Himself said "I was a stranger and ye took me in"... The kitchen of the abbot and the guests shall be by itself so that guests coming at uncertain hours, as is always happening in a monastery, may not disturb the brothers... He who has not been ordered to shall by no means join the guests or speak to them. But if he meets them or sees them, saluting them humbly, as has been said, and seeking their blessing, he shall pass by, saying that he is not allowed to speak with a guest.

CHAPTER 57: Concerning the craftsmen of the monastery

Artificers, if there are any in the monastery, shall practice with all humility their special arts, if the abbot permits it. But if any one of them becomes inflated with pride on account of knowledge of his art, to the extent that he seems to be conferring something on the monastery, such a one shall be plucked away from the art; and he shall not again return to it unless the abbot perchance again orders him to, he being humbled. But if anything from the works of the artificers is to be sold, they themselves shall take care through whose hands the works are to pass lest they presume to commit some fraud upon the monastery.

CHAPTER 66: Concerning the doorkeepers

At the door of the monastery shall be placed a wise old man who shall know how to receive a reply and to return one; whose ripeness of age will not permit him to trifle. Which doorkeeper ought to have a cell next to the door so that those arriving may always fine one present from whom they may receive a reply ... A monastery, moreover, if it can be done, ought so to be arranged that everything necessary,—that is, water, a mill, a garden, a bakery—may be made use of, and different arts be carried on, within the monastery, so that there shall be no need for the monks to wander about outside. For this is not at all good for their souls.

76

The Art of the Painter and Illuminator, from Theophilus' *On Divers Arts* (*De diversis artibus* Book 1)

An Essay upon Various Arts in three Books by Theophilus called also Rugerus, translated by Robert Hendrie, London, John Murray, 1847, pp. 2, 29, 45, 49.

Available online at Internet Archive

Theophilus was an eleventh–twelfth century monk who wrote three practical 'how-to' books: the first for painters, the second for glass workers (see #85), and the third for metal workers. While the author wrote in the Romanesque period, the artistic practices he describes have their roots in earlier periods. The sections quoted below help illustrate the amount of work a painter or illuminator in any period would have to do before ever setting brush to surface, since they had to make their own ink, glues, varnish, pigments, and gold leaf.

CHAPTER 1: Of the mixture of colors for the nude

The color which is called flesh color, with which the face and the nude are painted, is thus composed. Take ceruse, that is white which is made from lead [see chapter 39 below], and put it, not ground, but dry as it is, into a copper or iron vessel, and place it upon glowing coals, and burn it until it is converted into a yellow color. Then grind it, and mix with it white ceruse, and cinnabar [see chapter 36 below], until it is made like flesh. The mixture of these colors may be made according to your will; so that if you wish to have red colored faces, add more cinnabar; but if clear complexions, put more white; if pallid however, add for cinnabar a little green.

CHAPTER 24: Gold Leaf

Take Greek parchment, which is made from linen cloth, and you will rub it on both sides with a red color which is burned from sinoper, that is ochre, very finely ground and dry, and polish it with a beaver's tooth, or that of a bear or wild boar, very carefully, until it becomes shining, and that the color may adhere through the friction. Then cut up this parchment with scissors, into square pieces, to the size of four fingers, equally broad and long. Afterwards make a kind of purse of vellum parchment, of the same dimension and strongly sewed, ample enough that you may fill into it many pieces of reddened parchment. Which being done take pure gold and make it very thin with a hammer upon an anvil, very carefully, so that there be no fracture in it, and cut it into four parts to the measure of two fingers. Then place in this purse one piece of reddened parchment and upon it one piece of gold in the middle, and then parchment and again gold, and do this until you have filled up the purse, and so that the gold may always be placed in the middle. Then have a mallet cast from yellow brass, small towards the handle, and large in the flat part, with which you strike the purse upon a large and flat stone, not heavily, but moderately; and when you have frequently inspected it, you will consider whether you wish to make the gold thin[ner]...

CHAPTER 36: Of cinnabar

If you wish to make cinnabar, take sulfur, of which there are three kinds, white, black, and yellow; breaking which upon a dry stone, add to it two parts of quicksilver, in equal weight of the balance, and when you have carefully mixed it, place it in a glass bottle, covering it all over with clay, and close the mouth that the vapor may not exude, and put it near the fire to dry. Then place it among the burning coals, and presently, when it has begun to grow hot, you will hear a noise inside, the manner in which the quicksilver combines with the burning sulfur; and when the sound has ceased, immediately take off the bottle, and opening it, take out the color.

CHAPTER 39: Of ceruse and minium

But in making ceruse, make for yourself plates of lead thinned, and placing them together dry, in a hollow piece of wood, as the copper [described in another chapter]; hot vinegar or urine being poured over it, cover it. Then after a month raise the cover, and taking away whatever white there is, again replace it as before. And when you have sufficient [lead white or ceruse], and wish to make minium of it, grind the same ceruse upon a stone without water, and then placing it in two or three new pots, put it upon the hot coals; have also a thin curved iron rod at one end fitted with wood and flat at the top, with which you can sometimes stir and mix this ceruse: and you may do this until the minium becomes quite red.

77

A Walk through Medieval Rome, from *The Marvels of Rome* (III.1-6)

Mirabilia urbis Romae: The Marvels of Rome or a Picture of the Golden City, an English version of the Medieval Guide-Book with a supplement of illustrative matter and notes by Francis Morgan Nichols, London, Ellis and Elvey, 1889, pp. 70-74, 78-86.

Credit: Theophilus, "The Art of the Painter and Illuminator," *An Essay Upon Various Arts in Three Books,* trans. Robert Hendrie. Copyright in the Public Domain.

The Marvels of the City of Rome is a guidebook written in the 1140's by an unnamed canon of St. Peter's. It remained the authority on the visible antiquities of the city for several centuries. While its information regarding the antiquities themselves is questionable, it is quite useful as a description of what was still standing in Rome at this time. During the twelfth century, the population of Rome was concentrated in a very small area around what is now Vatican City on the west bank of the Tiber river. The rest of the walled city of Rome contained the fields, vineyards, and farms maintained by scattered monasteries, churches, and the palaces of nobility. The author uses these contemporary churches and palaces as a means of locating the ancient monuments. Reproduced below is the author's description of a perambulation from Old Saint Peter's in the Vatican to the Capitoline hill across the river.

One can somewhat follow this itinerary via the early fifteenth-century map of Rome reproduced on the cover of this book (Limbourg Brothers, Très Riches Heures du duc de Berry, folio 141v). Oriented with the south at the top, some of the identifiable landmarks are: Top center, just inside the wall is the Lateran, to the left is the pink temple of Castor and Pollux and an aqueduct leading to the Equestrian statue of Marcus Aurelius and a miniature Colosseum. The hill to the right is the Palatine with the Arch of Titus below. The hill below that with the gallows is the Capitoline. Below that is a small round building that represents the Pantheon. Below and a bit to the left of the Pantheon is a mound of earth within a circular enclosure which is the Mausoleum of Augustus. Bottom, outside the walls and to the left are two bridges across the Tiber River and the Mausoleum of Hadrian. The Vatican is in the lower right.

THE VATICAN AND THE NEEDLE

Within the Palace of Nero [i.e., Circus of Caligula] is the temple of Apollo that is called Saint Parnell or Petronilla [i.e., an earlier round church that became the apse of new St. Peter's], before which is the basilica that is called Vatican, adorned with marvelous mosaic and ceiled with gold and glass. It is therefore called Vatican because in that place the Vates, that is to say the priests, sang their offices before Apollo's temple, and therefore all that part of St. Peter's church is called Vatican. There is also another temple that was Nero's Wardrobe, which is now called Saint Andrew [i.e., earlier church that became the Sacristy, or room containing vestments, of new St. Peter's], near which is the memorial of Caesar that is the Needle [i.e., an Augustan obelisk] where his ashes nobly rest in his sarcophagus, to the intent that as in his lifetime the whole world lay subdued before him, even so in his death the same may lie beneath him forever...

THE BASIN AND THE GOLDEN PINECONE IN OLD SAINT PETER'S

In Saint Peter's Paradise [i.e., the atrium in front of the basilica] is a Basin that was made by Pope Symmachus, and equipped with pillars of porphyry, that are joined together by marble tablets with griffins and covered with a costly sky of brass, with flowers, and dolphins of brass gilt, pouring forth water. In the midst of the basin is a brazen Pinecone [originally from an ancient Roman fountain and still displayed at the Vatican in the Cortile della Pigna, or the Courtyard of the Pinecone], which, with a roof of gilded brass, was the covering over the statue of Cybele, mother of the gods, in the opening of the Pantheon. Into this Pinecone water out of the Sabbatine Aqueduct was supplied underground by a lead pipe and, being always full, gave water through holes in the nuts to all that wanted it, and by the pipe underground some part thereof flowed to the emperor's bath near the Needle...

THE MAUSOLEUM OF HADRIAN KNOWN AS CASTEL SANT' ANGELO

There is a castle that was the temple [i.e., mausoleum] of Hadrian, as we read in the sermon of the festival of Saint Peter where it says: 'The memorial of the emperor Hadrian, a temple built up of marvelous greatness and beauty', which was all covered with stones and adorned with diverse histories, and fenced with brazen railings round about, with golden peacocks and a bull, of which peacocks two were those that are at the Basin of the Paradise. At the four sides of the temple were four horses of gilded brass, and in every side were brazen gates. In the midst of the circle was the porphyry sepulcher of Hadrian, that is now at the Lateran before the Fullery, and is the sepulcher of Pope Innocent, and the cover is in Saint Peter's Paradise upon the Prefect Cencius' tomb. Below were gates of brass as they now appear. And in the porphyry monument of the blessed Helen is buried Pope Anastasius IV...

THE MAUSOLEUM OF AUGUSTUS

At the Flaminian Gate, Octavian made a castle that is called Augustum, to be the burying place of the emperors, which was incased in diverse kinds of stone. Within there is a hollow, leading into the circle by hidden ways. In the lower circle are the sepulchers of emperors, and in each sepulcher are letters saying after this fashion: 'These be the bones and ashes of Nerva emperor, and such and such was the victory he won', and before it stood the image of his god, as in all the other sepulchers. Amid the sepulchers is a recess where Octavian was wanting to sit and the priests there would do their ceremonies. And from every kingdom of the whole world he commanded that there should be brought one basket full of earth, which he put upon the temple to be a remembrance unto all nations coming to Rome.

OF DIVERSE PLACES BETWEEN THE SEPULCHER OF AUGUSTUS AND THE CAPITAL

In the top of the Pantheon, that is to say Santa Maria Rotunda, stood the golden Pinecone that is now before the door of Saint Peter's [n.b., the mistaken association of the bronze pinecone with the Pantheon's oculus may have arisen from the name of the region around the rotunda: Rione dell Pigna or region of the pinecone]. And the church was all covered with tablets of gilded brass, insomuch that from afar it seemed as it were a mountain of gold, whereof the beauty is still discerned in part. And in the top of the front of the Pantheon stood two bulls of gilded brass. Before the palace of Alexander [i.e., the Baths of Nero which were extended in the third century by the emperor Alexander Severus] were two temples of Flora and Phoebus. Behind the palace where the Shell now is, was the temple of Bellona. There was it written:

> *Old Rome was I, now new Rome shall be praised;*
> *I bear my head aloft, from ruin raised.*

At the Shell of Parione [possibly an ancient basin] was the temple of Gnaeus Pompeius [i.e., the theater of Pompey] of marvelous greatness and beauty, and his monument that is called Majorent was fairly adorned and was an oracle of Apollo, and there were other oracles in other places.

The church of Saint Ursus was Nero's Chancery. In the Palace of Antoninus [i.e., ruins around the column of Antoninus Pius] was the temple of Divus Antoninus. By San Salvatore, before Santa Maria in Aquiro, are the temple of Aelian Hadrian and the Arch of Pity [or Piety]. In the Campus Martius is the temple of Mars, where consuls were elected in the Calends of June, and they stayed until the Calends of January. If he that was chosen consul was clear of crime, his consulship was confirmed to him. In this temple did the Roman conquerors set the beaks of their enemies' ships, whereof were made works to be a sight for all nations. Near to the Pantheon was the temple of Minerva Chalcidica [probably near later church of Santa Maria sopra Minerva], where some pillars of marble are still seen. Behind San Marco [part of the Palazzo Venezia] is the temple of Apollo. In the Camillanum, where San Cyriaco is, was the temple of Vesta; in the Calcarari, the temple of Venus [probably ruins behind the church of S. Nicola dei Cesarini/Calcaria, now lost but originally in the Largo Argentina area]; in the Lady Rose's monastery [now S. Caterina dei Funari], the Golden Castle [i.e., Circus Flaminius] that was the oracle of Juno.

The Romanesque Period

78

On the millennium, from Raoul Glaber's *History in five books* (3.13)

Rodulfus (or Raoul or Ralph) Glaber was a monk who died in the middle of the eleventh century. He described divine omens, including rumblings of Mount Vesuvius, which occurred just prior to the turn of the last millennium and the subsequent widespread fear that the world was coming to an end. It did not, as he reports here, an occurrence which may even have contributed to a revival in architecture

So on the threshold of the aforesaid thousandth year, some two or three years after it, it befell almost throughout the world, but especially in Italy and Gaul, that the fabrics of churches were rebuilt, although many of these were still seemly and needed no such care; but every nation of Christendom rivaled with the other, which should worship in the seemliest buildings. So it was as though the very world had shaken herself and cast off her old age, and were clothing herself everywhere in a white garment of churches. Then indeed the faithful rebuilt and bettered almost all the cathedral churches, and other monasteries dedicated to diverse saints, and smaller parish churches.

79

Excerpts from *Pilgrim's Guide to Santiago de Compostela (Codex Calixtinus,* Book V)

William Melczer, *The Pilgrim's Guide to Santiago de Compostela*, New York, Italica Press, 1993, pp. 85, 94, 98–99, 118, 126.

A different translation can be found online at sites.google.com/site/caminodesantiagoproject/

The Pilgrim's Guide, *written in the mid-twelfth century, is essentially a tourist guide for pilgrims traveling to the shrine of the Apostle James in Compostela, Spain. Advice is given on routes, where to stay, where to find potable water, local people, and places to visit along the way—including the burial place of Isidore of Seville (see #73) who "decorated the entire holy Church with the flower of his writings." In the passages quoted below we learn of the French dislike of the Basques, the miraculous power of the relics of St. Giles, and to whom all the altars in the pilgrimage choir of the church of Santiago de Compostela are dedicated.*

CHAPTER 1. Of The Routes to St. James

There are four roads which, leading to Santiago, converge to form a single road at Puente la Reina, in Spanish territory. One crosses Saint-Gilles, Montpellier, Toulouse, and the pass of Somport; another goes through Notre-Dame of Le Puy, Sainte-Foy of Conques and Saint-Pierre of Moissac; another traverses Sainte-Marie-Madeleine of Vezelay, Saint-Leonard in the Limousin as well as the city of Perigueux; still another cuts through Saint-Martin of Tours, Saint-Hilaire of Poitiers, Saint-Jean-d'Angely, Saint-Eutrope of Saintes and the city of Bordeaux.

CHAPTER 7. The Quality of The Lands and The People Along this Road

The Navarrese and the Basques are very similar and show much the same characteristics in their food, garments, and language... They dress most poorly and eat and drink disgustingly. The whole household of a Navarrese, to be sure, the servant no less than the master, the maid no less than the mistress, eat from a single dish all the food mixed together; and they eat not with spoons but with their own hands and furthermore drink from a single cup. If you saw them eating, you would take them for dogs or pigs in the very act of devouring; if you heard them speaking, you would be reminded of the barking of dogs... This is a barbarous nation, distinct from all other nations in habits and way of being, full of all kind of malice, and of dark color. Their face is ugly, and they are debauched, perverse, perfidious, disloyal and corrupt, libidinous, drunkard, given to all kind of violence, ferocious and savage, impudent and false, impious and uncouth, cruel and quarrelsome, incapable of anything virtuous, well informed of all vices and iniquities. In malice they resemble the Getae and the Saracens, and are in everything inimical to our Gallic nation [i.e., France]. If they could, the Navarrese or the Basque would kill a Frenchman for no more than a coin.

CHAPTER 8. The Saintly Remains on This Road

Likewise, one must pay a visit with particular attentiveness to the most dignified remains of the most pious and Blessed Giles, confessor and abbot... Oh, what a beautiful and valuable labor it is to visit his tomb! The very day that one invokes him with all one's heart, no doubt one will be happily assisted. I myself have verified what I am saying. I have once seen somebody in the town of the saint who, the day he had invoked him, escaped, under the protection of the blessed confessor, from the house of a certain shoemaker Peyrot, this house, old and decrepit, soon after collapsed... Thus, a sick man wears his tunic and is restored to health; another man is bitten by a snake and, by his inexhaustible virtue, is healed; still another one, deranged in his mind, is delivered from the devil...

CHAPTER 9. The Characteristics of The City and The Church of St. James

The altars of the basilica correspond to the following order: first of all, next to the French portal, which is on the left, we have the altar of San Nicolas; then the altar of the Santa Cruz; then, in the ambulatory, the altar of Santa Fe, virgin; then the altar of San Juan, apostle and evangelist, brother of Saint James; then the altar of San Salvador in the large apsidal chapel; then the altar of San Pedro, apostle; then the altar of San Andres; then the altar of San Martin, bishop; and finally the altar of San Juan Bautista. Between the altar of Santiago and that of San Salvador, there is the altar of Santa Maria Magdalena at which morning masses are sung for the pilgrims.

80

What the Bayeux Tapestry text says

F.F.L. Birrell, *Guide to the Bayeux Tapestry*, published by the Victoria and Albert Museum Department of Textiles, London, 1921, pp. 14–18.

Available online at Smithsonian Institution Libraries and Internet Archives

Credit: F.F.L. Birrell, "Text from the Bayeux Tapestry," *Guide to the Bayeux Tapestry*, pp. 14-18. Copyright in the Public Domain.

The Bayeux Tapestry is a 230-foot-long embroidered linen that illustrates the 1066 Battle of Hastings and the events leading up to it. It consists of 50 scenes with Latin headings and was probably commissioned by William the Conqueror's relative Odo, the bishop of Bayeux. The Latin text is translated here. A full set of images of the tapestry can be found at the websites for the Bayeux Museum and Bibliotheca Augustana as well as Wikimedia and the Academy of Medieval European Martial Arts (www.aemma.org)

EDWARD REX
Edward the King

UBI HAROLD, DUX ANGLORUM, ET SUI MILITES EQUITANT AD BOSHAM
Where Harold, Duke of the English, and his soldiers ride to Bosham

ECCLESIA
The church [at Bosham]

HIC HAROLD MARE NAVIGAVIT
Here Harold crossed the sea.

ET VELIS VENTO PLENIS VENIT IN TERRA WIDONIS COMITIS
And with sails full of wind [they had no choice but to] land in the territory of
Count Guy [of Ponthieu]

HAROLD
Harold

HIC APPREHENDIT WIDO HAROLDU
Here Guy seizes Harold

ET DUXIT EUM AD BELREM ET IBI EUM TENUIT
And led him to Beaurain and held him there [as a prisoner]

UBI HAROLD [ET] WIDO PARABOLANT
Where Harold and Guy converse [about the ransom]

UBI NUNTII WILLELMI DUCIS VENERUNT AD WIDONE
Where the messengers of Duke William came to Guy

TUROLD
Turold [name of a squire or stable boy]

NUNTII WILLELMI
The messengers of William [ask for Harold's release]

HIC VENIT NUNTIUS AD WILGELMUM DUCEM
Here the messenger came to Duke William

HIC WIDO ADDUXIT HAROLDUM AD WILGELMUM NORMANNORUM
DUCEM
Here Guy led Harold to William, Duke of the Normans

HIC DUX WILGELM CUM HAROLDO VENIT AD PALATIU SUU
Here Duke William with Harold came to his Palace

UBI UNUS CLERICUS ET ÆLFGYVA
Where a certain clerk and Ælfgyva [? *uncertain event*]

HIC WILLEM DUX ET EXERCITUS EIUS VENERUNT AD MONTE
MICHAELIS
Here Duke William and his army came to Mont St. Michel [with Harold to
battle Conan, Duke of Brittany]

ET HIC TRANSIERUNT FLUMEN COSNONIS
And here they crossed the river Couesnon

HIC HAROLD DUX TRAHEBAT EOS DE ARENA
Here Duke Harold dragged them out of the quicksand

ET VENERUNT AD DOL ET CONAN FUGA VERTIT
And they came to Dol, and Conon turned in flight

REDNES. HIC MILITES WILLELMI DUCIS PUGNANT CONTRA
DINANTES ET CUNAN CLAVES PORREXIT
Rennes. Here the soldiers of Duke William fight against the men of Dinan,
and Conon reached out the keys [at the end of his lance in surrender]

HIC WILLELM DEDIT HAROLDO ARMA
Here William gave Harold arms [and knights him]

HIE [should be hic] WILLELM VENIT BAGIAS
Here William came to Bayeux.

UBI HAROLD SACRAMENTUM FECIT WILLELMO DUCI
Where Harold made an oath [of loyalty] to Duke William

HIC HAROLD DUX REVERSUS EST AD ANGLICAM TERRAM
Here Duke Harold returned to England

ET VENIT AD EDWARDU REGEM
And came to King Edward

HIC PORTATUR CORPUS EADWARDI REGIS AD ECCLESIAM SCI.
PETRI APLI [abbreviation for Sancti Petri Apostoli]
Here the body of King Edward is borne to the Church of St. Peter the Apostle

HIC EADWARDUS REX IN LECTO ALLOQUIT FIDELES
Here King Edward in bed addresses his vassals

ET HIC DEFUNCTUS EST
And here he is dead

HIC DEDERUNT HAROLDO CORONA REGIS
Here they gave to Harold the King's crown

HIC RESIDET HAROLD REX ANGLORUM
Here sits Harold King of the English

STIGANT ARCHIEPS [abbreviation for Archiepiscopus]
Archbishop Stigand.

ISTI MIRANT STELLA
These men are amazed at a star [probably Halley's comet]

HAROLD
Harold

HIC NAVIS ANGLICA VENIT IN TERRAM WILLELMI DUCIS
Here an English ship came into the land of Duke William [and he learns
Harold is now king]

HIC WILLELM DUX JUSSIT NAVES EDIFICARE
Here Duke William gave orders to build ships [for an invasion of England since Harold had sworn loyalty to him]

HIC TRAHUNT NAVES AD MARE
Here they draw down the ships to the sea

ISTI PORTANT ARMAS AD NAVES
These men carry arms to the ships

ET HIC TRAHUNT CARRUM CUM VINO ET ARMIS
And here they drag a cart with wine and arms

HIC WILLELM DUX IN MAGNO NAVIGIO MARE TRANSIVIT
Here Duke William crossed the sea in a great ship

ÆET VENIT AD PEVENESÆ
And came to Pevensey.

HIC EXEUNT CABALLI DE NAVIBUS
Here the horses exit from the ships

ET HIC MILITES FESTINAVERUNT HESTINGA UT CIBUM RAPERENTUR
And here the soldiers hurried to Hastings to find food

HIC EST WADARD
Here is Wadard [supervising]

HIC COQUITUR CARO
Here meat is cooked

ET HIC MINISTRAVERUNT MINISTRI
And here the servants served

HIC FECERUNT PRANDIUM
Here they made a feast

ET HIC EPISCOPUS CIBU ET POTU BENEDICIT
And here the Bishop blesses the food and drink.

ODO EPS [abbreviation for episcopus] WILLELM ROTBERT
Bishop Odo, William, Robert

ISTE JUSSIT UT FODERETUR CASTELLUM AT HESTENGA
The latter commanded that a rampart should be thrown up at Hastings

CAESTRA
The camp

HIC NUNTIATUM EST WILLELMO DE HAROLD
Here news of Harold [and his movements] is brought to William.

HIC DOMUS INCENDITUR
Here a house is burned

HIC MILITES EXIERUNT DE HESTENGA
Here the soldiers left Hastings

ET VENERUNT AD PRELIUM CONTRA HAROLDUM REGE
And came into battle against King Harold

HIC WILLELM DUX INTERROGAT VITAL SI VIDISSET HAROLDI EXERCITU
Here Duke William asks Vital if he had seen Harold's Army.

ISTE NUNTIAT HAROLDUM REGE DE EXERCITU WILLELMI DUCIS
This man informs King Harold concerning the army of Duke William.

HIC WILLELM DUX ALLOQUITUR SUIS MILITIBUS UT PREPARARENT SE VIRILITER ET SAPIENTER AD PRELIUM CONTRA ANGLORUM EXERCITU
Here William exhorts his soldiers to prepare themselves manfully and wisely for battle against the English army

HIC CECIDERUNT LEWINE ET GYRD, FRATRES HAROLDI REGIS
Here fell Leofwyne and Gyrth, brothers of Harold the King

HIC CECIDERUNT SIMUL ANGLI ET FRANCI IN PRELIO
Here fell together English and French in battle

HIC ODO EPS BACULU TENENS, CONFORTAT PUEROS
Here Bishop Odo, holding a staff, rallies the young troops

HIC EST WILELM DUX
Here is Duke William

E … TIUS [some letters missing]
Eustace

HIC FRANCI PUGNANT ET CECIDERUNT QUI ERANT CUM HAROLDO
Here the French fight and those who were with Harold fell

HIC HAROLD REX INTERFECTUS EST
Here King Harold was slain.

ET FUGA VERTERUNT ANGLI
And the English turned in flight.

81

The life of Saint Maurice, from Jacobus de Voragine's *The Golden Legend*

Jacobus de Voragine, *The Golden Legend, Readings on the Saints*, translated by William Granger Ryan, Volume II, Princeton, 1993, pp.188–190.

A different translation can be found online at Internet Medieval Sourcebook

Maurice is the first saint to be portrayed in Western Christian art as a person of color. His life, and martyrdom, is recorded in the very popular medieval text The Golden Legend, *a compilation of hagiographies by Jacobus de Voragine. The earliest image of the saint is a statue erected on the façade of the cathedral at Magdeburg dated to 1240–1250 (Fig. 34). While Jacobus wrote a little later in the early-1260s, there's no indication that he was influenced by the earlier statue.*

[The name] Maurice/Mauritius is derived from *mari*, meaning the sea or bitter, *cis* which means vomiting or hard, and *us*, a counselor or one who hastens. Or the name comes from *mauron*, which, according to Isidore [#73], is the Greek word for black. Saint Maurice had bitterness from dwelling in misery and being put far from his native land; he vomited in the sense that he rejected everything superfluous; he was hard and firm in bearing the torments of his martyrdom; he was a counselor in the exhortation he addressed to his troops; he was one who hastened by his fervor and the multiplication of his good works; and he was black in his contempt of self.

The passion of these saints was written and compiled by Saint Eucherius, bishop of Lyons.

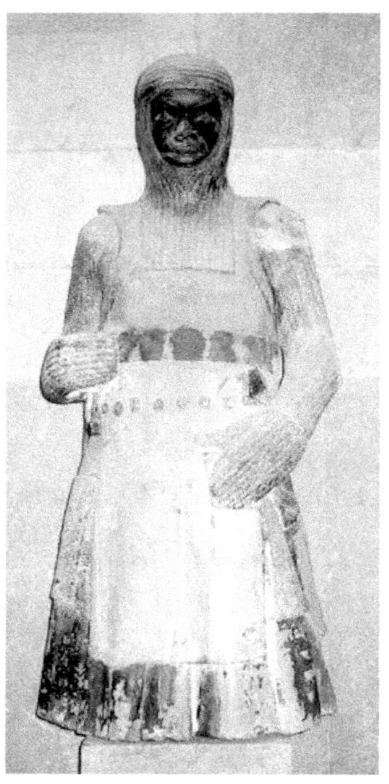

Fig. 34 Saint Maurice sculpture, Magdeburg Cathedral, Germany.

It is said that Maurice was the commander of the holy legion called "Theban." The soldiers were called Thebans after their city, the name of which was Thebes. This was the region toward the East, beyond the border of Arabia, a land powerful and wealthy, fertile and fruitful, and pleasantly wooded. The inhabitants of the region are said to be tall and sturdy, expert in arms, brave in warfare, shrewd and witty, and richly endowed with wisdom. The city had a hundred gates and was situated above the Nile River, which flows out of the earthly paradise and is called Gyon. Of this city it is said: "Behold old Thebes, lying crushed with her hundred gates."

Here James, brother of the Lord, preached the Gospel of salvation and perfectly taught the people the faith of Christ. Diocletian and Maximian, however, who began to reign in A.D. 277 [co-reign actually began in A.D. 286], were determined to wipe out the Christian religion and sent letters to this effect to all the provinces where Christians dwelt. They wrote: "If there was something to be decided or known, and the whole world was marshaled on one side and Rome alone on the other, the whole world would flee in defeat, and Rome would stand alone at the peak of knowledge. Why do you, poor little folk, resist her commands and draw yourselves up so stubbornly against her statutes? Therefore either accept belief in the immortal gods, or the immutable sentence of condemnation will be pronounced against you."

The Christians received these letters but sent the messengers back without an answer. Diocletian and Maximian were angry at this, and dispatched orders to all the provinces that all men capable of bearing the weapons of war should muster and should subdue all those who were rebelling against the Roman Empire. The emperors' letters were delivered to the people of Thebes, and these people, in obedience to God's command, rendered to Caesar the things that are Caesar's and to God the things that are God's. They recruited a choice legion of 6,666 soldiers and sent them to the emperors to help them in waging just wars—not therefore to suppress Christians but rather to defend them. The commander of this sacred legion was the illustrious Maurice, and its standard-bearers were Candidus, Innocent, Exuperius, Victor, and Constantine. Diocletian now sent Maximian, his associate emperor, to Gaul with an immense army, to which he attached the Theban legion. Pope Marcellinus had admonished the Thebans that they should rather perish by the sword than violate the Christian faith which they had made their own.

When the whole army had crossed the Alps and come to Octodurus, the emperor commanded that all who were with him should offer sacrifice to the idols and should unanimously take an oath against Rome's rebellious subjects, but particularly against Christians. When the holy soldiers hear this, they withdrew a distance of eight miles from the army and made camp along the Rhone in a pleasant place called Agaune. When Maximian learned of this, he sent soldiers to tell them to come quickly and offer sacrifice to the gods with the others. The Thebans answered that, being Christians, they could not do this. The emperor, fuming with anger, said: "An insult to heaven is added to the contempt directed at me, and as I am despised, so is the Roman religion! Let these willful soldiers know that I can avenge no only myself but my gods!" The emperor then sent his soldiers to deliver the order that either the Thebans were to sacrifice to the gods or every tenth one of them was to be beheaded. The saints then joyfully hastened forward, one after the other bending his neck to receive the headsman's deathblow.

Now Saint Maurice rose in their midst and addressed them: "I rejoice with you because you are all ready to die for the faith of Christ. I have allowed your fellow soldiers to be put to death because I saw you prepared to suffer for Christ, and I have kept the command the Lord gave Peter: 'Put your sword into its sheath' (John 18:11). Now that the bodies of our comrades form a barricade around us and our garments are reddened with their blood, let us follow them to martyrdom! Therefore, if you agree, let us send our answer to Caesar: 'We are your soldiers, Emperor, and we have taken arms to defend the commonwealth. There is no treason in us, no fear; but we will not betray the faith of Christ.'" Receiving this message, the irate emperor ordered a second decimation of the Thebans.

When that had been done, Exuperius the standard-bearer picked up a banner and, standing amidst the troops, said: "Maurice, our glorious leader, has spoken to us about the glory of our comrades. Now let me say that Exuperius, your standard-bearer, has not taken arms to resist dying for Christ! I say, let our right hands throw aside these carnal weapons and be armed with virtues, and, if it please you, let us send this reply to the emperor: 'We are you soldiers, O Emperor, but we freely profess that we are Christ's servants. To you we owe military service, to him our innocence. From you we have received wages for our work, from him the beginning of life itself. So for him we are prepared to suffer every torment, and we will never give up our faith in him!'" The impious emperor now commanded his army to surround the whole legion so that not one man should escape. The soldiers of Christ were therefore surrounded by the soldiers of the devil, struck down by murderous hands, trampled by horses' hooves, and consecrated to Christ as his precious martyrs.

Image credits

82

A reaction to church opulence, from St. Bernard of Clairvaux's *Apologia to Abbot William of St.-Thierry*

G. G. Coulton, *A Medieval Garner; Human Documents from the four centuries preceding the Reformation*, London, Constable and Co., 1910, pp.70–72.

Available online at Internet Archive

Bernard of Clairvaux (1090–1153) was a member of the Cistercian order, which had been founded in the eleventh century in opposition to the increasing opulence of the Benedictines. His letter here, to the Benedictine abbot William of St.-Thierry of about 1125, denounces all monastic luxury, especially the presence of art in the cloisters.

I say naught of the vast height of your churches, their immoderate length, their superfluous breadth, the costly polishings, the curious carvings and paintings which attract the worshipper's gaze and hinder his attention, and seem to me in some sort a revival of the ancient pagan rites. Let this pass, however: say that this is done for God's honor. But I, as a monk, ask of my brother monks… "tell me, ye poor (if, indeed, ye be poor), what doeth this gold in your sanctuary?" …I know not how it is that, wheresoever more abundant wealth is seen, there do men offer more freely. Their eyes are feasted with relics cased in gold, and their purse-strings are loosed. They are shown a most comely image of some saint, whom they think all the more saintly that he is the more gaudily painted. Men run to kiss him, and are invited to give; there is more admiration for his comeliness than veneration for his sanctity. Hence the church is adorned with gemmed crowns of light—nay, with lustres like cartwheels, girt all around with lamps, but no less brilliant with the precious stones that stud them. Moreover we see candelabra standing like trees of massive bronze, fashioned with marvelous subtlety of art, and glistening no less brightly with gems than with the lights they carry. What, think you, is the purpose of all this? The compunction of penitents, or the admiration of beholders? O vanity of vanities, yet no more vain than insane! The church is resplendent in her walls, beggarly in her poor; if she clothes her stones in gold, and leaves her sons naked; the rich man's eye is fed at the expense of the indigent. The curious find their delight here, yet the needy find no relief. Do we not revere at least the images of the Saints, which swarm even in the inlaid pavement whereon we tread?

But in the cloister, under the eyes of the Brethren who read there, what profit is there in those ridiculous monsters, in that marvelous and deformed comeliness, that comely deformity? To what purpose are those unclean apes, those fierce lions, those monstrous centaurs, those half-men, those striped tigers, those fighting knights, those hunters winding their horns? Many bodies are there seen under one head, or again, many heads to a single body. Here is a four-footed beast with a serpent's tail; there, a fish with a beast's head. Here again the forepart of a horse trails half a goat behind it, or a horned beast bears the hind quarters of a horse. In short, so many and so marvelous are the varieties of divers shapes on every hand, that we are more tempted to read in the marble than in our books, and to spend the whole day in wondering at these things rather than in meditating the law of God. For God's sake, if men are not ashamed of these follies, why at least do they not shrink from the expense?

The Gothic Period

83

Rebuilding St. Denis, from Abbot Suger's *On the Consecration of the Church of St. Denis* (2, 4)

Abbot Suger and its Art Treasures on the Abbey Church of St.-Denis. edited, translated and annotated by Erwin Panofsky, 2nd edition, Princeton, Princeton University Press, 1979, pp. 87, 89, 91, 101.

Abbot Suger (1081–1151) left two accounts of his rebuilding of the Abbey Church of St.-Denis: a booklet that describes the entire campaign from its conception to the consecration of the east end in 1144, and a record of the precious outfittings (see #84). In these excerpts from the first text, Suger explains why the original Carolingian building needed to be enlarged and recounts one of the many almost miraculous events that allowed him to do so.

Through a fortunate circumstance... —the number of the faithful growing and frequently gathering to seek the intercession of the Saints—the [old] basilica had come to suffer grave inconveniences. Often on feast days, completely filled, it disgorged through all its doors the excess of the crowds as they moved in opposite directions, and the outward pressure of the foremost ones not only prevented those attempting to enter from entering but also expelled those who had already entered. At times you could see... that no one among the countless thousands of people because of their very density could move a foot; that no one, because of their very congestion, could [do] anything but stand like a marble statue, stay benumbed or, as a last resort, scream. The distress of the women, however, was so great and so intolerable that you could see... how they cried out horribly as though in labor; how several of them, miserably trodden underfoot [but then] lifted by the pious assistance of men above the heads of the crowd, marched forward as though upon a pavement; and how many others, gasping with their last breath, panted in the cloisters of the brethren to the despair of everyone...

Through a gift of God a new quarry, yielding very strong stone, was discovered such as in quality and quantity had never been found in these regions. There arrived a skillful crowd of masons, stonecutters, sculptors and other workmen, so that—thus and otherwise—Divinity relieved us of our fears and favored us with Its goodwill by comforting us and by providing us with unexpected [resources]. I used to compare the least to the greatest: Solomon's riches could not have sufficed for his Temple any more than did ours for this work had not the same Author [God] of the same work abundantly supplied His attendants. The identity of the author and the work provides a sufficiency for the worker...

Upon consideration, then, it was decided to remove that vault, unequal to the higher one, which, overhead, closed the apse containing the bodies of our Patron Saints, all the way [down] to the upper surface of the crypt to which it adhered; so that this crypt might offer its top as a pavement to those approaching by either of the two stairs, and might present the chasses [reliquaries] of the Saints, adorned with gold and precious gems, to the visitors' glances in a more elevated place. Moreover, it was cunningly provided that—through the upper columns and central arches which were to be placed upon the lower ones built in the crypt—the central nave of the old [church] should be equalized, by means of geometrical and arithmetical instruments, with the central nave of the new addition; and, likewise, that the dimensions of the old side aisles should be equalized with the dimensions of the new side-aisles, except for that elegant and praiseworthy extension, in [the form of] a circular string of chapels, by virtue of which the whole [church] would shine with the wonderful and uninterrupted light of most luminous windows, pervading the interior beauty.

84

On the Decoration of St. Denis, from Abbot Suger's *On What Was Done Under His Administration* (27, 31–33)

Abbot Suger and its Art Treasures on the Abbey Church of St.-Denis, edited, translated and annotated by Erwin Panofsky, 2nd edition, Princeton, Princeton University Press, 1979, pp. 47, 49, 55, 57, 59, 63, 65.

A different translation is available online at www.history.vt.edu/Burr/DeAdmin.pdf.

Although St.-Denis was a Benedictine abbey, its church was open to lay folk and attracted them in large numbers. The rich embellishment of the church, such as described here, was the type of material display deplored by St. Bernard of Clairvaux (see #82). Suger's account of the decorations (circa 1144), however, speaks to a philosophical belief that contemplation of these expensive yet beautiful materials could lead the worshiper to a state of heightened spiritual awareness.

XXVII Of the Cast and Gilded Doors

Bronze casters having been summoned and sculptors chosen, we set up the main doors on which are represented the Passion of the Savior and His Resurrection, or rather Ascension, with great cost and much expenditure for their gilding as was fitting for the noble porch... The verses on the door, further are these:

> Whoever you are, if you seek to extol the glory of these doors,
> Marvel not at the gold and the expense but at the craftsmanship
> of the work.
> Bright is the noble work; but being nobly bright, the work

Should brighten the minds, so that they may travel, through the
   true lights,
To the True Light where Christ is the true door.
In what manner it be inherent in this world the golden door
   defines:
The dull mind rises to truth through that which is material
And, in seeing this light, is resurrected from its former submersion.

XXXI. Concerning the Golden Altar Frontal in the Upper Choir.

Into this panel, which stands in front of his most sacred body, we have put,
according to our estimate, about forty-two marks of gold; [further] a multi-
farious wealth of precious gems, hyacinths, rubies, sapphires, emeralds and
topazes, and also an array of different large pearls—[a wealth] as great as
we had never anticipated to find. You could see how kings, princes, and many
outstanding men, following our example, took the rings off the fingers of their
hands and ordered, out of love for the Holy Martyrs, that the gold, stones,
and precious pearls of the rings be put into that panel. Similarly archbishops
and bishops deposited there the very rings of their investiture as though in
a place of safety, and offered them devoutly to God and His Saints. And such
a crowd of dealers in precious gems flocked in on us from diverse dominions
and regions that we did not wish to buy any more than they hastened to sell,
with everyone contributing donations.

XXXII. Of the Golden Crucifix.

We searched around everywhere by ourselves and by our agents for an abundance of precious pearls and gems, preparing as precious a supply of gold and
gems for so important an embellishment as we could find, and convoked the
most experienced artists from diverse parts. They would with diligent and
patient labor glorify the venerable cross on its reverse side by the admirable
beauty of those gems; and on its front—that is to say in the sight of the
sacrificing priest—they would show the adorable image of our lord the savior,
suffering, as it were, even now in the remembrance of his passion. ... One
merry but notable miracle which the Lord granted us in this connection we
do not wish to pass over in silence. For when I was in difficulty for want of
gems and could not sufficiently provide myself with more (for their scarcity
makes them very expensive): then, lo and behold, [monks] from three abbeys
of two Orders—that is, from Citeaux and another abbey of the same order,
and from Fontevrault—entered our little chamber adjacent to the church
and offered us for sale an abundance of gems such as we had not hoped to
find in ten years, hyacinths, sapphires, rubies, emeralds, topazes. Their
owners had obtained them from Count Thibaut for alms; and he in turn had
received them, through the hands of his brother Stephen, King of England,
from the treasures of his uncle, the late King Henry, who had amassed them

throughout his life in wonderful vessels. We, however, freed from the worry of searching for gems, thanked God and gave four hundred pounds for the lot though they were worth much more.

XXXIII.

Thus, when out of my delight in the beauty of the house of God, the loveliness of the many-colored gems has called me away from external cares, and worthy meditation has induced me to reflect, transferring that which is material to that which is immaterial, on the diversity of the sacred virtues: then it seems to me that I see myself dwelling as it were, in some strange region of the universe which neither exists entirely in the slime of the earth nor entirely in the purity of heave; and that, by the grace of God, I can be transported from this inferior to that higher world.

85

Stained glass windows, from Theophilus' *On Divers Arts* (*De diversis artibus* Book 2)

An Essay upon Various Arts in three Books by Theophilus called also Rugerus, translated by Robert Hendrie, London, John Murray, 1847, pp. 127–129, 137–139.

Available online at Internet Archive

Credit: Theophilus, "Stained Glass Windows," *An Essay Upon Various Arts in Three Books*, trans. Robert Hendrie. Copyright in the Public Domain.

As mentioned in reading #76, Theophilus was an eleventh to twelfth-century monk who wrote three practical 'how-to' books on the arts. Here from the second book are some instructions for making a stained glass window.

CHAPTER 9: Of Dilating or Spreading out The Plates of Glass

When glowing, take a hot iron, and, splitting a part of the glass [muff or cylinder made from blown glass], place it upon the hearth of the glowing furnace, and when it has begun to grow soft, take the iron forceps and smooth piece of wood, and, opening it in that part in which is the division, you will dilate [i.e., spread it flat] and smooth it according to your will with the pincers. When it has become quite smooth, immediately taking it out, place it in the cooling oven, moderately warmed; and so that the plate may not lie down, but stand against the wall, next to which you will place another...

CHAPTER 17: On Composing Windows

When you wish to compose glass windows, first make for yourself a flat wooden table, of such breadth and length that you can work upon it two portions of the same window; and taking chalk, and scrape it with a knife over all the table, sprinkle water everywhere, and rub it with a cloth over the whole. And when it is dry, take the dimensions of one portion of the window in length and breadth, marking it upon the table with ruler and compass with a lead or tin [tip]; and if you wish to have a border in it, draw it with the breadth which may please you, and in the pattern you may wish. Which done, draw out whatever figures you will, first with the lead or tin, then with a red or black color, making all outlines with study, because it will be necessary, when you have painted the glass, that you join together the shadows and lights according to the [drawing on the] table. Then arranging the different tints of draperies, note down the color of each one in its place; and of any other thing which you may wish to paint you will mark the color with a letter. After this take a leaden cup, and put chalk, ground with water, into it: make two or three brushes for yourself from hair, either from the tail of the marten, or badger, or squirrel, or cat, or the mane of the donkey, and take a piece of glass of whatever kind you like, which is in every way larger than the place upon which it is superposed, and fixing it in the ground of this place, so that you can perceive the drawing upon the table through the glass, so trace with the chalk the outlines upon the glass.

CHAPTER 18: Of Dividing or Cutting Glass

Afterwards heat in the fire the dividing iron which should be thin throughout, but thicker at the end. When it glows in the thick part apply it to the glass which you wish to cut, and presently the commencement of a small fissure will appear. If, however, the glass be hard, wet it with saliva, with your finger, in the spot where you place the iron; being instantly cracked, draw the iron along where you wish to divide, and it is followed by the fissure. All the portions being thus cut, take the *riesel*-iron, which is a palm in length, curved at each extremity, with which you will equalize and join all parts together, each one in its place.

86

The Cult of Carts, from Robert de Torigni's *Chronicle*

Chartres Cathedral: Illustrations, Introductory Essay, Documents, Analysis, Criticism, edited by Robert Branner, New York, Norton, 1969, p. 93.

Chartres Cathedral burned twice in the twelfth century, once in 1134 and then again in 1194. This contemporary description by Robert de Torigni (died 1186) of the rebuilding of the west front in the 1140s stresses the participation of masses of townsfolk. This kind of almost fanatical piety was later referenced as the "cult of carts." More traditional beasts of burden, oxen, are honored with statues on the western towers of Laon cathedral (Fig. 35).

In this same year, primarily at Chartres, men began, with their own shoulders, to drag the wagons loaded with stone, wood, grain, and other materials to the workshop of the church, whose towers were then rising. Anyone who has not witnessed this will not see the like in our time. Not only there, but also in nearly the whole of France and Normandy and in many other places, [one saw] everywhere ...penance and the forgiveness of offenses, everywhere mourning and contrition. One might observe women as well as men dragging [wagons] through deep swamps on their knees, beating themselves with whips, numerous wonders occurring everywhere, canticles and hymns being offered to God.

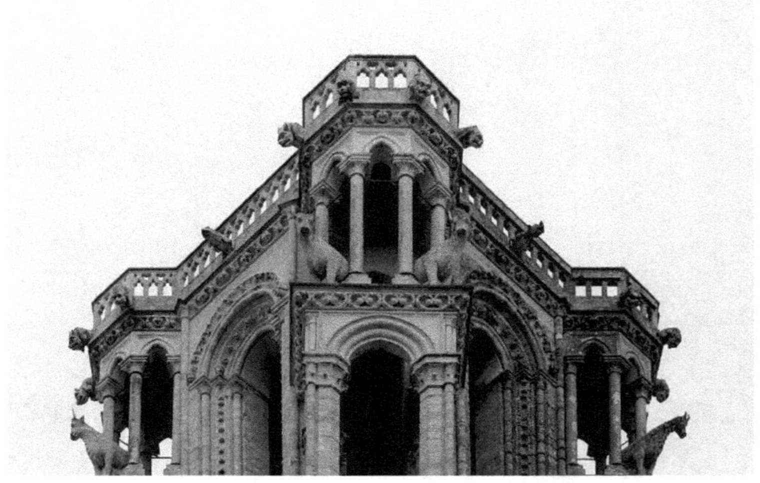

Fig. 35 Merged panorama of the sculpted oxen on the Laon Cathedral in France.

Image credits

87

Women and the Arts, from Christine de Pizan's *Book of the City of Ladies* (Part I, #41)

Finished in 1405, The Book of the City of Ladies *is a French prose work by Christine de Pizan. In it the author responds to medieval misogynistic statements by building an allegorical city comprised of famous women from the past (Fig. 36). She is guided in the endeavor by the three Virtues, the first of which is Lady Reason. In the passage below they consider the role of women in the arts.*

[Lady Reason]: 'What more can I say to prove to you that women are just as capable of learning arts and sciences as they are of inventing new ones? Believe me when I tell you that once they have learnt something, women are very quick to put their knowledge into action and to achieve great things. This is certainly true in the case of a woman called Thamaris, whose mastery of the art of painting was such that there was none to touch her while she was alive. Boccaccio says about her that she was the daughter of the painter Micon...

This Thamaris tossed aside all usual womanly tasks and devoted herself to learning her father's craft. She applied herself so well that during the reign of Archelaos over the Macedonians, the Ephesians commissioned Thamaris to paint a picture of the goddess Diana whom they worshipped. For a long time afterwards, this picture was held in very high esteem, as befitted a work

261

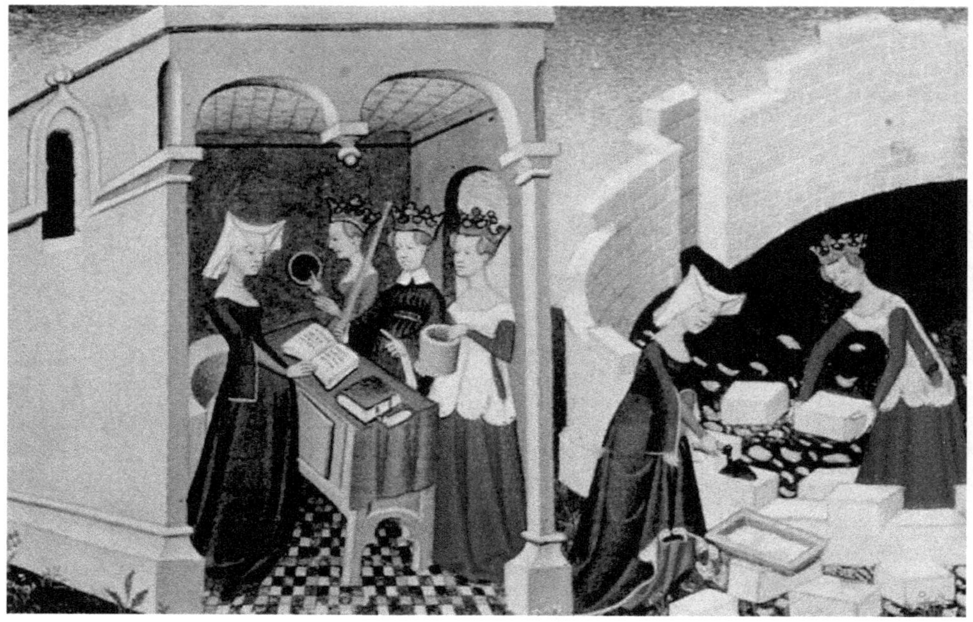

Fig. 36 Women at work, 15th century French illustration of Christine de Pizan's *Book of the City of Ladies*, Bibliotheque nationale de France (Fr.607 f.2).

of such great artistry, and was only displayed on feast days in honor of Diana. It was preserved for many years as a marvelous testament to this lady's skill and has ensured that even today her brilliance has not been forgotten.

Irene was another woman from Greece, who excelled herself in the art of painting to the point of surpassing all others of her time. She was a pupil of a painter called Cratinus, who was a master in his field, yet she became such a great expert that she completely outshone her teacher. Her contemporaries were amazed by her achievement and chose to commemorate Irene by dedicating a statue to her of a girl in the act of painting. They reserved an honorable place for this statue in a gallery of other figures which depicted the greatest past masters in a variety of disciplines. This was in accordance with a custom which the ancients had of revering those who outdid all others in a particular domain, be it in wisdom, strength, beauty or some other attribute, preserving their names for posterity by erecting statues to them in prominent places.

Marcia the Roman was a virgin who lived an exemplary life full of great virtue and morality. She too was another fine craftswoman in the art of painting, achieving such excellence in her field that she outstripped all men, including Dionysius and Sopolis who were thought to be the best artists in the world at that time. To put it briefly, she attained the very pinnacle of perfection in her field, according to the most authoritative sources. In order to leave behind her an indelible record of her expertise, one of this Marcia's most notable works was a brilliantly executed self-portrait done with the aid of a mirror which was so lifelike that anyone who saw it thought it was real. For many years, this picture was greatly treasured and pointed out to other craftsmen as a supreme specimen of their art.'

I then said to Reason: 'My lady, it is clear from these examples that those who were wise were held in much higher esteem in the past than nowadays and that the sciences themselves were much more highly thought of then than they are now. However, to go back to what you were saying about women who excelled in the art of painting, I know a woman called Anastasia working today who is so good at painting decorative borders and background land-scapes for miniatures that there is no craftsman who can match her in the whole of Paris, even though that's where the finest in the world can be found. Only Anastasia can execute such delicate floral motifs and tiny details and she is so well regarded that she is entrusted with finishing off even the most expensive and priceless of books. I know all this from my own experience as she has done some work for me which has been ranked amongst the finest creations of the greatest masters.'

Reason replied: 'I can well believe it, my dear Christine. Anyone who wanted could cite plentiful examples of exceptional women in the world today; it's simply a matter of looking for them.'

Image credits

Fig. 36: Zenodot Verlagsgesellschaft mbH, "Women at Work, Christine de Pizan's Book of the City of Ladies," https://commons.wikimedia.org/wiki/File:Meister_der_%27Cit%C3%A9_des_ Dames%27_002.jpg. Copyright in the Public Domain.

<h1 style="text-align:center">88</h1>

On Giotto, from Giorgio Vasari's
The Lives of the Artists

Lives of the most eminent painters, sculptors, and architects, translated from the Italian of Giorgio Vasari, with notes and illustrations, chiefly selected from various commentators by Mrs. Jonathan Foster, London, Henry G. Bohn, Volume I, 1855, pp. 93–95.

Available online at HathiTrust Digital Library

Giorgio Vasari was a sixteenth-century Italian painter, architect, and biographer. His book, The Lives of the Artists, *is the fundamental source of information for Italian Renaissance art. Vasari essentially traces the birth of the Renaissance to one artist, Giotto Bondone, who was active in the years around 1300. The following excerpt is from the beginning of his chapter on that artist.*

Giotto, seeing that he alone, although born amidst incapable artists, and at a time when all good methods in art had long been entombed beneath the ruins of war—yet, by the favor of heaven, he, I say, alone succeeded in resuscitating art, and restoring her to a path that may be called the true one. And it was in truth a great marvel, that from so rude and inapt an age, Giotto should have had strength to elicit so much, that the art of design, of which the men of those days had little, if any knowledge, was, by his means, effectually recalled into life. The birth of this great man took place in the hamlet of Vespignano, fourteen miles from the city of Florence, in the year 1276. His father's name was Bondone, a simple husbandman, who reared his child, to whom he had given the name of Giotto, with such decency as his condition permitted. The boy was early remarked for extreme vivacity in all his childish proceedings, and for extraordinary promptitude of intelligence; so that he became endeared,

265

not only to his father, but to all who knew him in the village and around it. When he was about ten years old, Bondone gave him a few sheep to watch, and with these he wandered about the vicinity, now here and now there. But, induced by Nature herself to the art of design, he was perpetually drawing on the stones, the earth, or the sand, some natural object that came before him, or some fantasy that presented itself to his thoughts. It chanced one day that the affairs of Cimabue took him from Florence to Vespignano, when he perceived the young Giotto, who, while his sheep fed around him, was occupied in drawing one of them from life, with a stone slightly pointed, upon a smooth clean piece of rock, and that without any teaching whatever, but such as Nature herself had imparted. Halting in astonishment, Cimabue inquired of the boy if he would accompany him to his home, and the child replied, he would go willingly, if his father were content to permit it. Cimabue therefore requesting the consent of Bondone, the latter granted it readily, and suffered the artist to conduct his son to Florence, where in a short time, instructed by Cimabue and aided by Nature, the boy not only equaled his master in his own manner, but became so good an imitator of Nature, that he totally banished the rude Greek [Byzantine] manner, restoring art to the better path adhered to in modern times, and introducing the custom of accurately drawing living persons from nature, which had not been used for more than two hundred years. Or, if some had attempted it, as said above, it was not by any means with the success of Giotto. Among the portraits by this artist, and which still remain, is one of his contemporary and intimate friend, Dante Alighieri, who was no less famous as a poet than Giotto as a painter, and whom Giovanni Boccaccio has lauded so highly... This portrait is in the chapel of the palace of the Podesta [the Bargello] in Florence.

89

On the Black Death, from Giovanni Boccaccio's *The Decameron*, "The First Day"

Giovanni Boccaccio, T*he Decameron*, 2nd edition, translated by G. H. McWilliam, London, Penguin Classics, 1995, pp. 5, 7, 13.

A different translation is available online at Internet Medieval Sourcebook

Credit: Giovanni Boccaccio, "On the Black Death," *The Decameron*, pp. 5, 7, 13, trans. G.H. McWilliam. Copyright © 1972, 1995 by G. H. McWilliam. Reprinted with permission by Penguin (UK).

Boccaccio (1313–1375) was an eyewitness to the horror of the bubonic plague and his description of it is reproduced here. In his Decameron, ten young people, who have fled Florence to a country villa in order to escape the plague, entertain themselves by telling ten stories over the course of ten days. In fact Giotto (see #88) is described in story 5 on day 6 as someone who "brought back to light an art which had been buried beneath blunders of those who, in their paintings, aimed to bring visual delight to the ignorant rather than intellectual satisfaction to the wise." This approach to art is the complete opposite of the medieval one established by Pope Gregory the Great (see #71). These changing attitudes, as well as the social leveling produced by the plague, mark the end of the medieval world and the beginning of the early modern era.

I say, then, that the sum of thirteen hundred and forty-eight years had elapsed since the fruitful Incarnation of the Son of God, when the noble city of Florence, which for its great beauty excels all others in Italy, was visited by the deadly pestilence. Some say that it descended upon the human race through the influence of the heavenly bodies, others that it was a punishment signifying God's righteous anger at our iniquitous way of life. But whatever its cause, it had originated some years earlier in the East, where it had claimed countless lives before it unhappily spread westward, growing in strength as it swept relentlessly on from one place to the next...

Its earliest symptom, in men and women alike, was the appearance of certain swellings in the groin or the armpit, some of which were egg shaped whilst others were roughly the size of the common apple. Sometimes the swellings were large, sometimes not so large, and they were referred to by the populace as *gavoccioli*. From the two areas already mentioned, this deadly *gavocciolo* would begin to spread, and within a short time it would appear at random all over the body. Later on, the symptoms of the disease changed, and many people began to find dark blotches and bruises on their arms, thighs, and other parts of the body, sometimes large and few in number, at other times tiny and closely spaced. These, to anyone unfortunate enough to contract them, were just as infallible a sign that he would die as the *gavocciolo* had been earlier, and as indeed it still was...

Some people were of the opinion that a sober and abstemious mode of living considerably reduced the risk of infection... Others took the opposite view, and maintained that an infallible way of warding off this appalling evil was to drink heavily, enjoy life to the full, go round singing and merrymaking, gratify all of one's cravings whenever the opportunity offered, and shrug the whole thing off as one enormous joke. Moreover, they practiced what they preached to the best of their ability, for they would visit one tavern after another, drinking all day and night to immoderate excess; or alternatively (and this was their more frequent custom), they would do their drinking in various private houses, but only in the ones where the conversation was restricted to subjects that were pleasant or entertaining. Such places were easy to find, for people behaved as though their days were numbered, and treated their belongings and their own persons with equal abandon. Hence most houses had become common property, and any passing stranger could make himself at home as naturally as though he were the rightful owner...

Ah, how great a number of splendid palaces, fine houses, and noble dwellings, once filled with retainers, with lords and with ladies, were bereft of all who had lived there, down to the tiniest child! How numerous were the famous families, the vast estates, the notable fortunes, that were seen to be left without a rightful successor! How many gallant gentlemen, fair ladies, and sprightly youths, who would have been judged hale and hearty by Galen, Hippocrates and Aesculapius (to say nothing of others), having breakfasted in the morning with their kinsfolk, acquaintances and friends, supped that same evening with their ancestors in the next world!

Acknowledgments

I would like to thank and acknowledge several people who helped and supported the production of this little book. For suggesting texts that should be included, thanks go to Michael Hoff, Ferdinanda Florence, and John Younger. For the friendliest of communications during the first edition, Kevin Hoffman, thank you. For feedback, encouragement, and help with translating a French text (#2), I am very grateful to Linda Marie Zaerr. I appreciate the validation provided by instructors who adopted this book and my mother who said she found it readable! Also, thanks are owed to my students who actually did the assigned reading and pointed out errors, particularly the double text for Notker the Stammerer. I also want to thank Boise State University for the sabbatical leave this last year which made a second edition possible.

Finally, I'd like to dedicate this book to my father. He saw the first edition, and even bought multiple copies to give as Christmas gifts one year, but not the second one. Miss you, Dad.

CPSIA information can be obtained
at www.ICGtesting.com
Printed in the USA
BVHW081741120919
558288BV00007B/355/P